NEXT LEVEL

GAMES REVIEW 2023

First published in Great Britain 2022 by Expanse
An imprint of HarperCollins*Publishers*
1 London Bridge Street, London SE1 9GF
www.farshore.co.uk

HarperCollins*Publishers*
1st Floor, Watermarque Building, Ringsend Road
Dublin 4, Ireland

Written by Ben Wilson
Foreword by Julia Hardy

This book is an original creation by Expanse

For a full list of credits for this book, please see page 254.

ISBN 978 0 0085 4102 6
Printed in Italy
001

This book is produced from independently certified FSC™ paper
to ensure responsible forest management.

For more information visit: www.harpercollins.co.uk/green

All games have age guidance and we recommend that parents and guardians of younger gamers are aware of these guidelines and the content of the games being played. This book is for a general audience and therefore reviews the year in gaming, covering a wide range of games from PEGI 3 to PEGI 18. While we have ensured the content of this book is suitable for a general audience, discretion is advised.

Expanse & HarperCollins are not responsible for content hosted online by third parties. Any links to websites were correct at the time of going to print. We recommend online activity for younger fans is monitored by parents and guardians.

NEXT LEVEL

GAMES REVIEW 2023

BY BEN WILSON

CONTENTS

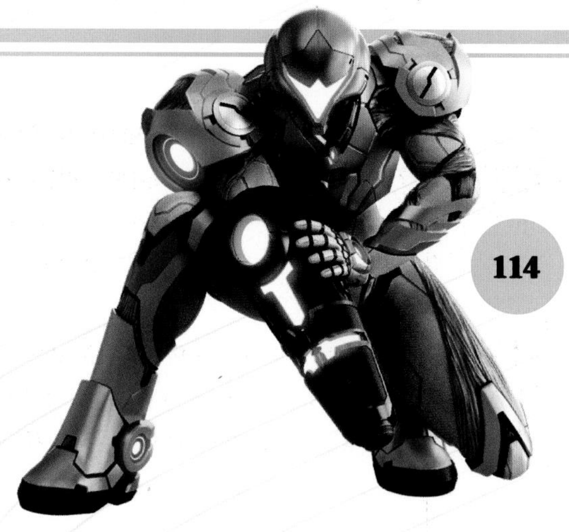
114

016

052

092

FEATURES

CHAPTER 03

CHAPTER 04

FOREWORD
BY JULIA HARDY

Video games are great. But you knew that already, that's why you're here. If it's possible, though, the past year has taught us that games can be even better than we ever imagined. I mean we knew they were amazing but now even your grandad totally gets it. From nana doing her gardening in Animal Crossing or family FIFA battles to decide who does the washing up. Just when everyone got to their limit of TV shows after being stuck inside for ages, it was video games that came to the rescue and saved our sanity.

Some of my favourite games of the past year have been so weird and varied: from terrifying card games (*Inscryption*) to never-ending respawning (*Returnal*), or playing music in space with bizarre-looking celestial creatures (*The Artful Escape*) and driving expensive cars I will never own (*Gran Turismo*), plus taking down robot dinosaurs (*Horizon Forbidden West*). There are beyond heaps and my pile of shame grows ever deeper.

One of the things I was super happy about this year was the no-build *Fortnite* mode. Which I guess a lot of you probably weren't all that bothered about, as I'm sure you're great at *Fortnite*. But the building side of it always perplexed me, as my HP pinged off me while I was stuck in what looked like a collection of B&Q sheds after a Tsunami. It is so *embarrassing*.

The other great thing that happened this year was the Steam Deck launching. I'm a fan of weird, quirky little (and big) indie games and of taking my Nintendo Switch everywhere, whether appropriate or not. Now I can take pretty much all the PC games out and about. I'll never have a dull bus ride, dinner or visit to my auntie's ever again. I mean, that would be true if I had one. The waiting lists are long! It is coming though. And soon I will never have to make eye contact with anyone ever again. Jkjk, it's important to look someone in the eye, every once in a while. Especially when ordering food as, otherwise, they might not understand just how hungry you are.

But enough about this year, I want to be excited about what's next ... and you are not going to be disappointed.

VR! It's the next logical step in gaming becoming more intuitive. In Tokyo, I played a Zero Latency VR experience in zombie horde mode. Imagine a big square room, VR backpacks like *Ghostbusters* and proximity alerts (so you don't bump into each other). Running around in a game world, taking out the undead felt AMAZING.

I could point my arm at the thing and shoot – or run away. And soon, with PlayStation doubling down on VR, plus all the other amazing VR kits like Oculus, there will be so much virtual reality fun to be had at home. It's never not funny making your dad do it, as he looks funny trying to do stuff anyway.

© NIC FORD

VR is a little way off from being in everyone's home so let's talk about some of the great games that are still to come over the next year.

A big one for me is *The Legend of Zelda: Breath of the Wild 2*. If you haven't played the first, you probably have just enough time to get it done before the sequel comes out (if you played it for as long as I did). It's god tier Nintendo as far as I'm concerned. A perfect game, full of fun, exploration, combat and just a really engaging world that other studios would dream of creating. And *Breath of the Wild 2* is going to be just as amazing, I can feel it. **crosses fingers**

The most hyped game is *Starfield*, mainly as it's hard to find an adult gamer who hasn't lost hundreds of hours on one of Bethesda's giant games, like *Skyrim* or *Fallout*. *Starfield* is going to be a huge open world RPG, set in space with "1000+ planets to explore". This means – yes, you guessed it – hundreds of hours of gameplay. If you're not old enough to play it yet, it's still a good thing, as it'll keep your gamer parents occupied for at least a whole year.

Next year, *Spider-Man* is going to be back and this time (hopefully) everyone that wants one will have a PS5 to play the new game on. Better start saving your spare cash or being *really really really* good to build up those parental bonus points that you can trade in for goods and services.

There are so very many more games still to come and things are only going to get even better, bigger and more bombastic as we slide into 2023 and beyond. Prepare yourself, your friends, and your hard drive memory for a truly epic year.

GLOSSARY

4K – Ultra HD! It's an even clearer picture than HD.

AAA – An AAA (or triple A) game is a big blockbuster release, like *Starfield*.

AI – Artificial intelligence. In gaming it means the computer plays a character in the game.

ACHIEVEMENT – Challenges or goals set by your platform, like Xbox or Steam, that you can complete in a game to earn points.

AMIIBO™ – Nintendo figurines and cards that you can buy. Tap them against your console and unlock new characters, weapons, actions and more.

AR – Artificial reality. A type of technology used with a headset that gives players a 360 gaming experience. See also VR.

AVATAR – A big blue alien. Also your playable character in a game, usually an avatar is customisable.

BACKWARDS COMPATIBILITY – When a new console is released, studios will make them backwards compatible so older games will work on newer platforms.

BATTLE ROYALE – A giant online multiplayer game, like *Fortnite*.

BETA – An early version of a game that's sometimes made available ahead of an official release so players can test out the gameplay and mechanics.

BOSS – The big bad enemy, much tougher than regular baddies. You usually come across a boss at the end of a level or the end of a game.

BUTTONMASHER – An insult for someone who isn't very experienced at gaming.

CAMPAIGN – Long-running games, like *The Elder Scrolls Online*, often have extended quests called campaigns, these are usually the main story mode of the game.

CCG – Collectible card game. Build a deck of cards and battle other players or the computer. *Hearthstone* and *Magic: the Gathering* are CCGs.

CEL-SHADED – An animation style that makes characters look cartoon-like while still being 3D. *Tiny Tina's Wonderlands* is cel-shaded.

CHECKPOINT – Get to checkpoint to save your progress. They're usually safe areas with no enemies around and quite often look like bonfires.

CLOUD – An online storage system. If you back up your game to the cloud it has been saved online.

CO-OP – Short for co-operative game. Where several players work together to complete a quest. Sometimes this is the same as the solo player campaign but you can play it with your mates.

COMBO – A sequence of buttons that, when pressed in the correct order, make characters perform new or special moves.

COSPLAY – Costume play. When mega fans dress up as characters from a game, TV show, book or movie they are cosplaying.

BATTLE ROYALE

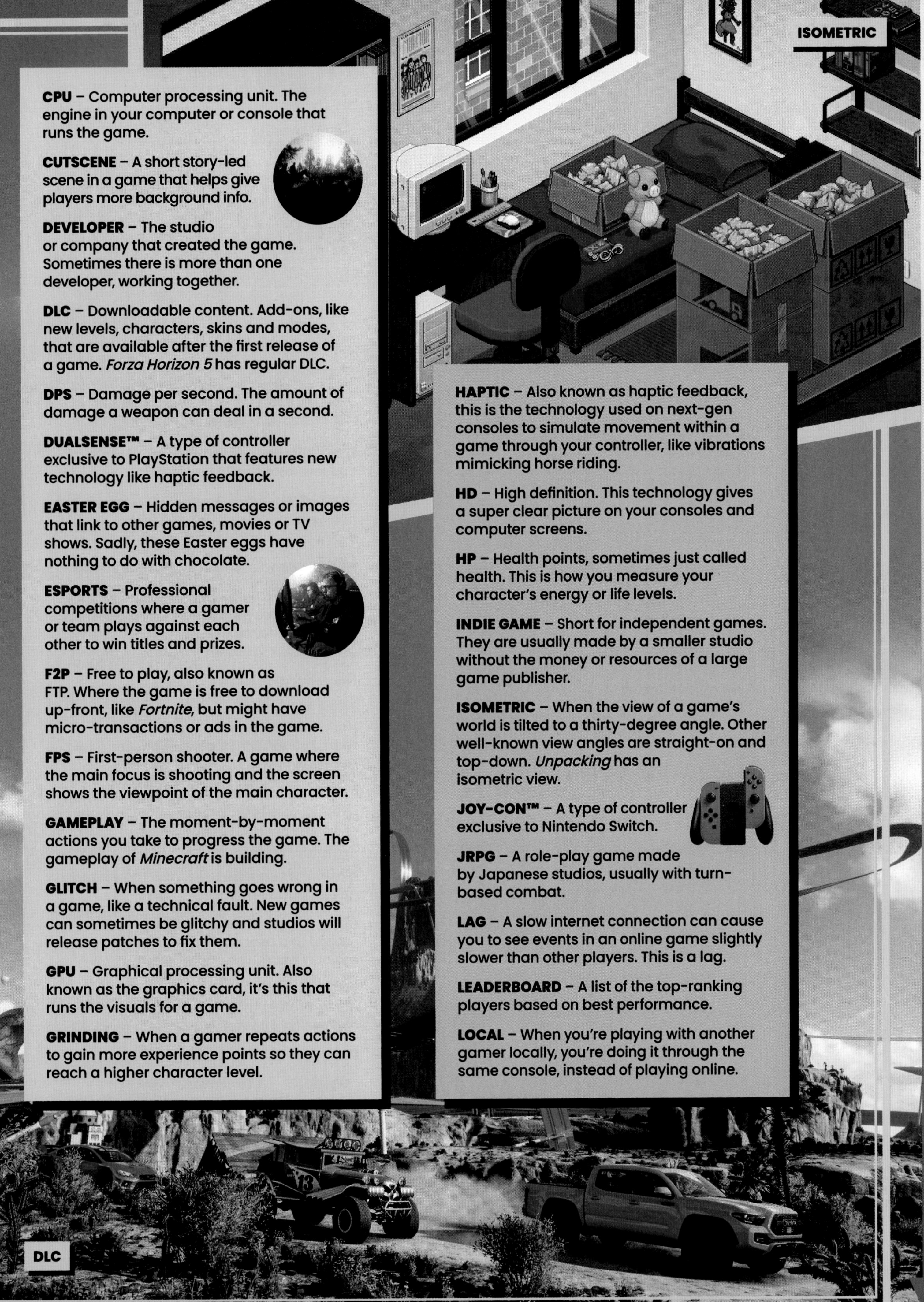

CPU – Computer processing unit. The engine in your computer or console that runs the game.

CUTSCENE – A short story-led scene in a game that helps give players more background info.

DEVELOPER – The studio or company that created the game. Sometimes there is more than one developer, working together.

DLC – Downloadable content. Add-ons, like new levels, characters, skins and modes, that are available after the first release of a game. *Forza Horizon 5* has regular DLC.

DPS – Damage per second. The amount of damage a weapon can deal in a second.

DUALSENSE™ – A type of controller exclusive to PlayStation that features new technology like haptic feedback.

EASTER EGG – Hidden messages or images that link to other games, movies or TV shows. Sadly, these Easter eggs have nothing to do with chocolate.

ESPORTS – Professional competitions where a gamer or team plays against each other to win titles and prizes.

F2P – Free to play, also known as FTP. Where the game is free to download up-front, like *Fortnite*, but might have micro-transactions or ads in the game.

FPS – First-person shooter. A game where the main focus is shooting and the screen shows the viewpoint of the main character.

GAMEPLAY – The moment-by-moment actions you take to progress the game. The gameplay of *Minecraft* is building.

GLITCH – When something goes wrong in a game, like a technical fault. New games can sometimes be glitchy and studios will release patches to fix them.

GPU – Graphical processing unit. Also known as the graphics card, it's this that runs the visuals for a game.

GRINDING – When a gamer repeats actions to gain more experience points so they can reach a higher character level.

HAPTIC – Also known as haptic feedback, this is the technology used on next-gen consoles to simulate movement within a game through your controller, like vibrations mimicking horse riding.

HD – High definition. This technology gives a super clear picture on your consoles and computer screens.

HP – Health points, sometimes just called health. This is how you measure your character's energy or life levels.

INDIE GAME – Short for independent games. They are usually made by a smaller studio without the money or resources of a large game publisher.

ISOMETRIC – When the view of a game's world is tilted to a thirty-degree angle. Other well-known view angles are straight-on and top-down. *Unpacking* has an isometric view.

JOY-CON™ – A type of controller exclusive to Nintendo Switch.

JRPG – A role-play game made by Japanese studios, usually with turn-based combat.

LAG – A slow internet connection can cause you to see events in an online game slightly slower than other players. This is a lag.

LEADERBOARD – A list of the top-ranking players based on best performance.

LOCAL – When you're playing with another gamer locally, you're doing it through the same console, instead of playing online.

MATCHMAKING – An automatic process that joins you up with other players online.

METROIDVANIA – A style of platforming game inspired by the classic Metroid and Castlevania series, focusing on exploration and revisiting previously-explored areas with new abilities.

MICRO TRANSACTIONS – Paid content within a game, like when you buy new skins, weapons and ammo.

MINI-GAME – Games within games! This can be a collection of mini-games, like *Fall Guys* or *Mario Party*, or a short game within a longer one, like Orlog in *Assassin's Creed: Valhalla.*

MMO – Short for MMORPG.

MMORPG – Massive multiplayer online role-play game. You can see why they shortened it! *World of Warcraft* and *The Elder Scrolls Online* are MMORPGs.

MOBA – Multiplayer online battle arena. *DOTA 2* and *League of Legends* are MOBAs.

MOD – Short for modification. Player-made updates or patches that give a game a new look or mechanic.

MULTIPLATFORM – When a game can be played on more than one console or platform, like PS5, Switch and PC.

MULTIPLAYER – Any game that's more than one player. They can be co-operative or combative, like *Overwatch*.

NES – Nintendo Entertainment System. A console from the 80s.

NEXT-GEN – Next-generation console. The new versions of gaming platforms, like PS5 or X-box Series X/S.

NOOB – People who are new to gaming.

NPC – Non-player character. Any character you come across in a game that isn't controlled by another human.

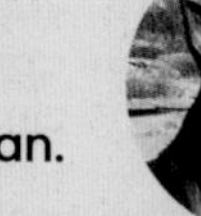

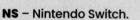

NS – Nintendo Switch.

OPEN WORLD – A game without a strict path to follow, where players are free to roam around the huge world to complete their objectives.

PATCH – Downloadable updates to fix bugs, glitches or ad content.

PLATFORMER – A type of game where you jump, bounce or run onto different platforms and objects across the screen to get to new levels.

PORT – A version of a game that's been moved to a new platform of console without major reworks, like a remaster.

PRO-GAMER – Someone who plays a game professionally, through eSports competitions.

PS – PlayStation.

PUBLISHER – The company who releases the game. They don't always create it themselves, that's a developer.

PVE – Player versus engine. When it's just you and the computer AI.

PVP – Player versus player. When you're against another human or group of humans. This can be online or local.

REMASTER

QTE – Quick time events. These are button prompts during cutscenes that require the player to act quickly to succeed.

RAGEQUIT – Are you getting frustrated about losing the game? Ragequitting is when you angrily leave a game after losing over and over again.

REBOOT – The latest entry in a classic franchise that's been designed for new audiences with modern technology.

REMASTER – A beloved game that has been redesigned with new graphics, like *Uncharted: Legacy of Thieves Collection.*

RESPAWN – When you come back to life after being killed in a videogame, you will usually respawn at a checkpoint.

ROGUE-LIKE – A style of game inspired by the Rogue series where all progress is lost when you die and levels are randomly generated with turn-based gameplay.

ROGUE-LITE – A style of game that's similar to rogue-like, but not all progress is lost when you die and there isn't turn-based gameplay.

RPG – Role-play game. A story-based game with a focus on in-depth worlds and quests.

RTS – Real-time strategy. A genre of game where players make moves at the same time instead of taking turns.

SANDBOX – A style of game with a focus on building from scratch, like Minecraft.

SEASON PASS – Players pay a set amount per season, or sometimes per year, to get exclusive access to add-ons and content.

SHOOTER – A style of game where the main focus is using weapons to take out enemies.

SIDE-SCROLLER – When the view of a game's world is side-on and the screen moves from left to right. *Teenage Mutant Ninja Turtles: Shredder's Revenge* is a side-scroller.

SNES – Super Nintendo Entertainment System. A console from the 90s.

SOULS-LIKE – A style of action RPG with high difficulty, inspired by *Demon Souls.*

SPEED-RUN – Trying to complete a game in as short a time as possible.

STREAMING – Filming yourself while playing a game and publishing it online at the same time.

TROLLING – Saying insulting things online to purposefully cause arguments.

TURN-BASED STRATEGY – A genre of game where players take turn making moves.

TWITCH – A live-streaming platform that a lot of gamers use to create and publish content online.

VR – Virtual reality. A type of technology used with a headset that gives players a 360 gaming experience. See also AR.

XBO – Xbox.

XP – Experience points. Players earn these by winning fights or completing quests and actions. Gain more XP to reach higher character levels.

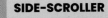

SIDE-SCROLLER

01

July - September

This quarter was packed full of big events, exciting eSports and new game releases, and we've got them all here for you. Check out fan-favourite adventures like *Psychonauts 2*, catch up on all the Gamescom teasers and learn absolutely everything there is to know about VR headsets in our handy guide!

GAMING HIGHLIGHT
Psychonauts 2
Page 22

NEWS FLASH

Get to Grips with Gamescom

The Ultimate Annual Gaming Show

Special Guest
As well as games journalist Geoff Keighley, *Saints Row* player character actor Bryce Charles (below right) joined in the announcements and introduced a trailer for the new game.

■ Welcome to the biggest games show in Europe! Gamescom teases the upcoming year and usually sees more than 350,000 gamers travel to Germany. 2021 was a little different though, due to the pandemic, and this year's show was entirely online. Over four days, games studios dropped dramatic announcements, previewed cool new tech, let players sample early versions of games and hyped up their new releases. Microsoft hosted its own Xbox Conference, while Sony featured in the show's Opening Night Live kick-off.

Horizon to Horizon

Sony snuck fresh *Horizon: Forbidden West* footage into Opening Night Live and Microsoft wowed audiences with the reveal of the *Forza Horizon 5* cover cars. They confirmed cloud gaming for Xbox Series X and S, with more than 100 titles coming to the service before 2022. The Xbox conference also showcased new videos of *Psychonauts 2, Microsoft Flight Simulator* and *Dying Light 2: Stay Human*, suggesting a bright future for the team in green.

The Numbers of Gamescom | **5.8 million** Viewers of the show's Opening Night Live event • **13 million** People who tuned into Gamescom • **180** Countries who watched Gamescom • **373,000** Attendees at the last in-person Gamescom show • **2009** The show's first year, replacing Germany's annual GC show in Leipzig • **255** Indie developers partnered with the show, along with 60 major companies.

Saints Row's Heavenly Unveiling

Gamescom always launches with a big first event: Opening Night Live. It sets the tone not just for the rest of the show, but the next twelve months in games. Video game journalist Geoff Keighley introduced hot new footage of *Halo Infinite* and *Call of Duty: Vanguard*. The reels for *Far Cry 6* and *Death Stranding: Director's Cut* were also huge draws for the millions watching online. The biggest announcement of all kicked off the evening: a reboot for *Saints Row*. The new game will relocate the *GTA*-rivalling series to a fictional American southwest city named Santo Eliso.

Gamescom's Big Winners

Each year a panel of judges hand out awards for the most exciting new titles previewed at Gamescom. Below are a selection of 2021's winners:

Best Xbox Game:
Halo Infinite

Best PlayStation Game:
Elden Ring

Best Action Game:
Far Cry 6

Best Sports Game:
Riders Republic

Best Strategy Game:
Age of Empires IV

Best Announcement:
Saints Row

The Legend of Zelda: Skyward Sword HD

Developer Nintendo **Publisher** Nintendo **Platform** NS

Stat Attack

One year after release, the remastered version has already sold over 3.6 million copies. Only seventy thousand fewer than the original sold in total!

Hyper Link

- Link was partially inspired by Peter Pan and first appeared in the 1986 NES release, *The Legend of Zelda*.
- The original *Skyward Sword* marked Nintendo's first ever use of a live orchestra in a video game.
- Zelda's harp tune 'Ballad Of The Goddess' is the same piece of music as 'Zelda's Lullaby' from *Ocarina of Time* – but played in reverse.

■ ***The Legend of Zelda*** **has been a fan-favourite franchise for decades. The original** ***Skyword Sword*** **first came out in 2011 and has been remastered with newer graphics. Remaking old classics is a trend that even Hollywood is taking part in, think** ***Dune*** **or** ***Ghostbusters*****. It's thanks to this that Nintendo decided to give the iconics game a second life for new players to enjoy.**

Nintendo Switch has a ton of gorgeous games but the remaster of *Skyward Sword* is one of their best. As well as amazing graphics, this remake has some gameplay updates that make all the difference. Its combat system beats the original, with the Joy-Con™ used to control blade swipes and whip snapping. Some long-standing fans found those Wii controls off-putting so there's now a right-stick option too. Three save files now replace the original single option and autosave is also included. If experienced players want an even harder challenge they can now avoid hints. Plus, the impatient will be happy – dialogue and cutscenes are now skippable.

These clever updates are perfect for the wonder that is *The Legend of Zelda*. The rerelease highlights all the best bits of the ten-year-old game and is sure to stay fresh for another decade.

Skyloft Conversion

Link's origin story, set on and below the floating islands of Skyloft, scored numerous Game of the Year awards upon its original Wii release in 2011. This Switch remaster delivers on the decade of hype and hope that followed it. More linear than previous Zelda games, your focus is on completing quests, puzzles and battles. Players travel across the three massive hubs of Faron Woods, Eldin Volcano and Lanayru Desert, and are steered by conversations with memorable characters like infatuated funnyman Groose and scrap-shop owner Gondo.

Skyward Sword *introduces lots of new creatures to the world of* Zelda. *How many can you find?*

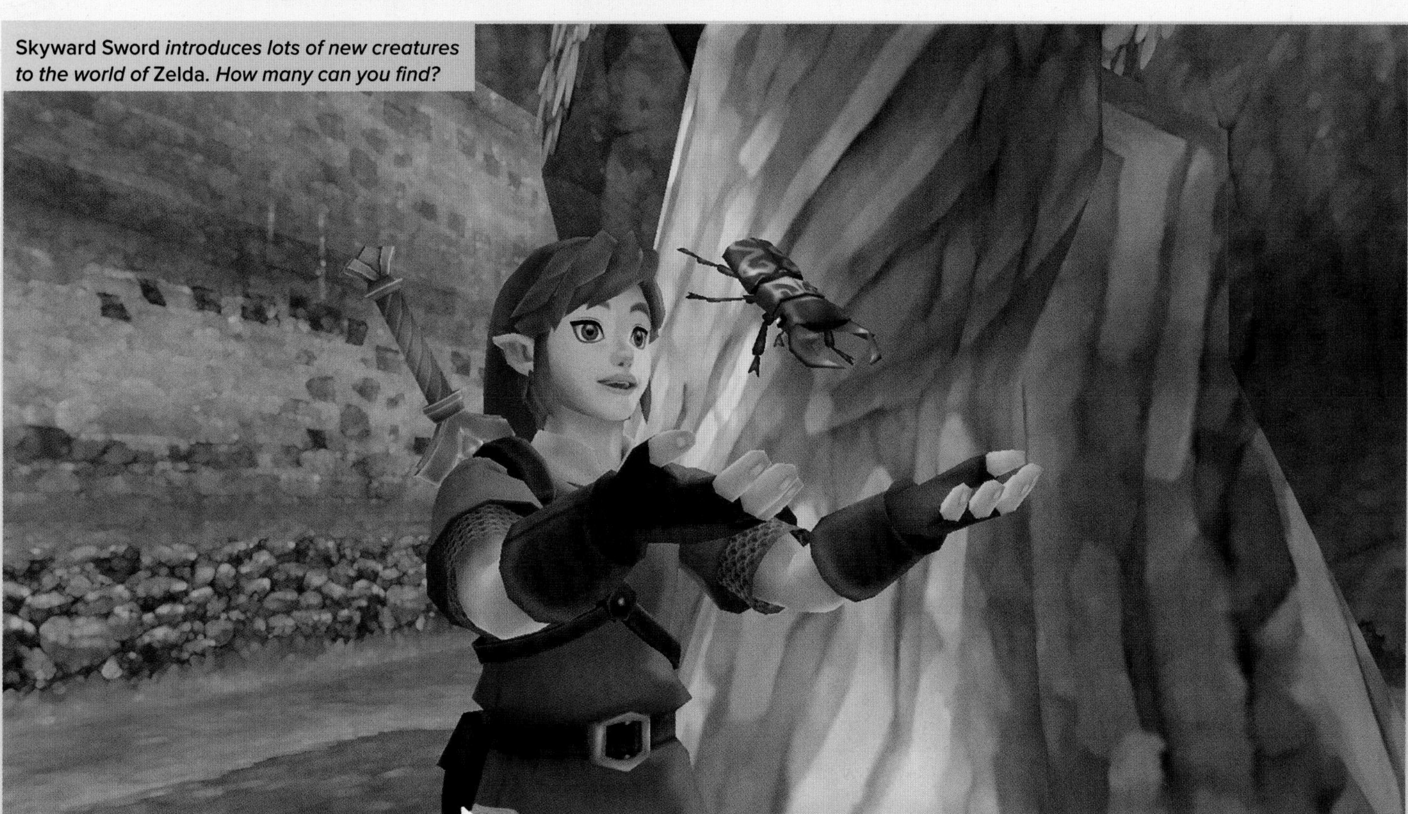

Link to the Fast

The new *Legend of Zelda: Skyward Sword HD* remake works with an Amiibo™ figure that grants in-game fast travel. It depicts Zelda cuddling up to a Loftwing and instantly moves Link from The Surface to The Sky (or vice versa) when tapped against a controller's NFC touchpoint. It's one of the best uses of Amiibo™ toys since they came out in 2014.

SWOOSH! Combat options, like sword fights, are improved with right-stick control.

Microsoft Flight Simulator

Developer Asobo Studio **Publisher** Xbox Game Studios
Platform MAC, PC, XBX/S

■ The king of aerial exploration has landed on Xbox! This latest version gives players the chance to fly anywhere on the planet. The game is great for experts, with all the take-off, landing and gawping-out-of-windows detail found in the incredible PC version. It also cleverly mixes in pre-set long-haul trips called Discovery Flights. These tailor-made experiences let you jump straight into touring Everest or cruising over Rio de Janeiro, and are a perfect intro for new pilots.

The game has a huge amount of different planes to fly, giving aerial experts a chance to try out something new.

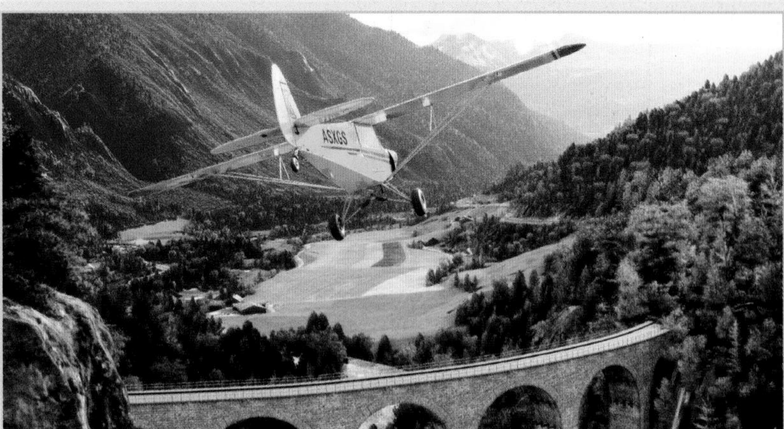

You'll spend a surprising amount of time staring out of the window at the beautiful real-world scenery. See how many famous landmarks you can spot!

Did You Know?
Microsoft Flight Simulator debuted on IBM PC in 1982, and you could fly a Cessna 182 over Chicago, LA, New York or Seattle.

DLC

There's a new story add on called **Life is Strange: True Colors Wavelengths** that focuses on side character Steph Gingrich. It's set between **True Colors** and **Before the Storm** and acts as an intro to Steph.

Life is Strange: True Colors

Developer Deck Nine **Publisher** Square Enix **Platform** NS, PC, PS4, PS5, XBO, XBX/S

■ All seems well for Alex Chen when she moves to a tranquil Colorado mining town after eight years in foster care. Then her brother Gabe is killed in a landslide, and investigating the accident falls on her. Each adventure in the *Life is Strange* series is built on one character having a special ability, and Alex's is superhuman empathy. Her ability enables her to read and change emotions causing characters to glow in different colours depending on how they are feeling. Talking to Alex's neighbours changes both story and scenery, as you're able to view the surrounding world as they see it.

Decisions of the Heart

The town of Haven Springs forms a believable backdrop for your wanderings, with a cute community vibe and small-town quirks: the local record shop doubles as a radio station. The game's personal nature also goes beyond Gabe's death as there are two characters you can choose to romance – one male, one female. You can also dress Alex in any of the twenty-four outfits that are unlocked, giving the game a more unique vibe. It's a bittersweet tale full of charm, depth and empathy, fronted by a character who's relatable despite her power.

Flying Colours

Erika Mori signed up for an adult acting class to break the monotony of her job as a management consultant and was cast as Alex Chen shortly after.

The lives of Ryan, Alex and Gabe are intricately linked, and through exploring Haven Springs, you're able to unpick those ties.

The game offers two romance storyline options. Will you choose to date Ryan or Steph?

Bustafellows

Developer Nippon Cultural Broadcasting Extend
Publisher PQube **Platform** ANDROID, IOS, NS, PC

■ Time-travelling, flirting and solving a mystery. *Bustafellows* has all three! The game fits into the Otome genre, a Japanese simulation where the story is uncovered by dating the other characters. You play as journalist Teura, who can pick between a crooked lawyer, hitman hunter, plastic surgeon, autopsy specialist and self-proclaimed underground boss to progress the story. Forging strong relationships is the key to stopping one of these new friends from dying. The animation is stunning, and setting a Japanese visual novel in an American city makes for a very cool blend of backgrounds.

Dating Rules

● Some voiced lines aren't subtitled but you can tap Y to access the full translation log.

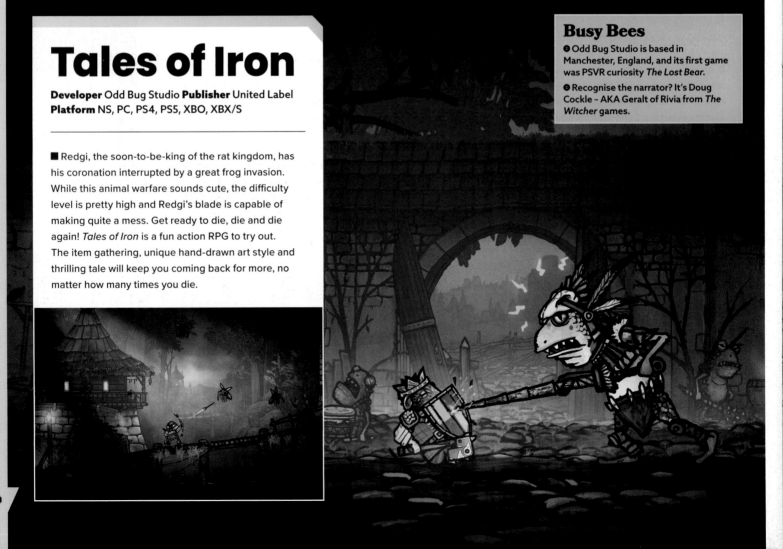

Tales of Iron

Developer Odd Bug Studio **Publisher** United Label
Platform NS, PC, PS4, PS5, XBO, XBX/S

■ Redgi, the soon-to-be-king of the rat kingdom, has his coronation interrupted by a great frog invasion. While this animal warfare sounds cute, the difficulty level is pretty high and Redgi's blade is capable of making quite a mess. Get ready to die, die and die again! *Tales of Iron* is a fun action RPG to try out. The item gathering, unique hand-drawn art style and thrilling tale will keep you coming back for more, no matter how many times you die.

Busy Bees

● Odd Bug Studio is based in Manchester, England, and its first game was PSVR curiosity *The Lost Bear*.

● Recognise the narrator? It's Doug Cockle – AKA Geralt of Rivia from *The Witcher* games.

Top Tip
Rayton's whip is well worth mastering – it's a great long-range weapon and can be charged-up in order to unleash rockets.

F.I.S.T.: Forged In Shadow Torch

Developer TiGames **Publisher** Bilibili **Platform** NS, PC, PS4, PS5

■ ***F.I.S.T.*** **is an exciting new sidescroller by Shanghai-based indie developer TiGames. There are a ton of studios releasing *Castlevania* and *Metroid* inspired games and *F.I.S.T.* beats many of them to the punch – and drill, and electrified whip.**

Those three weapons are a big part of *F.I.S.T.: Forged in Shadow Torch*. As well as thumping, player character Rayton's iron fist can be used to grab opponents who are blocking you before slinging them across the screen. Data disks are found on enemies and you earn upgrades. The upgrades are vital for frantic boss battles and make smashing goons all the more fun, too.

Temple of Boom

F.I.S.T.'s huge map is great for those new to gaming, with a marker pointing out where you need to go and stats that tell you how much of each area you've cleared. Levels vary from run-down streets to ancient temples. It makes for a fitting PS5 tribute to those 1980s classics.

Retro Genres

● Sub-genre *Metroidvania* is a mix of 1980s sidescrollers *Metroid* and *Castlevania*. Featuring huge, markable maps that hide secrets for higher levels.

Rayton goes up against enemies armed with high-tech limbs of their own – luckily the iron-clad bunny can take a punch.

BOOM! Rayton can use his three different weapons to blast through enemies' shields.

July-September

GAME SPOTLIGHT

Did You Know?

A platformer is a genre of game that's focused on movement. The player character needs to jump from level to level to collect rewards.

Hall Of Fame

The highlights of Tim Schafer's kitsch-yet-cool past:

MONKEY ISLAND 2: LECHUCK'S REVENGE (1991)

DAY OF THE TENTACLE (1993)

FULL THROTTLE (1995)

GRIM FANDANGO (1998)

PSYCHONAUTS (2005)

BRÜTAL LEGEND (2009)

STACKING (2011)

THE CAVE (2013)

Psychonauts 2

Developer Double Fine **Publisher** Xbox Game Studios **Platform** MAC, PC, PS4, XBO, XBX/S

■ Game designer Tim Schafer is a legend in the indie games world. He co-designed the 1990 classic *The Secret of Monkey Island* and became famous for mixing solid gameplay and kooky themes. *Psychonauts* is the perfect blend of both. It reinvented the traditional cartoon platformer by including psychic powers such as clairvoyance and levitation. The sequel, *Psychonauts 2* is just as creative.

Snake Charmer

As in the 2005 game, you play as Raz – a tiny acrobat who is shunned by his family because of his psychic abilities. Raz is fascinated by the nerdy Psychonauts espionage agency and the storyline unfolds with Raz entering the minds of other characters. He's hunting for the evil Maligula, who can command water serpents using hydrokinesis. The choices you make in conversations help to steer the storyline, while every environment varies wildly from the last, making for a fun and totally unpredictable game.

As well as those weird and wild stages, *Psychonauts 2* is packed with quirky characters and funny one-liners. Still need a reason to play? Then listen out for the voices of Hollywood stars Jack Black as Helmut Fullbear and Elijah Wood as Nick Johnsmith.

What's more unpredictable than a swarm of bees in a forest? Explore lots of interesting areas in Psychonauts 2.

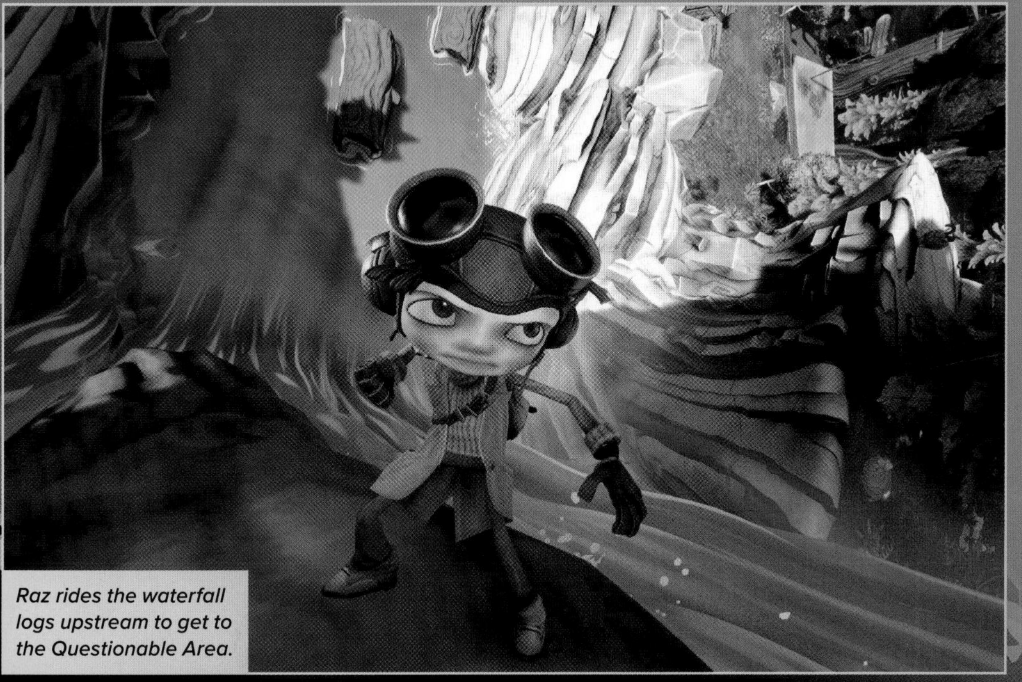

Raz rides the waterfall logs upstream to get to the Questionable Area.

Dinner with a Difference

Psychonauts 2 is a game full of unusual highlights. The best levels include PSI King's trippy, 1960s-style Sensorium and the jam-packed food-factory vibe of Compton's Cook Off. It's really funny, too. At one point Raz's friend Lili tells a theme-park worker that the duo are VIPs, only to be met with sarcasm: "Oh, does that stand for Vertically-Impaired Preteens?"

Cast List

Raz

This is Razputin Aquato's third *Psychonauts* game (including VR title *Rhombus of Ruin*). New powers include thought control and slowing time. He's one super-powered ten-year-old!

Donatella

Raz's mum played no part in the first game, but she has a big role in *Psychonauts 2*. As well as Raz, she has four other kids: Frazie, Mirtala, Queepie and Dion.

Dr Loboto

The original *Psychonauts'* insane dentist returns, still with odd-coloured eyes and dastardly motives. Ever heard the phrase 'madcap surgeon'? His crazy headwear is a play on the idea.

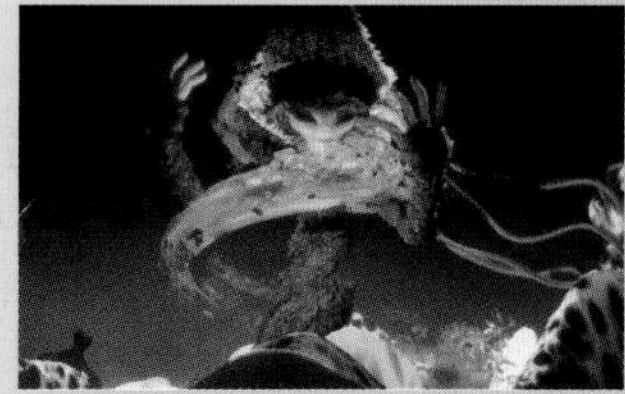

Maligula

Psychonauts 2's big boss packs five powers, including astral projection. Her name is likely inspired by third Roman emperor Caligula, who was just as power mad.

BACK TO REALITY

How Many Headsets?

There were a whopping **11.2 million headsets sold in 2021** and **8.7 million of those were by Meta**. That's the equivalent of everyone in Austria walking around with a Meta Quest 2 on their head.

PlayStation VR

TRENDS

Back to Reality

Check Out Our Guide to the Biggest Trends

■ Is there anything more futuristic than virtual reality headsets? There are now headsets for every type of gamer. Maybe you play on an app or through a console, there's something fun for everyone to try. On the more accessible end of the scale is Valve's HTC Vive, which emerged on PC a few months ahead of PSVR. Google Cardboard also offers a VR experience that works on most smartphones through a number of Android and iOS apps. Nintendo's family fun Labo Kit was released in 2019 and requires a Switch to play. While at the other end of the scale, there are expansive, fully immersive hardware sets, which offer gaming experiences that simply weren't possible ten years ago.

How it Started

A decade has already passed since a Kickstarter campaign for Oculus Rift raised $2.4 million – inspiring Meta (previously known as Facebook) to buy the entire company for $2 billion two years later. That inspired Sony to begin work on Project Morpheus, which would eventually be released as PSVR in 2016 and triggered a trend that continues to grow stronger.

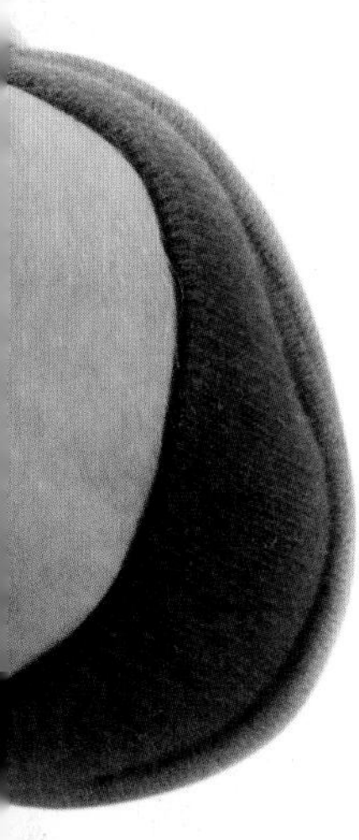

Oculus Rift Development Kit 2

BACK TO REALITY

Virtual Reality Round-Up

Don't know where to start? Take a look at some of the biggest virtual reality options that are in development:

HTC Vive Cosmos

Developer: HTC

The first thing to know about Vive is that you need a powerful computer to drive the pixels to your headset. The second is that there are a range of products. Cosmos – an affordable option – comes with motion controllers and feels good too, with foam-padded arches. Beat Saber and Elite Dangerous VR are among its must-plays.

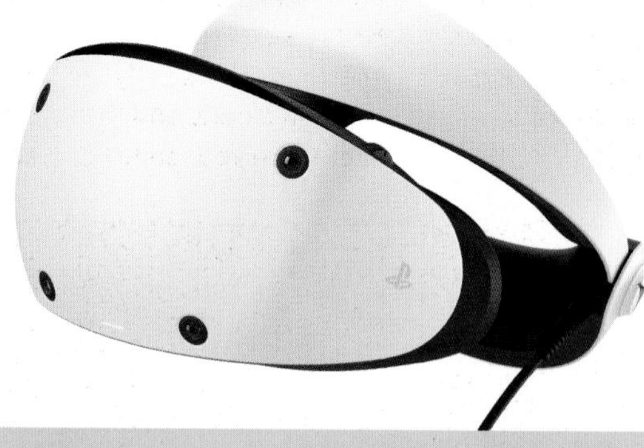

PSVR

Developer: Sony

Over the past year, we've seen Sony promise a ton of new virtual reality experiences with the PSVR 2 headset. *Hitman 3* now includes a murderous first-person sandbox and *Lone Echo II* lets players experience the zero-G atmosphere in an abandoned space station. But, you'll have to wait for the PSVR 2 for PS5 games that support next-gen VR play.

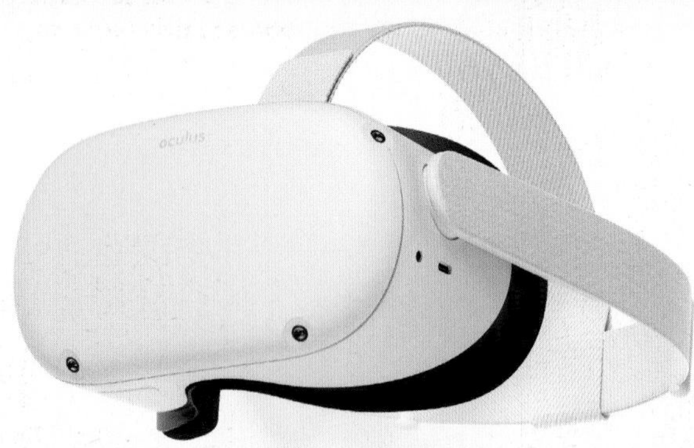

Oculus Quest 2

Developer: Meta Technologies

With Oculus Rift being phased out, Quest 2 is the main VR focus for Meta. Rift needed a PC to work but that's optional for Quest 2. It delivers everything using a headset, controllers and a smartphone app. The headset is light and adjustable with lots of accessories. *Resident Evil 4*, *I Expect You To Die 2* and *Totally Baseball* are some new titles.

Labo VR

Developer: Nintendo

Nintendo has created a very different type of virtual reality for new players looking to sample VR. Labo does the job in a very original way. You assemble sheets of cardboard into shapes, which then come to life onscreen. This build-your-own process is all part of Labo VR's curiously relaxing experience.

Five VR Games to Try

Hitman 3

Enjoy complete freedom from a first-person perspective. Assassinate foes with tricks both fresh and familiar. Most tasks, such as opening doors and grabbing items are done using button presses rather than your hands, but it's still a fun and immersive way of killing time – and targets.

Iron Man VR

While *Iron Man VR* isn't canon to the Marvel Cinematic Universe, it still lets you be Tony Stark for a few hours. Just without the option to spend all his millions on decking out your bedroom with gadgets. Put on the headset and throw punches, fire energy blasts, fly through clouds and customise your suit.

Lone Echo II

400 years in the future, you're an android on-board an abandoned space station. You must solve puzzles and avoid enemies by experimenting with the objects around you. It's brilliantly physical, almost everything in the environment is interactive – from wrist-mounted thrusters to an electric toothbrush.

Farpoint

Farpoint was the first game to use PSVR Aim, a gun-shaped controller specifically designed for shooters. It was released in 2017 and isn't the longest or deepest adventure. But the mechanics of alien encounters feel great, making for a straightforward VR starting game, despite its age.

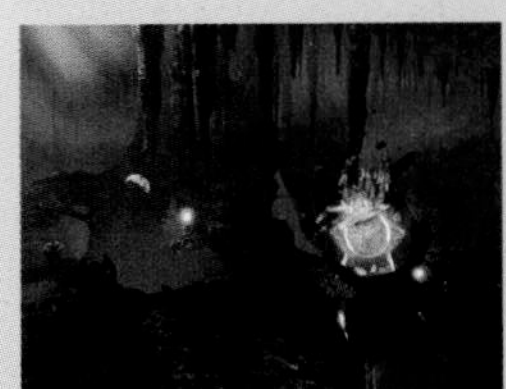

Beat Saber

Another oldie-but-goodie. It's a neon-themed rhythm movement game where you slash colour-coded blocks in time to the beat of songs. You use two motion controllers to slice in time with the music. There are also DLC additions that include music by Lady Gaga, Green Day and Imagine Dragons.

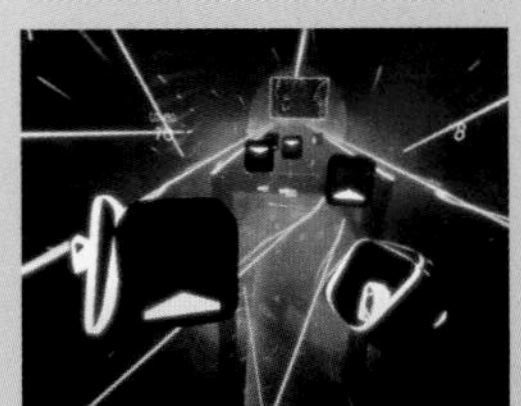

Take Your Time

For obvious reasons (muscle ache!), VR games tend to be quite short but there are a few long ones to try out, if you can stand up for that long. *Assetto Corsa VR*, *Fallout 4 VR* and *DiRT Rally VR* all take over seventy-five hours to fully complete.

STATE OF PLAY

Heroes of the Year

Gaming's Biggest Superstars

Link

Game Legend of Zelda: Skyward Sword HD
First Appearance The Legend of Zelda
Occupation Adventurer Knight
Height 164 cm **Age** 17 (approx)
Hair Colour Light Brown **Eye Colour** Blue
Home Skyloft **Voiced by** Takashi Ōhara

Nintendo's iconic RPG hero has been assorted heights and ages since his 1986 introduction, but *Skyward Sword* is based on his teenage years. As for Link's abilities, where do you begin? He survives being struck by lightning, wields swords two times his size, uses bombs to destroy solidified magma and defeats monsters and demons for a day job. What a guy.

Colt Vahn

Game Deathloop **First Appearance** Deathloop **Occupation** Assassin
Height 170 cm (approx) **Age** 45 (approx) **Hair Colour** Black
Eye Colour Brown **Home** The Motherland **Voiced by** Jason E. Kelly

Deathloop's hero is deadly with a range of weapons. Colt's reprise skill also lets him resurrect twice before the super shooter's time-loop resets. The assassin can use abilities, AKA slabs, owned by the targets he's hunting down across Blackreef. He's so cool that there are already strong rumours of a *Deathloop* sequel or prequel.

Kena

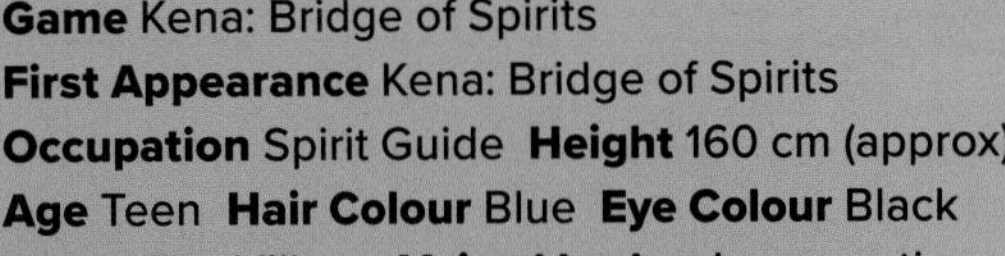

Game Kena: Bridge of Spirits
First Appearance Kena: Bridge of Spirits
Occupation Spirit Guide **Height** 160 cm (approx)
Age Teen **Hair Colour** Blue **Eye Colour** Black
Home The Village **Voiced by** Ayu Larassanti

Bridge of Spirits' lead character has plenty of skill at her disposal. In addition to steering souls to the afterlife. Kena's dexterity with a staff unleashes a delightful array of attacks. Her pulse ability acts as a shield when on defence. She can also command cute-yet-deadly spirit critters called the Rot to move objects or distract enemies.

Island in the Sky

The inspriation for iconic location Skyloft was based on Mont Saint-Michel, a small island off the coast of Normandy, in France.

Aloy

Game Horizon Forbidden West
First Appearance Horizon Zero Dawn
Occupation Machine Hunter
Height 168 cm
Age 20 (approx)
Hair Colour Red
Eye Colour Green
Home The Embrace
Voiced by Ashly Burch

Horizon's machine-smashing main character is based on a range of awesome heroes. We're talking Ygritte from *Game of Thrones*, Sarah Connor from *Terminator* and *Alien*'s Ellen Ripley. The ginger arrow-slinger is an incredibly skilled warrior and hunter, and her newest outing is simply unmissable.

Ghost of Tsushima: Director's Cut

Developer Sucker Punch Productions **Publisher** Sony **Platform** PS4, PS5

Did You Know?
A movie adaption is on the way, by *John Wick* director Chad Stahelski.

■ **Jin Sakai is a samurai trying to take back the island of Iki from a Mongol invasion. On this quest, players can roam around on foot or horseback, wielding a katana, bow and grappling hook. *Ghost of Tsushima* is a beautifully designed game, making exploration just as addictive as combat.**

The PS5 director's cut edition looks incredible in 4K and running at 60 FPS. There are other upgrades for the next-gen consoles too. Adaptive triggers mean you feel the tension in holding L2 and R2 to draw back your bow. Plus, the DualSense™ controllers add different vibrations or pulses for a variety of movements, like travelling on horseback. There's also a new horse charge ability that's fun to try out, letting players plough through waves of enemies in a simple, slo-mo blur.

This Charming Man

Like the original PS4 edition, Sakai's journey around Iki remains fight-focused with most missions ending in fisticuffs. Or rather, swordicuffs. Iki gives players a huge choice in side quests, which award charms that can be used to improve combat and stealth abilities. Plus weapons can be upgraded at merchant shops found around the island.

DLC
The multiplayer pack **Ghosts of Tsushima Legends** is free if you already own the game. It adds a new map, Blood and Steel, where players can team up with four real-life friends to take on Oni invaders.

Jin and Bear It

The action in the Director's Cut has switched from Tsushima to Iki and there are also two new Mythic Tales. The Tale of Black Hand Riki concerns a mad pirate who has stolen Jin's cursed sarugami armour. While The Legacy of Kazumasa Sakai lets players dig into Jin's relationship with his father through playable memories. No spoilers! But it's a real highlight to the story.

Jin Sakai's journey across Iki provides chance upon chance to develop your sword skills.

Dramatic encounters with Sakai's past give the additional stories depth and intrigue.

Exploring the island of Iki is a delight and a huge bonus to the Director's Cut.

The History of Sucker Punch

Rocket: Robot on Wheels
The Washington-based studio landed on Nintendo 64 in 1999 with this platformer, where players solved puzzles using realistic physics.

Sly Cooper
A third-person platformer that wowed PS2 gamers in 2002 with its stealthy one-hit kills. It was followed by two equally beloved sequels.

inFamous
In 2009, players were given electrical powers and set loose on an open world. You could then choose whether to be good or evil. The games were so successful on PS3 that Sony bought the studio. The series spawned five games in total.

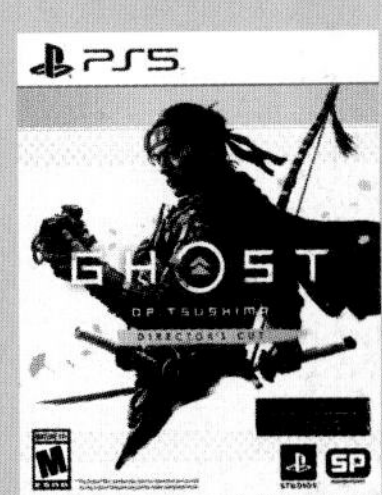

Ghost Of Tsushima
Medieval sandbox inspired by classic Japanese cinema, such as *Seven Samurai* and *Sanjuro*. Tsushima is the name of the game's stunning island setting.

Did You Know?
Despite being made by a two-person team, 100,000 people played *Death's Door* in its first week after release.

Death's Door

Developer Acid Nerve **Publisher** Devolver Digital
Platform NS, PC, PS4, PS5, XBO, XBX/S

■ Explore a charming cemetery and collect the souls of the dead as a bounty hunter crow. *Death's Door* is a moody adventure game starring cute, Ghibli-style characters. You'll need fast fingers! Combat is swift but requires skill too – you're often dealing with unexpected hazards (like disappearing floor tiles) at the same time as fighting off an unusual collection of twisted foes. Acid Nerve crafted *Death's Door* in the image of *Legend of Zelda* and as a result, unlockable items uncover fresh secrets in previously played levels. The gothic setting is balanced by touching moments of hope and humour.

Get ready for some weird and wacky bad guys to fight! A yeti, a witch with a pot on her head and a giant fighting frog are just a few.

There's a super quirky world to explore, filled with colourful details and even more colourful characters. Like Pothead, the man cursed with a pot for a head.

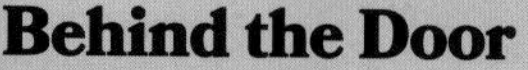

Behind the Door

● Publisher Devolver Digital are a US-based team focused on indie games such as upcoming rogue-like *Wizard with a Gun*.

Fuga: Melodies of Steel

Developer CyberConnect2 **Publisher** CyberConnect2
Platform NS, PC, PS4, PS5, XBO, XBX/S

■ When the peaceful village of Petit Mona is attacked by enemies, twelve kids in a giant tank called The Taranis are its only defenders. *Fuga* is a turn-based strategy RPG and a prequel to PS1's *Tail Concerto* (1998) and *Solatorobo*, which hit Nintendo DS in 2011. The game tasks you with picking which child controls each gun turret – the tank has three to choose from. Along the way, you'll learn and master skills, uncovering mysteries about their new mobile home. Imagine exploring a steampunk take on WW2-era France, where battles are broken up by conversations between a likeable band of childish animal heroes.

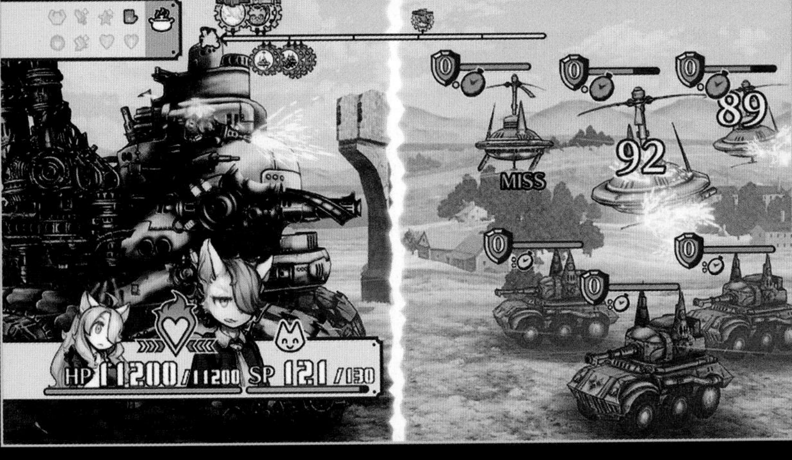

Deadly but Dark

The Taranis' main weapon is the destructive Soul Cannon – but using it means choosing a child to sacrifice. Noooo!

Eldest Souls

Developer Fallen Flag Studio **Publisher** United Label
Platform NS, PC, PS4, PS5, XBO, XBX/S

■ Mankind is stuck in an ancient war against the Old Gods and only one warrior and his giant sword stands against them. *Eldest Souls* is a classic souls-like game, featuring relentless combat and a monstrous difficulty curve. There are ten bosses to take down and each one requires multiple attempts to conquer them. As players try and try again, they learn their enemies' moves and need to change their approach to emerge victorious. If ten bosses sounds like a low number, rest assured that even experienced players clock in at around fifteen hours to complete the game.

Check Out

The souls-like genre is relatively new, and inspired by the death-focused Demon's Souls *(2009) and* Dark Souls *(2011).*

Did You Know?
This is the first ever *Sims* game to feature llamas as a functioning animal.

The Sims 4: Cottage Living

Developer Maxis **Publisher** EA
Platform MAC, PC, PS4, PS5, XBO, XBX/S

■ Nearly a decade after its original release, *The Sims 4* just keeps growing. *Cottage Living* is the first expansion pack to land on PS5 and Xbox Series X. It drops you into the fictional yet cosy English village of Henford-on-Bagley. Players can show off their prize cow at the Finchwick Fair, chat with locals in the Gnome's Arms, grow their own produce and befriend nearby animals – just beware of fiendish foxes with an eye on the chicken coop. Another brilliant addition to the huge real-life sim.

eFootball 2022

Developer Konami **Publisher** Konami
Platform ANDROID, IOS, PC, PS4, PS5, XBO, XBX/S

■ For twenty years, *Pro Evolution Soccer* fell short of the rival football sim *FIFA*. Game studio Konami finally retired the series following *PES 2020* to try something new. Its successor, *eFootball 2022*, is the first major free-to-play football sim in console history. There will be new seasonal updates every Autumn, instead of a completely new game to download. It's had a tricky start, so let's hope to see some classic *PES* features return in 2023.

Still in the Game
The game traces its history before *PES*, right back to 1995 kick-about *Goal Storm* on PS1.

DLC

Pick between two DLC packs. The **Music Pack** features three exclusive original game remixes. The **Cosmetic Pack** includes new clothing, icons and boosts for our blue hero.

Sonic Colours Ultimate

Developer Blind Squirrel Games **Publisher** Sega
Platform NS, PC, PS4, WII, XBO

■ Hedgehog, blue body, white hands, red sneakers ... it's gotta be the Fastest Thing Alive! In *Sonic Colours Ultimate*, the main gameplay is pretty true to the original 2010 release. You race through 3D levels set across an intergalactic theme park, freeing alien-like Wisps from old foe Dr Eggman. There are also new powers, modes and graphics – 4K resolution and 60FPS. The sharpened character design and background art is a delight to play through. It's bright, colourful and rapid to the point of breathlessness, with some levels lasting a minute or less. There's also no way for Sonic to die, which make this a great option for newer gamers.

Each Wisp has their own power and the Cyan Wisp allows Sonic to transform into the Cyan Laser.

There are a ton of bizarre zones to zoom through in the game, like the Sweet Mountain.

Did You Know?

Sonic was very nearly an armadillo – and the rejected mascot eventually entered his series as Mighty the Armadillo.

F1 2021

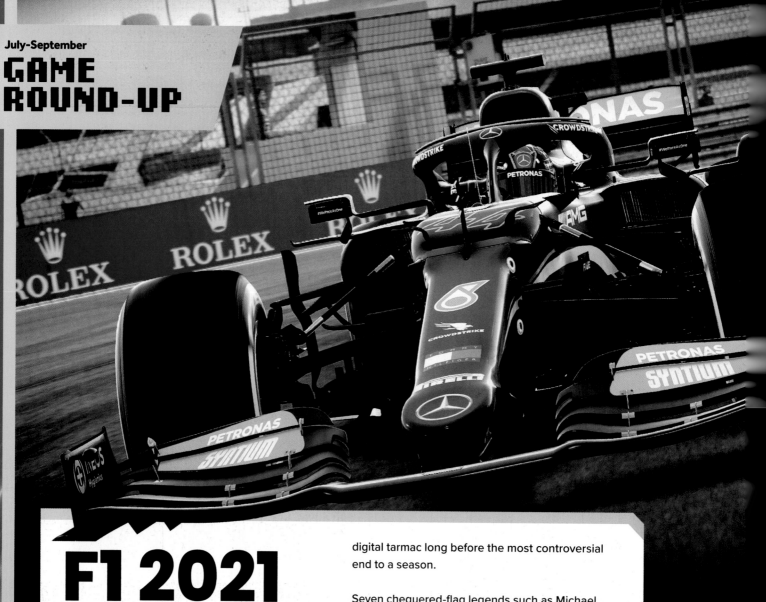

Developer Codemasters **Publisher** EA
Platform PC, PS4, PS5, XBO, XBX/S

■ *F1 2021* is speeding ahead of real-life racing, giving players the chance to race in the four events that were cancelled in the F1 season: Marina Bay, Melbourne, Montreal and Suzuka.

F1 2021 has been letting players pit Lewis Hamilton and Max Verstappen against one another on the digital tarmac long before the most controversial end to a season.

Seven chequered-flag legends such as Michael Schumacher, Ayrton Senna and Lewis Hamilton are also selectable in MyTeam. This is where you're able to hire drivers, choose sponsors and try to beat the big guns in winning world titles. Just pick your team name carefully, as it can't be edited later.

Jump-start Your Career

Long-standing F1 fans aren't left behind. Career mode now enables two people to play, either as teammates or rivals, with customisation options covering your driver's look, helmet, number and even their podium celebration.

Ready, Set, Go!

❶ Recognise the tannoy voices? Several of the announcements are voiced by Podcaster Chris Scullion from Tired Old Hack and YouTuber Chain Bear F1.

Feel the need for speed in this intense cockpit view. The race track will zoom past you in a blur of colour.

Watch real-life racers like Charles Leclerc speed their way up the leader boards in the fastest cars.

An Awkward Friendship

A fascinating new addition is Braking Point story mode. It's set across the 2019, 2020 and 2021 campaigns. You start out as an aspiring British F2 star, Aiden Jackson, who secures a Formula One contract, only to bump Dutch teammate Casper Akkerman during their first race. Braking Point lets you play as both drivers.

That drama spurs the mode along across the next two seasons and seventeen chapters. Enjoy Netflix show *Formula 1: Drive to Survive?* Then you're going to love this too.

Check Out

Fancy yourself as the next Christian Horner or Toto Wolff? *F1 Manager 2022* gives players the chance to lead their own F1 team.

The infamous French Grand Prix is just one of the many real-life competitions you get to race through.

Aston Martin driver Sebastian Vettel finished the season tied in third place with Valtteri Bottas in the live driver ratings.

Top Eight

F1 2021 features live driver ratings – here's how the elite finished the season.

LEWIS HAMILTON: 94

MAX VERSTAPPEN: 93

VALTTERI BOTTAS: 90

SEBASTIAN VETTEL: 90

FERNANDO ALONSO: 89

CHARLES LECLERC: 89

LANDO NORRIS: 89

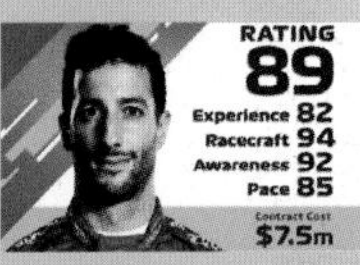

DANIEL RICCIARDO: 89

Sweet Sweet Fantasy

Celebrate Over Three Decades of Final Fantasy

It's been a super busy time for *Final Fantasy* fans. *Final Fantasy XIV* had a spectacular ending with the *Endwalker* expansion pack. Then *Final Fantasy VII Remake Intergrade* dropped on PS5. Plus, *Stranger of Paradise: Final Fantasy Origin* had an alternate universe retelling of the very first game from 1987.

If you think those games are exciting, the *Final Fantasy Pixel Remaster* series has also been released. Square Enix, the publisher of the games, dropped the first six *Final Fantasy* titles onto Steam with updated pixel graphics, fresh audio, quick saves and the ability to move diagonally.

Delicious Sprites

Staying true to the original was a priority. Artist Kazuko Shibuya returned to redraw every character sprite in HD. The studio also brought back composer Nobuo Uematsu to make new arrangements for the unmistakable background music. Some tweaks occurred but no changes were made to the now-legendary stories.

The six games form a huge slice of gaming history, with lots of landmark moments to look out for. Chocobos first appear in *Final Fantasy II*, as does fan-favourite recurring character Cid. They're all must-plays if you own a PC and love RPGs.

Pixel Art!

Kazuko Shibuya worked on *Final Fantasy* artwork from the very first game in 1987, including the famous opening screen. This makes her one of the most prolific female game designers in the world!

Know Your Pixel Remasters

A brief history of the first six Final Fantasy games ...

FINAL FANTASY I

The very first *Final Fantasy* arrived on Nintendo Entertainment System (NES) in 1997. A team called the Warriors of Light seeks to restore light to four elemental crystals and save the world by overcoming four Elemental Fiends. It's one of the most influential series ever made and has been the inspiration for hundreds of games.

FINAL FANTASY II

A new band of four comes together to ward off evil. The first sequel introduced Firion, Maria, Guy and Leon. *Final Fantasy II* arrived on Japanese computers in 1988. It wasn't available for the rest of the world to play until PlayStation remade the game in 2003.

FINAL FANTASY III

Another team work to take down the Cloud of Darkness and its evil wizard Xande. *Final Fantasy III* brought the Job system to the series. Japan got to experience it in 1990, but everyone else had to wait. Nintendo DS created a port for players to plug into their consoles in 2006.

This Year's Final Fantasy

Page 99

Final Fantasy VII Remake Intergrade

Page 148

Final Fantasy XIV: Endwalker

Page 190

Stranger of Paradise: Final Fantasy Origin

FINAL FANTASY IV

The series' famous Active Time Battle system arrives, which changed the future of gaming. Dark knight Cecil and a bunch of allies seek to stop crystal-chasing sorcerer Golbez. This Super NES game did make it to America, where it was confusingly renamed *Final Fantasy II*.

FINAL FANTASY V

Your party is led by an adventurer named Bartz and the recurring character Gilgamesh becomes a henchman of Exdeath. *Final Fantasy V* hit Japan's Super Famicom in 1992. It took another seven years for the game to become available outside of Japan.

FINAL FANTASY VI

The *Final Fantasy* series grows up and introduces mature topics in this new release, such as a magical arms race. There's also now an exciting steampunk theme. Gamers can choose between fourteen permanent playable characters – all customisable with weapons, armour and Relics.

Trivia

● The soundtrack to *NBA 2K22* changed throughout the real-life season. Every week the First Fridays feature added new tracks from an eclectic mix of artists including hip-hop, pop, rock and more. Beenie Man, Lil Nas X, Thundercat and Drake are among the names on its track list.

HEAD TO HEAD

NBA 2K22

Developer Visual Concepts **Publisher** 2K Games
Platform MAC, NS, PC, PS4, PS5, XBO, XBX/S

Background I *NBA 2K22* is a slam dunk. It's such a strong game that rival *NBA Live* stopped releasing new games four years ago. This is the basketball giant's 23rd edition. It first came out on the Dreamcast console in November 2000. Back then it featured Allen Iverson on the cover and was owned by Sega, rather than 2K.

Features I MyTeam is *NBA 2K22*'s card-collecting, team-building mode. MyNBA delivers the best career mode around, with a crazy amount of detail – right down to choosing a sports scientist and sleep doctor. MyCareer has a quest-based story for your created player. The W, the expanded WNBA option in MyCareer, is a big step forward for sports games.

Gameplay I *NBA 2K22* looks incredible. So much detail has gone into player faces, tattoos and sweat mechanics. Yes, we said sweat mechanics! It plays fantastically too, with a real focus on believable dribbling and passing. Good defence requires you to know your b-ball, so it's worth brushing up on the rules.

There's nothing like landing a basket after an intense round of blocking from the other side's defence.

Player faces are so detailed in NBA 2K22*, this could almost be a photo from a real-life game. See your team mates react to missing a pass or winning a point.*

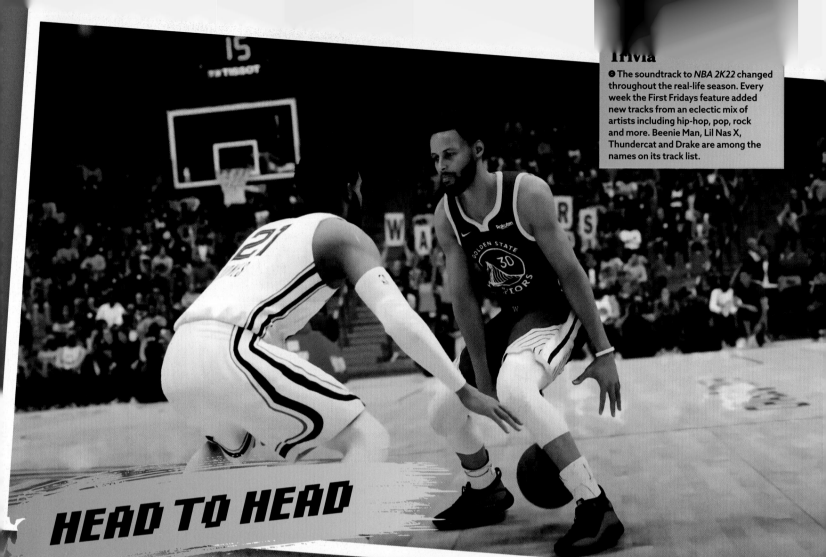

Madden NFL 22

Developer EA Tiburon **Publisher** EA Sports **Platform** PC, PS4, PS5, XBO, XBX/S

Background | EA's huge American Football series has been around since 1988 and has sold more than 130 million copies. It takes its name from the legendary former coach and commentator John Madden, who was involved in its development.

Features | *Madden NFL 22* focuses on Ultimate Team, where players build a fantasy line-up from digital cards, then lead it into action. Face of the Franchise provides the chance to experience the NFL as a rookie. Superstar KO is a co-operative eliminator mode with crazy rules. Want a full management career? Try Franchise Mode.

Gameplay | *Madden*'s Gridiron is faster than the real thing. Online matches often escalate into quarterbacks throwing the length of the field. Its best feature is Superstar X-Factors. Skills are given to star players to separate them from the competition – so triggering Patrick Mahomes' 'Bazooka' enables him to sling the ball eighty-three yards.

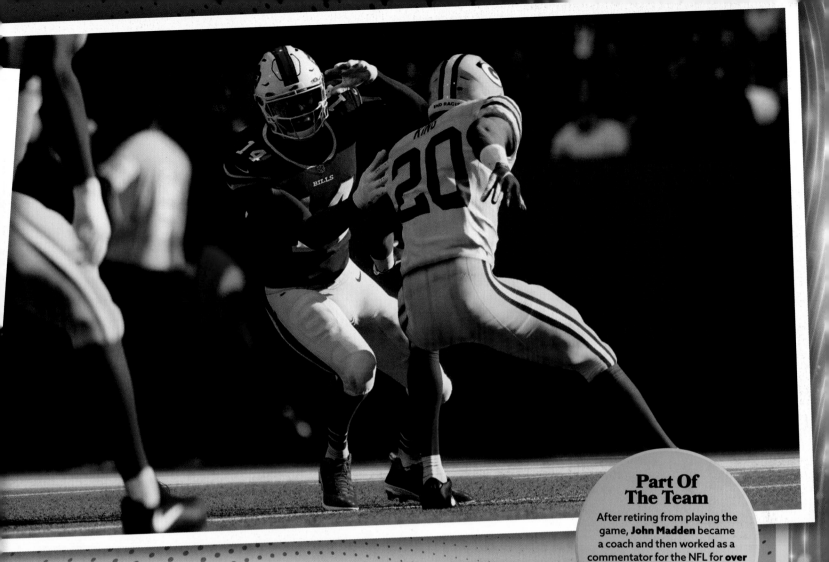

Part Of The Team

After retiring from playing the game, **John Madden** became a coach and then worked as a commentator for the NFL for **over forty years**. He gave his voice and expertise to *Madden NFL* right from the very beginning.

Trivia

This is the first *Madden* game to include home field advantage, where playing in your own stadium gives you special bonuses and visiting teams have handicaps. When you play in Buffalo, the away team struggles to control its kicks, and in Seattle, the fans turn into squiggly lines to represent noise from the home crowd's '12th Man'.

Get ready to play with the best of the best that the NFL has to offer.

The playing fields in Madden NFL 22 *have a ton of true-to-life additions, like chants from the crowds and cameramen.*

THE INSIDER TAKE

Developers Share Highlights from a Memorable Year

Lauren Scott
Senior Systems Designer on Psychonauts 2

What's the best thing you played in the last year?
I'm tempted to say *Elden Ring*, but I also got into a pretty deep stint of *RimWorld*. That game really sucks you in. As a systems designer, it presses all the right buttons.

What element of Psychonauts 2 are you most proud of?
The upgrade system. It was a solution to a tough design problem, and we had the courage to build it late in development. It represents a proud team moment, working together to make the game as good as it was meant to be.

What game are you most looking forward to?
I have always been a *Final Fantasy* fan, so I have my fingers crossed that *FFXVI* will ship within the next year!

Domenico Celenza
Producer on Hot Wheels Unleashed

What's the best thing you played in the last year?
I have a huge backlog, so I'll go with a not-so-recent game: *Inscryption*. I really liked the atmosphere, meta-story and plot twists.

What element of Hot Wheels Unleashed are you most proud of?
How we managed to create a proper *Hot Wheels* game, not a generic arcade racer. I like to think that the whole video game is a representation of what we were imagining as kids while playing with our beloved orange tracks.

What game are you most looking forward to?
Return to Monkey Island. I have good memories of playing the original games as a kid. When the nostalgia kicks so hard, you cannot avoid the hype.

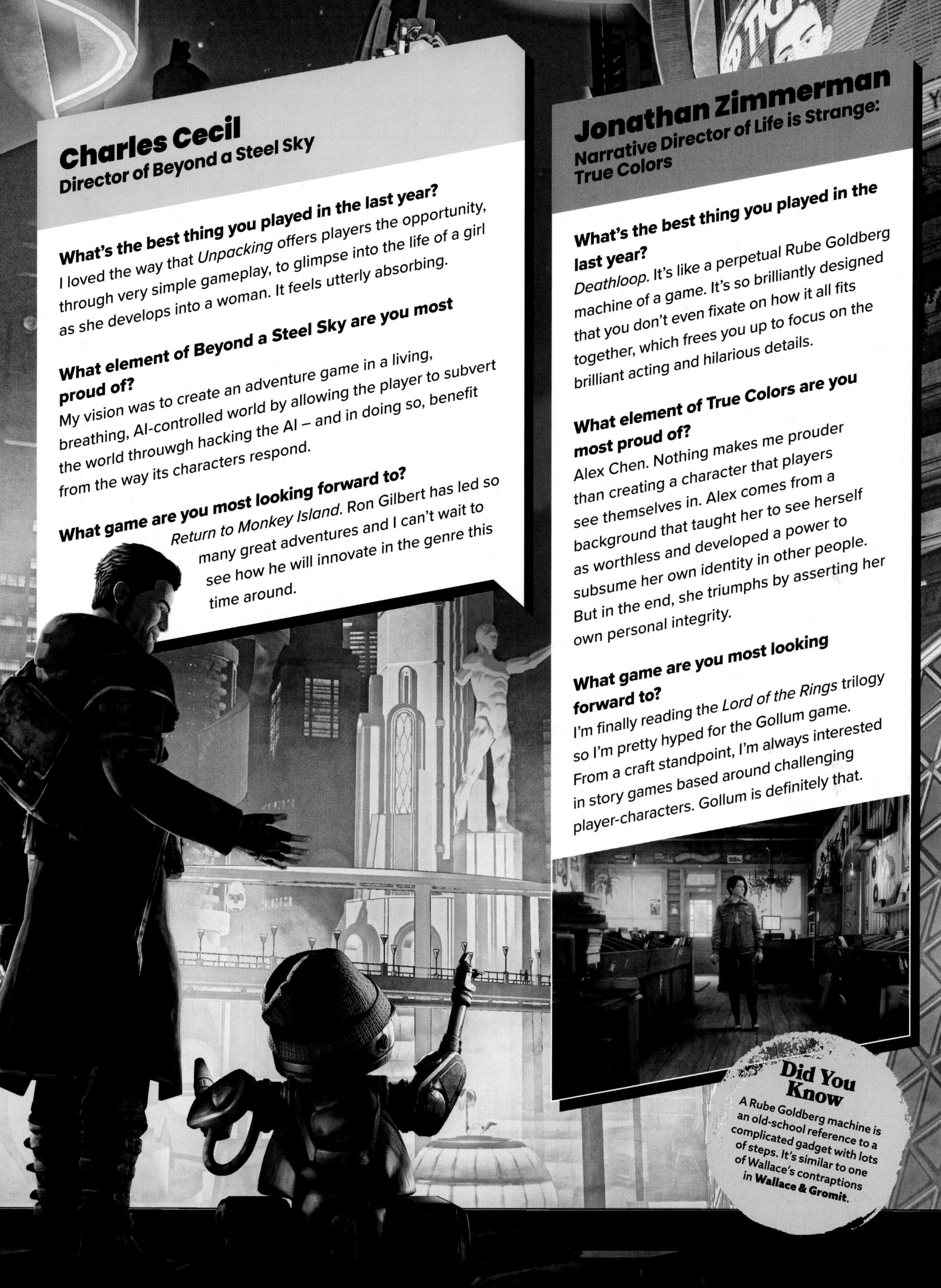

Charles Cecil
Director of Beyond a Steel Sky

What's the best thing you played in the last year?
I loved the way that *Unpacking* offers players the opportunity, through very simple gameplay, to glimpse into the life of a girl as she develops into a woman. It feels utterly absorbing.

What element of Beyond a Steel Sky are you most proud of?
My vision was to create an adventure game in a living, breathing, AI-controlled world by allowing the player to subvert the world throuwgh hacking the AI – and in doing so, benefit from the way its characters respond.

What game are you most looking forward to?
Return to Monkey Island. Ron Gilbert has led so many great adventures and I can't wait to see how he will innovate in the genre this time around.

Jonathan Zimmerman
Narrative Director of Life is Strange: True Colors

What's the best thing you played in the last year?
Deathloop. It's like a perpetual Rube Goldberg machine of a game. It's so brilliantly designed that you don't even fixate on how it all fits together, which frees you up to focus on the brilliant acting and hilarious details.

What element of True Colors are you most proud of?
Alex Chen. Nothing makes me prouder than creating a character that players see themselves in. Alex comes from a background that taught her to see herself as worthless and developed a power to subsume her own identity in other people. But in the end, she triumphs by asserting her own personal integrity.

What game are you most looking forward to?
I'm finally reading the *Lord of the Rings* trilogy so I'm pretty hyped for the Gollum game. From a craft standpoint, I'm always interested in story games based around challenging player-characters. Gollum is definitely that.

Did You Know
A Rube Goldberg machine is an old-school reference to a complicated gadget with lots of steps. It's similar to one of Wallace's contraptions in **Wallace & Gromit**.

Tales of Arise

Developer Bandai Namco **Publisher** Bandai Namco
Platform PC, PS4, PS5, XBO, XBX/S

■ Bandai Namco has built this long-running fantasy series around a huge cast of playable characters and six are on tap in *Tales of Arise*. The main character is Alphen, who wears an iron-mask and has a case of amnesia. Alphen's packing a Blazing Sword, a furious temper and isn't able to feel pain.

Crawl or Nothing

Tales of Arise follows the enslaved Dahnan race learning to fight back against their oppressors. The Renas have been in control for three centuries and believe themselves god-like. This serious theme makes for a serious game, which is split into two halves. The first half is focused on finding the team, posing questions and working out which characters work best together by taking out enemies. The second half mixes in answers, twists and an extended dungeon crawl.

Tales of Arise keeps you hooked to the end in order to wrap up every story. The ending – no spoilers! – is a great pay off. There's no wonder Bandai Namco have been publishing this game series for over two decades! JRPG fans will want to make sure their party is as levelled up as possible for the final challenge.

DLC

There are over twenty different DLC packs for **Tales of Arise**. Pick out new themed costumes, buy extra Hootle Dolls, level up, discover adventuring artifacts and tons more!

Six of the Best

Alphen is the main man in *Tales of Arise*, but the entire party of six adds their own unique combat skills. Rifle-wielding Shionne is a deadly shot from distance, martial-artist Law's melee skills are irreplaceable in close quarters and mother-figure Kisara dishes out heavy attacks with a shield. While Rinwell's use of Astral Artes mean she's a valuable long-range fighter, and Dohalim – the party's only Renan – has some strong healing spells.

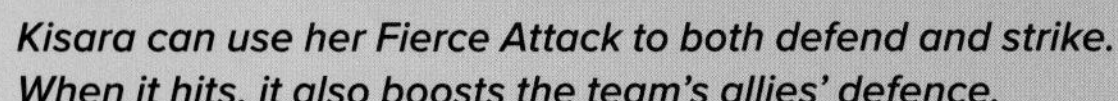

Kisara can use her Fierce Attack to both defend and strike. When it hits, it also boosts the team's allies' defence.

Must-use Perks

Flaming Edge

Alphen can unleash a furious, screen-clearing attack with his Blazing Sword. It doesn't cost any Artes Gauge but he will pay the price in HP.

Sniper Blast

Shionne is explosive. Hold down the button to throw a bomb and she slings extra ammo after releasing it, making the blast even more forceful.

Magic Charging

While controlling Rinwell, press and hold the Artes button to delay and charge your magic attack. It will make it even more powerful once you let go.

Rod Extension

Perfect-evade an enemy attack with Dohalim and his senses become heightened. He can then attack with greater range and land more critical hits.

The Forgotten City

Developer Modern Storyteller **Publisher** Dear Villagers
Platform NS, PC, PS4, PS5, XBO, XBX/S

■ *The Forgotten City* takes place in a small town within the Roman Empire where villagers are controlled by this rule: "The many shall suffer for the sins of the one." Should you or any other citizen commit a crime, beautiful gold statues come to life and freeze everyone. The aim is to uncover where this golden rule came from. Players can go back in time to explore, solve puzzles and win fights. Just don't get caught!

When in Rome

The Forgotten City was initially a mod for *The Elder Scrolls V: Skyrim*. It became so popular that writer Nick Pearce quit his day job to turn it into a full game. It's set in a super detailed recreation of ancient Italy and one of the main joys is simply gawping at architecture or chatting to townsfolk. Doing so throws up moral challenges, like deciding if you should meddle with time to save lives. There are funny moments too, try introducing yourself to characters who don't recognise you for the third, fourth time or fifth time.

Stat Attack

The original *Skyrim* mod notched three million downloads and a Writers' Guild Award in Nick Pearce's homeland of Australia.

Did You Know?

A mod – short for modification – is an extra piece of tech created by players to alter how a game looks or plays.

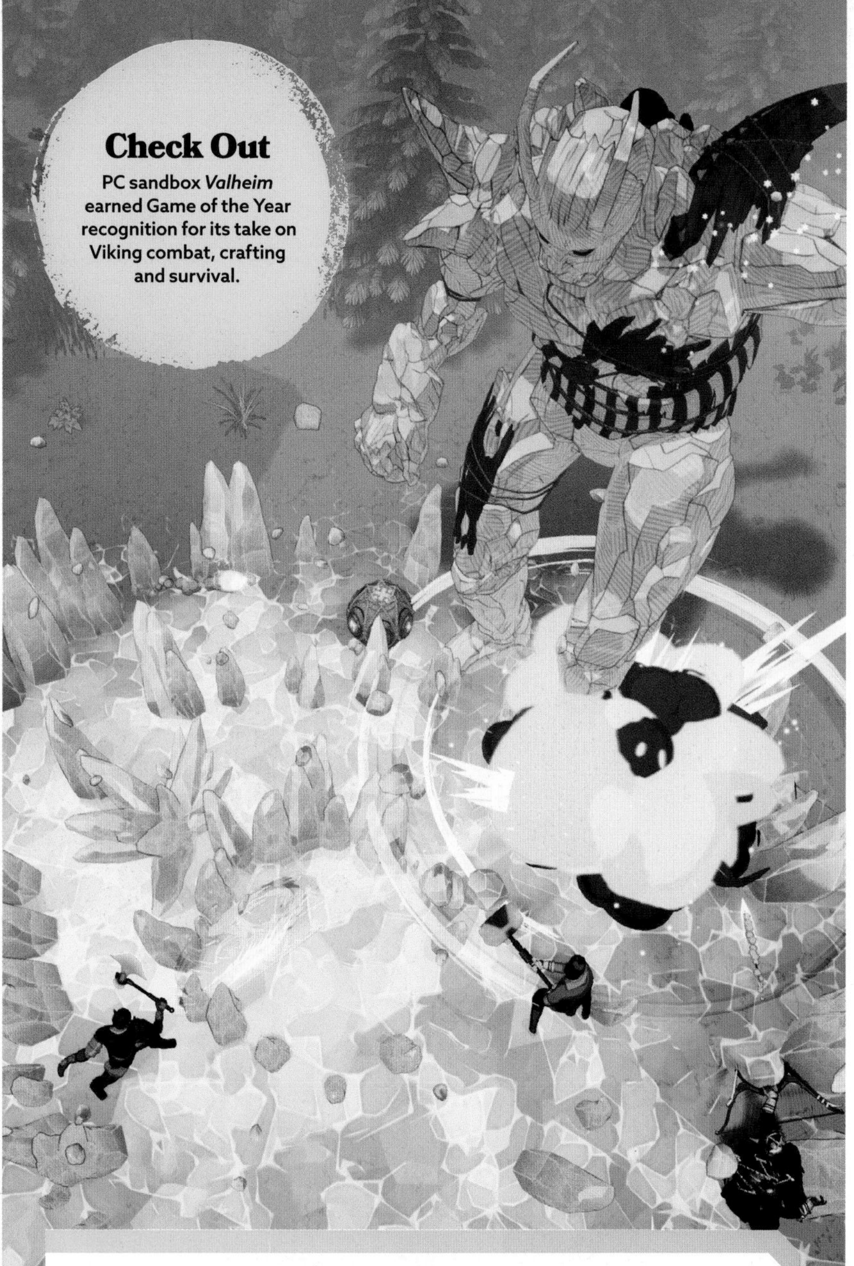

Check Out
PC sandbox *Valheim* earned Game of the Year recognition for its take on Viking combat, crafting and survival.

Tribes of Midgard

Developer Norsfell **Publisher** Norsfell **Platform** PC, PS4, PS5

■ Stop the end of the world, also known as Ragnarök, a Norse mythological story that will forever be a winner. You don't have to battle the apocalypse alone in *Tribes of Midgard*. Up to ten players compete together to fend off the deathly beasts who invade your village every night. Worlds are auto-created to ensure a constant state of freshness. The daytimes can be used to stockpile useful supplies, as players scan the world for resources to craft into potions, armour and weapons.

In Sound Mind

Developer We Create Stuff
Publisher Modus Games
Platform NS, PC, PS4, PS5, XBO, XBX/S

■ *In Sound Mind* is an interactive horror with a fun character development twist. You play as a troubled therapist named Desmond Whales, who finds cassette tapes from tortured patients. The tapes teleport you into mini-sandbox dreamscapes full of puzzles to be solved and scares to overcome. Each mini-game has a mix of platforming and shooter elements, giving every patient's mind a unique identity. The patients' inner torments are cleverly turned into end-of-level bosses for you to beat.

Deathloop

Developer Arkane Studios
Publisher Bethesda Softworks **Platform** PC, PS5

■ ***Deathloop* takes the on-trend theme of time travel and builds a first-person shooter around it. Set in the 1960s, you play assassin Colt Vahn, who needs to take down eight targets before midnight when the day will reset and everyone will forget what just happened. Everyone, that is, other than Colt and his smart rival Julianna Blake, who can be controlled by another player in a fun online option.**

Your targets all live on the island of Blackreef. It's split into four districts: Updaam, Karl's Bay, Fristad Rock and The Complex. The days are also broken up into four chunks: morning, noon, afternoon and night. Because targets are spread across those areas and time zones, you need to work out how to force them all closer together. This makes *Deathloop* an investigation sim and puzzler as much as it is a shooter.

Four to the Floor

Weapons are outrageous! The fourpounder is a powerful hand cannon, which can be tweaked with bullets that unleash toxic gas or cause heads to explode. Your targets also have their own weapons, powers and quirky personalities. Even when computer-controlled, Julianna is a constant unknown quantity too. You never tire of picking around the brilliantly realised world for clues and secrets. You can see why *Deathloop* won Best Game Direction and Best Art Direction at The Game Awards.

Island Locations

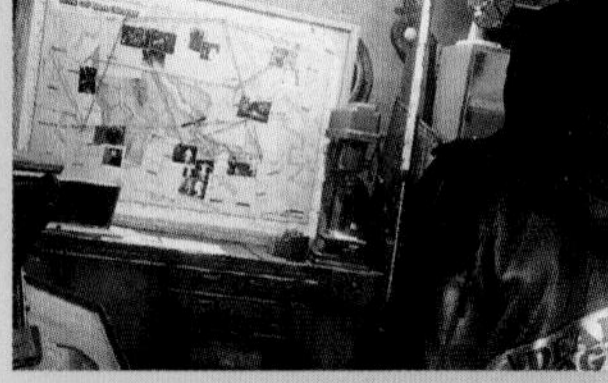

The Complex

The first area you visit after the how-to. It contains the research labs of two of your targets.

Karl's Bay

An obsessive cult resides amid the shabby aircraft hangars here and the members are not on your side.

Fristad Rock

Listen out for the community's favourite ballad 'City Lights / Ode to Somewhere' as you explore Fristad Rock.

Updaam

Home to an everlasting mansion party hosted by one of your targets, rich egomaniac Aleksis Dorsey.

Top Tip

Violence isn't always the answer in **Deathloop**. You can play stealthily or find creative solutions to your problems. The slabs are a great way to get ahead without bloodshed.

The game provides players with some truly bizarre settings. Fancy crashing a millionaire's party? How about raiding an aircraft hangar?

Julianna – the only other character whose memory doesn't reset when the loop does. And she can be controlled by another player, proving a difficult rival to beat.

Complex Exploration

You earn abilities that improve your chances each time the loop restarts. There's a similar element in previous Arkane games *Dishonored* and *Prey*. Even the basic powers - known as slabs - are ace, but it's in improving them that the real fun begins. The aether slab, for instance, starts off by making you invisible unless enemies are in close proximity, but can be boosted as you progress. Upgrade it to erase slab and you can kill an enemy without leaving a trace, whereas the ghost upgrade enables you to remain unseen while standing still.

The sepulchra breteira sniper rifle is one of the legendary golden weapons for players to find.

What in the Weird?

Wild and Weird Gaming Stories From Across the World

Far Cry 6 Taunts Players by Email

A ton of marketing emails before the release of any major game is standard if you're on a major publisher's database. But being heckled after you've already bought the game in question? That's new! Ubisoft kicked off this messaging mayhem following the release of *Far Cry 6*. Players received taunts in their inbox after taking a break from the game. "Surely you can do better than this," read some of them, mocking the gamer for their play-time. "I will remove you from history. No one will know your name," wrote El Presidente in another.

Swap Chocolates for a Computer

Every player has at least one game on their Christmas list. But would they be up for constructing those games from scratch? Build-your-own kit-makers Eight posed this very question using its Electronic Games Advent Calendar. Behind each window is a gaming component. When they were all connected together on Christmas Eve, you ended up with twenty-four retro favourites like *Wire Maze*, *Simon Says* and *Code Breaker.* Hopefully there was a stock of batteries waiting under the tree too. A vital element for every Christmas!

Sega Builds the Fastest PC Around

Sega has built its brand around speedy mascot Sonic, so news of it building the fastest gaming PC shouldn't be surprising. Until you hear that they did it literally. The Japanese giant assembled a PC-on-wheels that moves at speeds of 100km/62mph. They worked with Intel, ASRock, G-Force and remote-control car driver Masami Hirosaka. It packs a fairly decent spec too, with an Intel Core i9-12900K processor, 32GB of dual-channel RAM and 2TB SSD. Sadly you can't buy one, though. Sega gave it away in a sweepstake.

Xbox and Gucci Build $10,000 Console

How does an Italian designer celebrate turning twenty? By teaming up with a massive gaming publisher to create a $10,000 console, of course! That's what happened when Gucci marked its big birthday by releasing a bespoke Xbox Series X. Just 100 were available, all with a laser-cut monogram motif and two black, red and blue Gucci-themed controllers. The entire bundle came in a designer case with 'Good Game' emblazoned in large green letters. Despite the price, it sold out in two days.

STATE OF PLAY

The Best of FORTNITE

Epic's sandbox enjoyed a monster year! These were some of the highlights ...

Record Numbers

2021 was insanely busy for **Fortnite**. Not only did they add a ton of cool new skins, but the **number of registered users** for the bonkers battle royale soared to **350 million.**

Solid as The Rock

The year in *Fortnite* brought the hotly anticipated launch of Chapter 3, the island of Chapter 2 was flipped around and new weapons included the forceful ranger assault rival. Best of all, we got two massive Hollywood favourites. Dwayne 'The Rock' Johnson was added as The Foundation. Joining him was Spider-Man! The Marvel legend's addition came with a fully explorable Daily Bugle building. What's more, you could swing around the island for the first time by finding a new type of loot, called web shooters. But you only get eighty uses, so try not to *thwip* them all away.

Cool Crossovers

Fortnite maker Epic loves to give gamers a crossover. *Uncharted* was the most exciting. We got new maps with buried treasure, Nathan Drake and Chloe Frazer outfits and fresh weapons like the second hand saber pickaxe. A link-up with the NBA added uniforms for all thirty major basketball teams. Also, the game got its first ever anime collaboration, with *Naruto*. That added characters like Naruto and Sasuke and a new map: the beautiful Hidden Leaf Village.

Our Fave New Fortnite Skins

1. **Spider-Man**
2. **The Foundation**
3. **Indiana Jones**
4. **Ronin**
5. **Nathan Drake**
6. **Darth Vader**
7. **Haven**
8. **Unpeely**
9. **Eivor Varinsdottir**
10. **Gumbo**

Fortnitemares on Halloween

Players found both tricks and treats on Halloween. Fresh content arrived every day in October, like iconic Universal Studios characters *The Mummy* and Frankenstein's monster. Gamers could add some spookiness to their battle royale fun with old and new Halloween outfits. Plus, the Shortnitemares movie theatre broadcast ghoulish short films for the third year in a row.

Grande Designs

The biggest music stars in the world are queuing up to be in *Fortnite*. Ariana Grande dropped two *Fortnite* outfits and performed in-game as part of the Rift Tour. *Dance Monkey* queen Tones And I was another who joined the fun. She showcased songs from her debut album exclusively in *Fortnite*. A Dance Monkey Emote was also added to the Item Shop.

2003

What Games Were Big Twenty Years Ago?

■ Love Ultimate Team? Twenty years ago there was no such thing. Indeed, most sports fans didn't even consider *FIFA* to be the best football game! But while 2003 was a very different time on the sporting front, *Zelda* and *Mario Kart* were just as massive then as they are now ...

Pro Evolution Soccer 3

If you ask a football fan what the best ever game was, they'd find it hard to pick between *FIFA* and *Pro Evolution Soccer 3*. PES scores top marks in devoted fans' minds. There was no need for right-stick trickery to nail skills, while passing and shooting felt truly real. Its cover was memorable for different reasons. It featured super-famous Italian ref Pierluigi Collina. Why was this odd? He wasn't actually in the game itself!

GTA Double Pack

The highest-rated game of 2003 was two for the price of one. *GTA Double Pack* combined a pair of open-world classics into one collection. *Grand Theft Auto* III switched the car-stealing action to a third-person view and created an impressive version of New York named Liberty City. *GTA: Vice City* moved south to Miami. Set in 1986, it featured awesome neon backdrops and tunes from the era. Reviewers adored this double pack on PS2 and Xbox.

What's in a Name?

A major theme in 2003's bestselling games **Pokémon Ruby & Sapphire** is the relationship between land and sea. The two default male names in the game are **Landon** and **Sean**. The Japanese names are also direct translations of the words.

Game Boy Advance

The **Game Boy Advance** (GBA) series is one of the bestselling consoles of all time, **with 81.5 million sales worldwide**. The original **GBA** was released in 2001, before the updated **GBA SP** in 2003, followed by the **GameBoy Micro** in 2005.

Biggest-selling Games of 2003

01. Pokémon Ruby / Sapphire
Publisher Nintendo

02. Mario Kart Double Dash
Publisher Nintendo

03. Final Fantasy X-2
Publisher Square

04. PES 3
Publisher Konami

05. Super Mario Advance 4
Publisher Nintendo

06. Madden NFL 2004
Publisher EA Sports

07. Mario Party 5
Publisher Nintendo

08. Enter The Matrix
Publisher Atari

09. The Legend of Zelda: The Wind Waker
Publisher Nintendo

10. GTA: Vice City
Publisher Rockstar Games

The Legend of Zelda: The Wind Waker

The tenth *Legend of Zelda* was set on a group of islands within the Great Sea. Link was still the main man, along with a pirate captain named Tetra and a talking boat. Yes, a talking boat! It was called King of Red Lions and let Link travel between islands using the wind. See what they did with the name? If you were smart, you could use tools and items for different things. So a grapple hook would also function as a crane for recovering sunken treasure. Cool!

Mario Kart Double Dash

Twenty years on, this still feels like a unique game in the *Mario Kart* series. Why? Two characters in one kart! One steered while the other used items, and you could switch positions at any time. Twenty now-familiar faces appeared, and eleven of these were brand new. Until Double Dash, Daisy, Waluigi, Baby Luigi and Baby Mario had never appeared in a *Mario Kart* before. It was the second-biggest selling game of the year, even though it didn't come out until November.

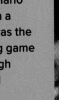

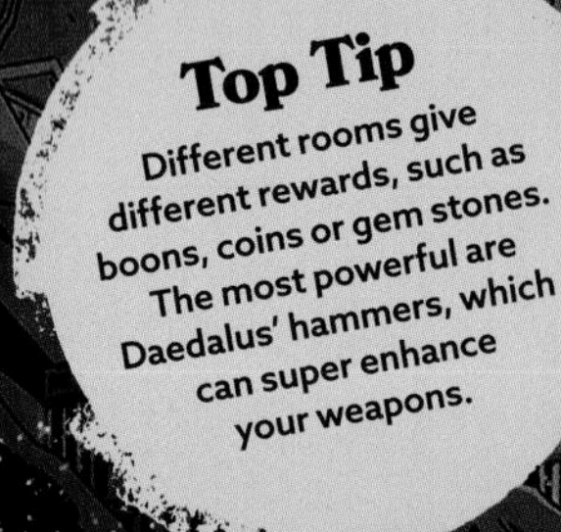

Top Tip
Different rooms give different rewards, such as boons, coins or gem stones. The most powerful are Daedalus' hammers, which can super enhance your weapons.

Hades

Developer Supergiant Games
Publisher Supergiant Games
Platform NS, PC, PS4, PS5, XBO, XBX/S

■ Who hasn't woken up on a Sunday morning and thought, "I quite fancy being an underworld prince today?" It's okay, no-one is judging you. Supergiant's popular dungeon crawler pretty much encourages this self-belief. As Hades' son Zagreus, you dodge obstacles and fight through waves of undead hordes in order to escape hell and return to the mortal world.

Something in the Ares

You only get one life, so are guaranteed to die many times. Which feels pretty appropriate, given the setting. Yet each time that happens, you hold on to character upgrades and relationships with NPCs, meaning you have a better shot of escaping on your next try. You also have six different weapon types to choose from and powers on offer from Olympian deities. Ares (God of War) grants boons that inflict super damage, while Dionysus (God of Wine) enables you to give enemies a hangover.

Levels are randomly generated so there's a freshness to every single run. And the only thing more certain than death in *Hades* is that you *will* come back for more.

Family Misfortunes

You start fresh with each run and the world is constantly changing around you. Characters once found close to Tartarus, the first biome you fight through, mysteriously disappear. Their fate will only be revealed through conversations with other NPCs. Bump into a boss that you've already defeated and they may reference that loss. The one consistent theme is Zagreus' sarcasm clashing perfectly with his dad's stern personality. It's a bizarre blend of soap opera and rogue-lite.

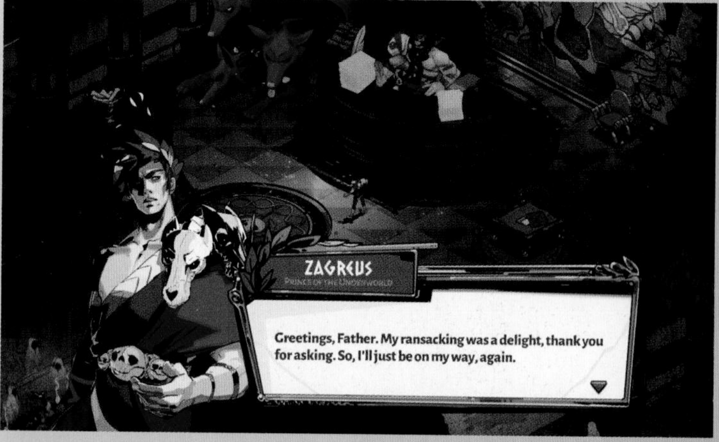

ZAGREUS
Greetings, Father. My ransacking was a delight, thank you for asking. So, I'll just be on my way, again.

Players see a lot of wretched thugs while fighting their way through Tartarus.

Immortal Combat

Hades' battles are awesome. You dash, you dodge, you smash through ghosts and witches and snakes made of bones in flurries of violent, screen-clearing action. Then on the next run you get taken out by a boss and rethink the play. The moments where you get to breathe are spent talking to other underworld characters and the rich mix of personalities keep you coming back to the game.

Unexpected partners Theseus and The Minotaur are the heroes of Elysium.

Gods of Olympus

Eight of the deities who can grant boons in **Hades**:

APHRODITE

ARES

ATHENA

CHAOS

DIONYSUS

HERMES

POSEIDON

ZEUS

Such a fast-paced game doesn't give a lot of time to reflect, so take any brief pause in action to admire the beautiful world. Zagreus looks out over the realm of Hades *before embarking on his next attempt to take down all of its subjects.*

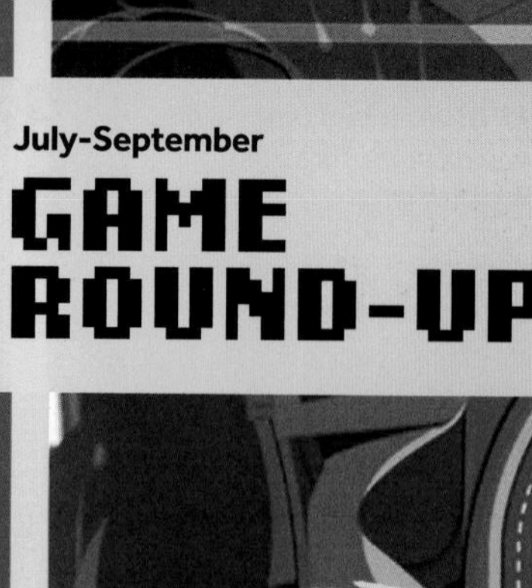

Top Tip
Avoid buying expensive equipment with your saved marbles, as most items can be found in chests or earned by completing side quests.

Cris Tales

Developer Dreams Uncorporated/Syck **Publisher** Modus Games
Platform NS, PC, PS4, PS5, XBO, XBX/S

■ Changing the future is a pretty big theme at the moment. *Cris Tales*' take on that is to split the screen into three. The past is on the left, the present in the centre and the future on the right. Players, acting as time mage Crisbell, can then alter their enemies' lives by sending them back or forward in time. It's an adventure with a dark side too, as you discover the grim futures of the cities you're exploring. *Cris Tales*' hand-drawn art style mixes in Colombian culture for a gorgeous experience, and has three different endings based on your heroic (or evil) choices.

It's in beautiful Narim that Crisbell discovers she has time mage powers.

View the past, present and future all at once as you make choices that change the game.

Check Out

If you enjoyed *Outer Wilds* and are looking for something similar, *Subnautica: Below Zero* is a game that sees you exploring the oceans of alien planet 4546B.

Outer Wilds: Echoes of the Eye

Developer Mobius Digital
Publisher Annapurna Interactive
Platform PC, PS4, XBO

■ The first game in this adventure series, *Outer Wilds,* was one of 2019's weirdest indie hits. Players had twenty-two-minute loops to journey across a pocket solar system. Each time chunk brought new info about an extinct alien race called the Nomai. You uncovered these secrets by exploring and completing logic puzzles. *Echoes of the Eye* adds terrifying moments of horror to the original's theme. An eerie spacecraft called *The Stranger* is the main playground. It contains a river, reservoir, canyon and starlit cove, all of which contain answers – and frights.

Greak: Memories of Azur

Developer Navegante Entertainment
Publisher Team17
Platform NS, PC, PS4, PS5, XBO, XBX/S

■ *Greak: Memories of Azur* is a stunning indie adventure from the publisher behind old-school 2D platformers *Worms* and *Lemmings*. It looks incredible and features a dreamy soundtrack. There are three sibling characters: melee expert Greak, floating mage Adara and hookshot-slinging Raydel. They are instantly likeable. You can easily switch between the charming trio using the D-pad. This is vital to solving puzzles and beating the toughest enemies.

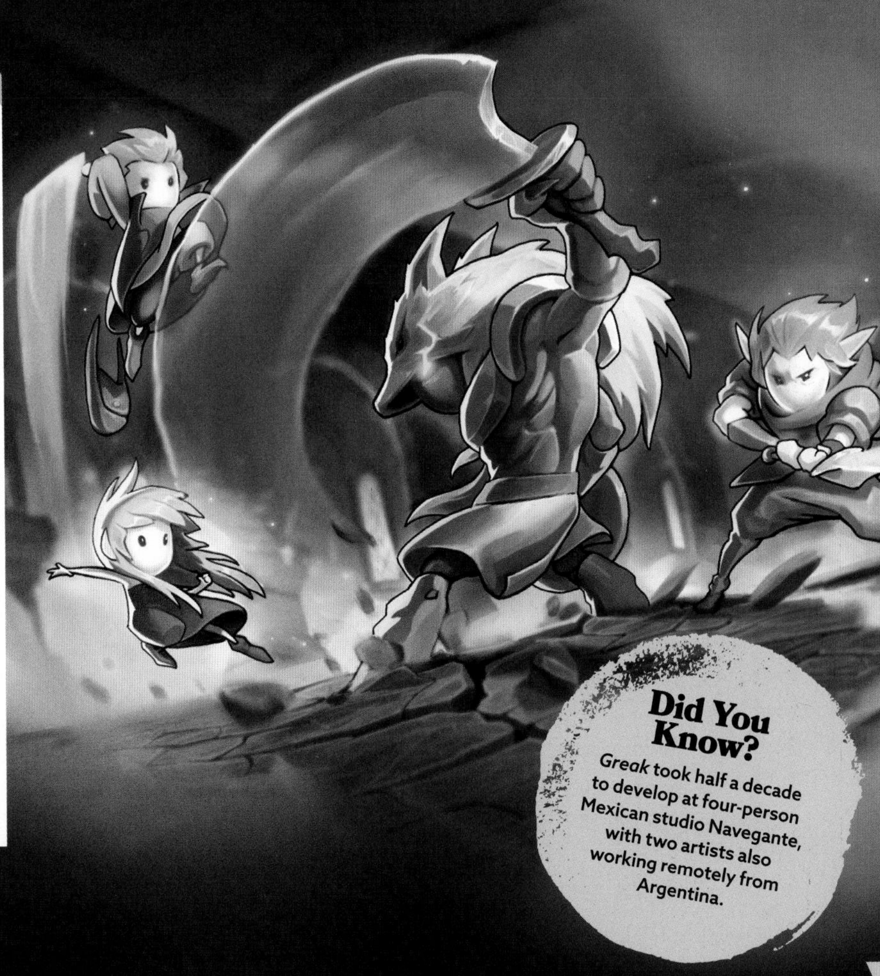

Did You Know?

Greak took half a decade to develop at four-person Mexican studio Navegante, with two artists also working remotely from Argentina.

The Great Ace Attorney Chronicles

Developer Capcom **Publisher** Capcom
Platform NS, PC, PS4

■ This collection brings *The Great Ace Attorney: Adventures* and *The Great Ace Attorney: Resolve* to worldwide HD screens for the first time. The two huge Japanese games tell one even bigger story set in the early twentieth century. As an uptight lawyer named Ryunosuke Naruhodo, you search crime scenes for clues, then bring cases to court. A lot of the fun comes from talking to the jurors, suspects and allies. The hapless-yet-hilarious English detective Herlock Sholmes is one of the top characters.

Top Tip
Finding it all too tough? Switch on the 'story mode' option to have cases play out automatically.

Elementary, My Dear

● The games are filled with a collection of eccentric characters. Such as Barok van Zieks, Ryunosuke's tough rival lawyer. Fan fave is Iris Wilson, the child genius and author of The Adventures of Herlock Sholmes.

Sholmes isn't just a detective that helps Ryunosuke on his cases, he's also a real-life wax figure! In The Great Ace Attorney he's hired to pretend to be a statue.

TOEM

Developer Something We Made **Publisher** Something We Made
Platform MAC, NS, PC, PS5

■ The last year has been ace for cute indie games and photo modes have been a huge hit. *TOEM* combines the two in a calming photo adventure game by tiny indie Swedish studio Something We Made. Players steer a little man through hand-drawn black-and-white levels taking snaps and lapping up the lovely acoustic soundtrack. There are also puzzles to solve as you explore the world, but even that part of the game is mostly gentle.

Check Out
Eastward is a similarly chilled adventure but with a darker side, available for PC and Switch.

Game of Tones
● *Game of Thrones'* Lena Headey fronts an impressive voice cast as the all-powerful Tastemaker.

The Artful Escape

Developer Beethoven & Dinosaur
Publisher Annapurna Interactive
Platform MAC, NS, PC, PS4, PS5, XBO, XBX/S

■ Do you want to be a space rockstar? This cool platformer lets you journey through a cosmos of 1970s-style levels as Francis Vendetti, a musician trying to find his sound. The guitar is your tool in this spacefaring adventure. Hammering X causes Francis to rock out riffs which affect the world around him and help him continue his trip across the galaxy. Boss battles come in the form of impressing alien overlords with button-matching performances. It's bright and thunderous fun that plays like no other game.

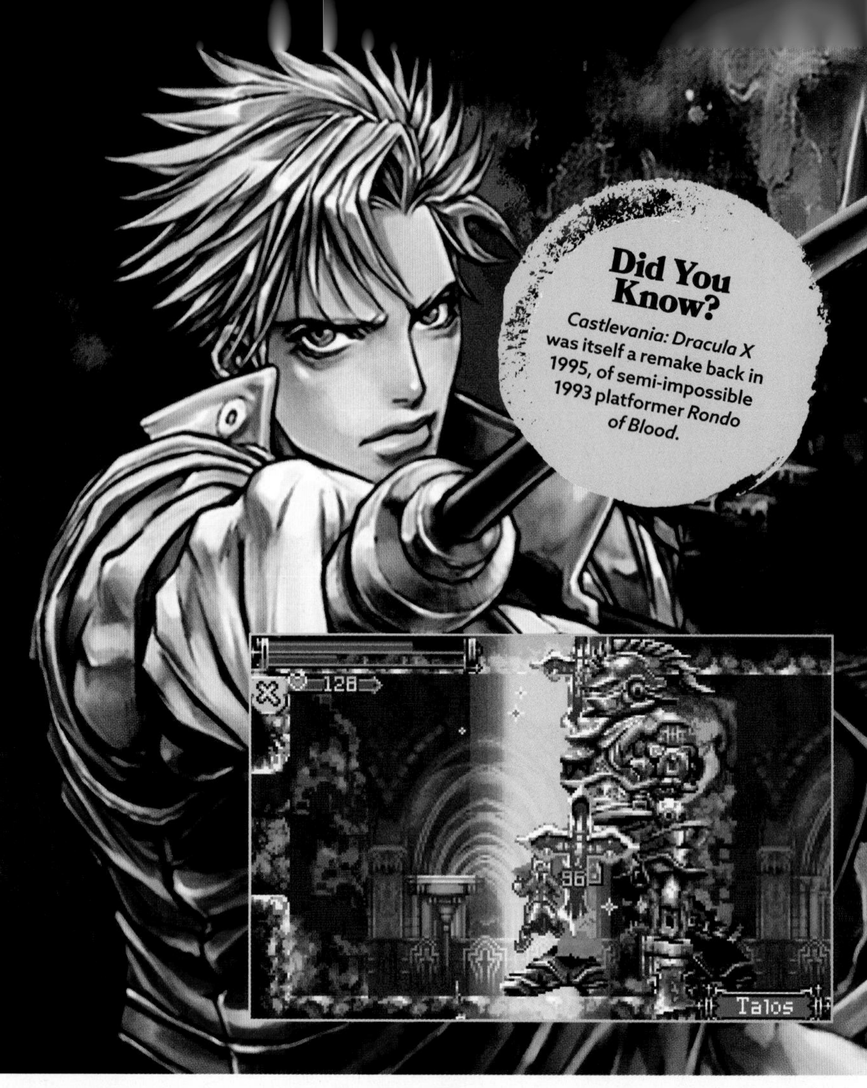

Did You Know?
Castlevania: Dracula X was itself a remake back in 1995, of semi-impossible 1993 platformer *Rondo of Blood*.

Castlevania: Advance Collection

Developer Konami **Publisher** Konami
Platform NS, PC, XBO

■ Want to play the games that inspired exploration-packed adventures like *F.I.S.T.*? This bundle delivers *Dracula X* (1995), *Circle of the Moon* (2001), *Harmony of Dissonance* (2002) and *Aria of Sorrow* (2003) in one single download. Quick saves and the ability to rewind mid-level are some of the new features in this modern-day release of the gothic classics. This vampire-stalking collection also includes an encyclopedia and full soundtracks from all four of the games.

Top Tip
Look for sections of track that don't have a checkpoint, as there's often a cheeky shortcut to be found.

Hot Wheels Unleashed

Developer Milestone
Publisher Milestone
Platform NS, PC, PS5, PS4, XBO, XBX/S

■ *Micro Machines* meets *Trackmania* in the racing game that turns toy cars into dreamy drives. Its main mode, City Rumble, offers a map filled with races, time trials and boss battles. The courses range from the surface of a pool table to the top of a skyscraper. The *Hot Wheels* toy range has a huge list of famous vehicles on sale and the game has the best ones. Now's your chance to power around in retro rides from *Back to The Future, Knight Rider* and *Teenage Mutant Ninja Turtles*.

WarioWare: Get It Together

Developer Nintendo **Publisher** Nintendo **Platform** NS

■ You can't host a Mario party without, well, *Mario Party* but the plumber's arch-rival wants you to consider it. Like the king of Nintendo family gatherings, the heart of Wario's first solo game is a collection of mini ones. The mini-games range from silly to bizarre. Bounce Back challenges you to keep a ball in the air as it slowly deflates. In Pit Stop, players tweeze the armpit hair of a Greek god. Possibly the weirdest game, Gold Digger, requires players to search for snot inside a giant – and annoyingly active – nose.

Someone Call 222

There are 222 mini-games in all, and in a neat new twist, many require the skill of a particular character. This is where the story mode comes in. Completing chapters grants you new characters, who can be used across all modes. Finishing the story opens up four-player party games, similar to *Mario Party*. The micro-games here are much zanier and speedier, at just a few seconds apiece. In a very meta twist, you can help Wario find the bugs in a video game he's created,

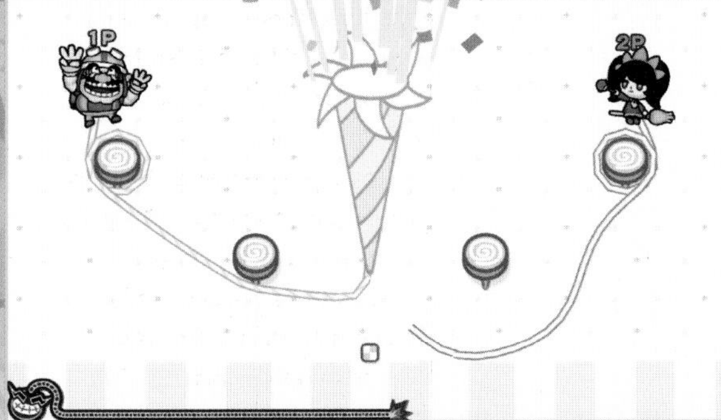

Pop Goes the Party gives players the chance to see Wario celebrate his birthday.

Avoid that heart-breaking moment when the ice-cream falls to the floor. SPLAT!

Wario's Pals

Even bad guys have good mates, like these best buds:

YOUNG CRICKET

18 VOLT

MONA

JIMMY-T

ASHLEY

ORBULON

RED

MASTER MANTIS

Gotta Play Em All

Even More Games to Try Out

■ These impressive games are still fighting for console time after their big releases. If you're looking for an even longer to-play list then check them out!

Games Within Games

Keen-eyed **Ratchet & Clank: Rift Apart** players may spot the arcade game in Zurkie's Bar featuring scenes from the 2011 spin-off **Ratchet & Clank: All 4 One**.

Ratchet & Clank: Rift Apart

Creator Insomniac Games added a must-own PS5 game in 2021 with *Ratchet & Clank: Rift Apart*. The sequel combines the best elements from past games in the series, then adds new character Rivet and a clever multiverse setting. It offers hour after hour of platforming perfection.

Disco Elysium: The Final Cut

You play as an amnesiac detective who can select from twenty-four different skill sets in a world that truly feels alive. Interrogating suspects and solving murders is just part of the fun in this incredibly deep and believable RPG. You can also do karaoke, write poetry and even equip specific morals and empathy using the detective's Thought Cabinet.

Mass Effect: Legendary Edition

PC, PS4 and Xbox One owners got a very special treat in May. A collection of *Mass Effect 1*, *Mass Effect 2* and *Mass Effect 3*, remastered with new graphics and tech upgrades. Commander Shepard is fully customisable throughout the sci-fi trilogy, and *Mass Effect 3*'s female character is now also in the first two games.

Hitman 3

Elite assassin Agent 47 makes his PS5 and Xbox Series X debut in this stealthy sandbox. It introduces six new locations: Berlin, Chongqing, Dubai, Dartmoor, Mendoza and Romania's Carpathian Mountains. There are numerous ways to pick off your targets, from dagger and fibre wire to silent-yet-deadly guns.

Returnal

Time loops were a big theme in 2021, and *Returnal* was one of the trendsetters. You control space pilot Selene in this sci-fi shooter set on shape-shifting alien planet Atropos. The fun time twist means that whenever she dies, time rewinds to her original crash landing. The storyline splits in two depending on one key decision.

Resident Evil Village

The classic survival-horror series gets a more action-focused makeover in its first next-gen game. Ethan Winters is the main character, searching for his kidnapped daughter amid a village of werewolf-like foes. Longstanding hero Chris Redfield also plays a major role but you'll have to play to find out more!

NEWS FLASH

Everything You Need to Know About eSports

Get to Know the Games, the Teams and the Top-paying Contests

■ eSports has never been so hot or offered such eye-popping rewards. Think of *League of Legends, Dota 2* and *Counter-Strike: Global Offensive*. These are truly massive eSports events, offering millions of dollars in prize money and watched by fans across hundreds of countries. If you want to become an eSport expert, then check out our guide to the biggest events and best players.

Fortnite Fighters

A **Fortnite World Cup** was introduced in 2019, and took place at New York's Arthur Ashe Stadium. **Kyle 'Bugha' Giersdorf was the winner, winning £3 million** with 2.3 million watching from home.

Overwatch On Hold

Overwatch is another eSport that saw its World Cup go on hiatus in 2020 and 2021. Before then, there had been four tournaments between 2016 and 2019, with the USA winning three and South Korea one.

10 Essential eSports Events

01 The International

Dota 2's world championship has earned a reputation for offering the biggest prizes. In 2021, the Bucharest-based event lived up to it by breaking the record for the largest award. Over $40 million was on offer, with $18.2 million of that going to the winners. Russia's Team Spirit took the prize, beating Chinese squad PSG.LGD 3-2 in the final.

02 FIFAe World Cup

The real football World Cup only takes place every four years. Luckily, we get one every year in EA's virtual sport. Germany's Mohammed Harkous won the competition's 15th event in 2019, beating the reigning champion Mossad Al Dossary 3-2 in the final.

03 Free Fire World Series

Incredibly, 2021's most-watched sports tournament in terms of peak viewers didn't involve *League of Legends* or *Dota 2*. Instead, mobile battle royale *Free Fire* was the most viewed. It had a peak of 5.41 million viewers tuning in at once. The event took place at Marina Bay in Singapore and was won by Thai team EVOS Phoenix.

Esports History

eSports have been around longer than you think. **The Intergalactic Spacewar Olympics** was the first ever eSports event. Twenty-four players competed in spaceship-based dogfights. It took place at California's Stanford University in 1972.

04 PGL Major Stockholm

Majors are the biggest event in the *Counter-Strike: Global Offensive* calendar. Last year, twenty-four teams competed for an overall reward of $2,000,000. Insane! Astralis were the defending champions, and they'd won four majors already, but they failed to make the quarterfinals this time. After thirteen days of competition, Ukrainian team Natus Vincere won the prize without dropping a single map.

05 Worlds

The League of Legends World Championship takes place towards the end of each year. Teams compete for the Summoner's Cup. China's Edwards Gaming beat Korea's DWG KIA in the 2021 final and won a cool $495,000. 2021's championship was the biggest eSports event in history. Fans watched 174.8 million hours of competition. That would be like watching every episode of *The Simpsons* over 400 times.

Top 10 eSports Tournaments by Prize Money

1. **$40 million** The International (Dota 2)
2. **$30.4 million** Fortnite World Cup (Fortnite)
3. **$7.7 million** World Champion Cup (Honor of Kings)
4. **$7.1 million** PUBG Global Invitational (PUBG)
5. **$6.4 million** Worlds (League of Legends)
6. **$4.6 million** Call of Duty League Championship (Call of Duty)
7. **$4.4 million** PUBG Global Championship (PUBG)
8. **$4 million** Fall Skirmish Series (Fortnite)
9. **$3.5 million** Overwatch League Playoffs (Overwatch)
10. **$3 million** Dota 2 Asia Championship (Dota 2)

Accidental Esports

The first ***PUBG* eSports** tournament was a happy accident. To celebrate the game passing two million sales, developer Bluehole announced a 2017 Charity Invitational to raise money for Gamers Outreach Foundation.

06 PUBG Global Championship

PlayerUnknown's Battlegrounds tournament is a long one! Elite teams go head-to-head for five weeks in order to survive the island-based battle royales. Thirty-two teams headed to Incheon in South Korea to fight for the $2million prize fund. Chinese team New Happy were crowned champions after an intense dogfight against Heroic.

07 Hearthstone Grandmasters World Championship

Blizzard's epic card-battling game has switched to online finals. Taipei hosted the last in-person World Championship in 2019. 2021 brought an all-Japanese final, with Wataru 'Posesi' Ishibashi beating 2020 title holder Sato 'Glory' Kenta to claim the $200,000 prize.

08 ALGS Championship

The Apex Legends Global Series Championship was all played out online in 2021. That wasn't the only difference this year: there were five regional winners rather than a single world champion. That didn't stop publisher EA paying out a huge total of $1.5 million in prize money. After 125 hours of tournament time were crammed into one single month, Team Kungarna won the North American prize.

© REUTERS / Alamy Images

© REUTERS / Alamy Images

09 Rocket League Championship Series

Sadly, there was no Rocket League World Champion in 2020 or 2021. Events in Dallas and Georgia were cancelled due to the pandemic. The sport remains massive though, with a $529,000 prize on offer the last time the tournament went ahead. NRG beat Renault Vitality to win, and they remain a huge force in the racing-footy hybrid.

Top 10 Purpose-Built eSports Arenas

1. **Three Gorges Harbor Esports Stadium (China)**
   6,000 seats
2. **Hangzhou Esports Centre (China)**
   4,087 seats
3. **Esports Arena Arlington (USA)**
   2,500 seats
4. **Gwangju Esports Arena (South Korea)**
   1005 seats
5. **HyperX Arena (USA**
   1000 seats
6. **Fortress Melbourne (Australia)**
   1000 seats
7. **Yota Arena (Russia)**
   1000 seats
8. **Esports Arena Orange County (USA)**
   880 seats
9. **Gfinity Arena (UK)**
   600 seats
10. **Full Sail University Fortress (USA)**
    500 seats

10 The Six Invitational

The Rainbow Six Siege Tournament is usually based in Montreal. It moved to Sweden for a year during the pandemic. After three consecutive top-four finishes, United States squad TSM finally ascended to the top of the elite in February 2022. They had only made the tournament as qualifiers, but they beat Russia's Team Empire in the Stockholm-based final.

Odd Year Out

Starcraft II had its own World Championship series from 201 to 2019, which was considered t game's highest tier of competiti South Korean players won it every year other than 2018, when **Finland's Joona 'Serral' Sotala snagged victory.**

Five eSports Teams You Need to Know

Natus Vincere

The Ukraine-based team may not be the highest-earning on these pages, but there's a good chance they're the most loved. The PGL Major Stockholm winners downed their controllers in early 2022 to serve their country, delivering humanitarian aid in Kyiv and distributing clothing to children in hospitals and orphanages. Whatever the future holds, they've etched their names into history.

FaZe Clan

Celebrity connections run high for the LA-based eSports brand. Musician Pitbull, basketball star Jamal Murray and actor Chris O'Donnell all invested in recent times. FaZe also has a clothing line with Premier League football team Manchester City. They started out playing *Call of Duty*, but these days is a contender at *CSGO* (*Counter-Strike: Global Offensive)* and *Rainbow Six* too.

Team Liquid

Team Liquid was founded in the Netherlands in 2000, the most successful brand in eSports has raked in $40 million in prize money. It's a major player at every *Dota 2*, *Counter-Strike: Global Offensive* and *League of Legends* event. Over the years, they've also dabbled in *Street Fighter* and *Super Smash Bros*. Its newest team, for free-to-play FPS (first person shooter) *Valorant*, was formed in 2020.

OG

For a long time, the Red Bull-sponsored team were focused solely on *Dota 2*. Maybe because they were champions! They charged to victory in The International 2018 and 2019. More recently, they've branched out into *Counter-Strike: Global Offensive* and *Valorant* too. Co-founder Johan 'N0tail' Sundstein is still with the team, but former partner Tal 'Fly' Aizik left to play for PSG Talon.

Evil Geniuses

Evil Geniuses started playing *Quake* in 1997. They then moved from Canada to Seattle and racked up prize money in *Dota 2* and *Counter-Strike: Global Offensive*. They've also been a major player in *Call of Duty*, winning the World League Championship in 2018. Like the other teams here, Evil Geniuses already assembled a *Valorant* line-up, so expect that to be eSports' next big thing.

Five Players with a Hall-of-Fame Future

Oleksandr 's1mple' Kostyliev

Back in 2016, Ukraine's *CSGO* heavyweight helped Team Liquid become the first North American team to make a major final. He then joined his homeland squad Natus Vincere in the next season. S1mple helped the team win in New York, Shanghai, Cologne and Katowice, before snaring the ultimate prize in 2021: victory at the PGL Major Stockholm. He was rated the number one *Counter-Strike: Global Offensive* player in the world last year and won the Game Award for Best eSports Player.

Johan 'N0tail' Sundstein

N0tail co-founded Team OG – the only team to be named World Dota 2 Champions twice. As of February 2022, he had amassed $7.18 million in eSports earnings – making him the most successful player of all time. He was on the winning team at The International in 2018 and 2019, and also won Major tournaments in Frankfurt, Manila, Boston and Kyiv. The Dane is so famous that, aged just twenty-five, he was featured on Forbes' Thirty Under Thirty list.

Jesse 'JerAx' Vainikka

Most professional sports players wait until their late-thirties to retire. *Dota 2*'s star player called it a day at just twenty-seven, having won two versions of The International alongside N0tail. Thankfully, his downtime was short-lived. Vainikka returned in November 2021 as a member of Evil Geniuses. He's scored career earnings of $6.48 million, using a gamer tag that combines his name with that of a favourite character: Cyrax from *Mortal Kombat.*

Kyle 'Bugha' Giersdorf

Dota 2's prize money is so big that thirty-four of the top thirty-five earners in eSports come from that game. The exception is *Fortnite* player Bugha, who's earned $3.1 million by smashing everyone at Epic's bonkers blaster. He won the Fortnite World Cup in 2019 and was named Best eSports Player at the Game Awards as a result. Epic gave Giersdorf his own in-game skin in July 2021, putting him in the same league as Neymar, Ariana Grande and Spider-Man.

Sasha 'Scarlett' Hostyn

As of March 2022, eSports' most successful female player had earned $425,000 and scored forty-one tournament victories over her decade-long career. The Canadian is nicknamed 'Korean Kryptonite' and 'Queen of Blades'. Most of her success has been in *StarCraft II* but she's also competed in *Dota 2.* China's Xiaomeng 'Liooon' Ling, who hammered both male and female rivals to win the 2019 Hearthstone Grandmasters, ranks second to Hostyn.

Coming In Clutch

S1imple is a prime example of a clutch player, able to pull off huge plays at the most important moments. As NaVi's number one sniper, he has been **voted MVP of nineteen different tournaments.**

IT'S IN THE GAME

EA Vancouver

■ The studio that makes FIFA hasn't always belonged to EA. Before 1991, it was known as Distinctive Software, and made games like *4D Sports Tennis*. In the three decades since then, its focused on ice hockey (*NHL*), basketball (*NBA Live*) and golf (PGA Tour). Its campus is just outside Vancouver, in Burnaby. As well as editing suites and a special effects studio, it has theatres, arcades and a full-sized astroturf football pitch. Huge!

Biggest Series: FIFA

The world's biggest sports sim started out in 1993 as *FIFA International Soccer*. It had no club team or real names, but was the year's bestselling game despite only coming out in December. They've released a sequel every year, and overall the series has sold more than 325 million copies.

Have You Played?

FIFA 22

NHL 22

UFC 4

Grand Slam Tennis 2

PREPARE TO DIE

FromSoftware

■ The *Elden Ring* studio found fame with *Demon's Souls* and *Dark Souls*. But it was making games long before that perfect pair. As far back as 1994, in fact, when it released labyrinth explorer *King's Field*. Robot shooter *Armored Core* is another cult fave. Its president is development legend Hidetaka Miyazaki. He's the director of the *Souls* series and won a Lifetime Achievement Award at the 2018 Golden Joysticks.

Have You Played?

Elden Ring

Sekiro: Shadows Die Twice

Dark Souls III

Demon's Souls

Biggest Series: Souls

The medieval fantasy series is famed as the hardest around. That's why so many love it: there's no feeling quite like finishing *Demon's Souls*. Incredibly, negative feedback from the Japanese press on its initial release meant publisher Sony didn't bother with a Western version. Word of its brilliance spread globally. Phew, or we may never have got *Elden Ring*.

DLC

Over the first year of launch there were four DLC drops. **The Endeavour Pass** is a 12-month add-on to your game purchase – it included all four DLC drops plus cosmetic items like weapons and armour.

Aliens: Fireteam Elite

Developer Cold Iron Studios **Publisher** Focus Home Interactive **Platform** PC, PS4, PS5, XBO, XBX/S

■ Placing new *Alien* games within the story of what's gone before can be a headache, so here's a quick history lesson. *Fireteam Elite* follows on from the original film trilogy, picking up where *Alien 3* left off, although it's mostly based on the second movie *Aliens*. It's set in 2202, twenty-three years after the films, and isn't related to Gearbox's *Aliens: Colonial Marines* or Creative Assembly's *Alien Isolation*. Got that? Don't worry, there won't be a test!

Bug-man's Holiday

This co-op shooter sends you to planetoid LV-895 to clean up the joint. The planet is absolutely covered in Xenomorphs. It's best enjoyed alongside two other real-life players, although there's no local multiplayer option. If online isn't your jam, the AI can control your fellow marines.

If you've seen the movies then it's a strong nostalgia trip. There are gunfights in rusting corridors and eerie caves. Enemies come at you from every direction – including the ceiling. Basic ones go up in a hilarious explosion of green goo, and you'll need to work together to take down the tougher creatures, like *Dying Light* meets *Ghostbusters*. The sheer variety of guns you collect and classes you unlock will help you defeat even the most monstrous of Xenomorphs.

Fight side-by-side with a team of real-life players as you're attacked from all angles.

Hive and Let Die

There are five classes to choose from in *Fireteam Elite*, such as technician (great at close combat and able to place an auto-turret) and demolisher (wielder of massive firepower – including rockets). Both these classes use flamethrowers to unleash fiery chaos, but the L56A3 Smartgun is even better. It has a 200-bullet capacity and rips through enemies faster than you can say "eat this".

Did You Know?

The legendary drinking-bird bobblehead from *Alien* can be found in the Crew Quarters area of *Fireteam Elite*.

Extra-terrestrial Alternatives

Alien (1982)

The first *Alien* spin-off game was only on the Atari 2600 and played a bit like *Pac-Man* – if Pac-Man was armed with a flamethrower.

Alien Trilogy (1996)

PS1, Saturn and PC shooter where you played as iconic movie character Ripley, exploring thirty levels and taking down three alien queens.

Alien: Colonial Marines (2013)

An intense first-person blaster made with Syd Mead, the concept artist from the *Alien* movies. It's available on PC, PS3 and Xbox 360.

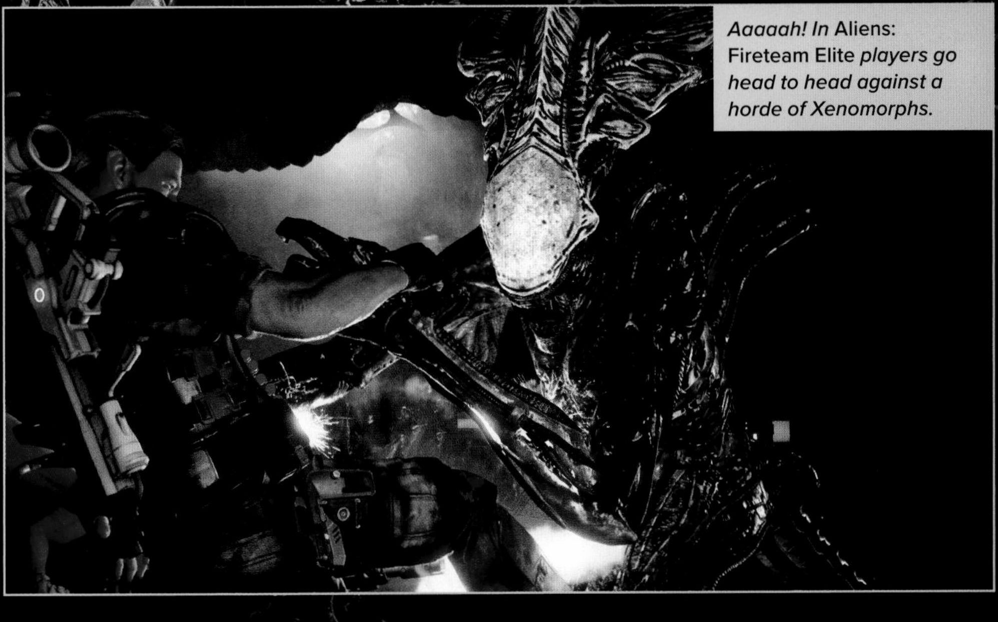

Aaaaah! In Aliens: Fireteam Elite *players go head to head against a horde of Xenomorphs.*

Alien: Isolation (2014)

Ripley's daughter Amanda is this survival horror's lead character. In *Isolation*, your enemy is entirely unpredictable – making every play a rush of nerves and adrenaline.

Top Tip
Look out for red circles in the world around you – these can be used to generate a shield.

Boomerang X

Developer DANG! **Publisher** Devolver Digital **Platform** NS, PC

■ **A boomerang with four lethal edges is your only weapon as you slash and slice through shadowy squids and poisonous spiders on a mysterious island. *Boomerang X* is played from a first-person perspective and is completely linear. Upgrading your sharp toy is the key to getting ahead here. Kill two enemies at once to earn the shotgun blast, kill three enemies at once with the shotgun blast to get the laser beam, and so on.**

Foul Furry Foes

Enemies are both disgusting and relentless. Enter an arena, smash the giant crystal above you and enjoy hell unfolding on all sides. Foes fly or swarm at you in waves and you need to pick off ones marked by a yellow indicator to advance to the next wave. Each of the twelve levels feels uniquely random and colourful. As these get wilder, so do your skills – slowing down time or using the boomerang in physics-defying ways.

Enemies that must be killed to gain entry to the next level have a handy yellow glow.

Kena: Bridge of Spirits

Developer Ember Lab **Publisher** Ember Lab
Platform PC, PS4, PS5

■ Are you in the mood for feel-good Pixar vibes? Then *Kena: Bridge of Spirits* is your game. It's a charming, third-person adventure where you use Kena's magical abilities to guide restless spirits into the afterlife. This delicate theme is beautifully handled. It reminds you that not all successful games need a devious twist. Even combat is unspeakably cute, as you swipe foes down with your bow or command loveable sprites called Rot to swarm enemies.

Another Life

- Early prototypes featured the Rot as the enemy, and Kena wasn't involved at all.
- Kena is a teenager in *Bridge of Spirits*, but was originally devised as an eight-year-old.

Hot Gear

- Eight bikes are available, including the 2019 Kawasaki Ninja ZX-10RR and 2021 BMW M1000 RR.
- Incredibly detailed DLC includes a Japanese manufacturers' pack with four designs and seventy-six spare parts.

RiMS Racing

Developer RaceWard Studio
Publisher Nacon
Platform NS, PC, PS4, PS5, XBO, XBX/S

■ This bike sim looks insanely lifelike, especially when you're careering around tracks like Silverstone in the rain. RaceWard Studio has boosted that authenticity too. You're able to check every aspect of your vehicle mid-race. Plus, you can pull into the pits to fix creaking parts. Helmet-owning experts will love the level of detail. Out on the track it's a fabulous drive.

Streets of Rage 4: Mr X Nightmare

Developer Lizardcube **Publisher** DotEmu **Platform** NS, PC, PS4, XBO

■ *Streets of Rage* is a hugely retro, iconic Sega Mega Drive beat-'em-up. Yet, incredibly, it took twenty-six years for anyone to create a sequel to 1994's *Streets of Rage 3*. The follow-up finally landed and this expansion introduces three additional playable characters and an exciting new Survival mode.

Joining old favourites Axel (blonde hair, blue eyes, fists of fury) and Blaze (brown hair, red boots, kickass demeanour) are Max, Estelle and Shiva. Like the returning protagonists, each has unique traits that add replay-ability. A run with the cumbersome yet powerful Max feels very different to scooting through levels as Shiva, who is unable to pick up weapons and instead kicks them across the screen.

Blaze of Glory

Survival mode challenges you to play as many stages as possible on a single life. The longer you last with a single character, the more moves are unlocked. Once you've earned enough moves, you can customise move-sets. Those tweaks then carry over into the main game, and bring even more characters. It's a smart way of adding longevity to this side-scrolling throwback.

Each different player character comes with their own skills and abilities. Try a run with each of them to find your fave.

All the Rage

- *Streets of Rage* originally emerged in Japan in August 1991, where it was known as *Bare Knuckle: Furious Iron Fist*.
- All three new characters first appeared in the Mega Drive series – for instance, Shiva was a boss in *Streets of Rage 2*.

Synth Riders

Developer Kluge Interactive
Publisher Kluge Interactive **Platform** PS VR

■ You'll be madly waving your arms around your living room in PS VR's breathless rhythm-action riot. Your flurrying fists control glowing balls – one purple, one blue – that need to hit colourful notes as they hurtle towards the headset. Notes in yellow must be nailed with both hands, green ones are up to you, giving players a chance to freestyle. The end result leaves you feeling like a DJ, a street dancer and an orchestra conductor all-at-once. DLC packs from Muse and the Daft-Punk-influenced Caravan Palace help to amplify this sensation.

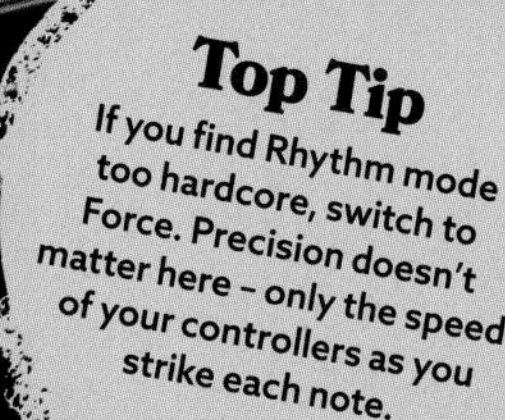

Top Tip
If you find Rhythm mode too hardcore, switch to Force. Precision doesn't matter here – only the speed of your controllers as you strike each note.

Humankind

Developer Amplitude Studios **Publisher** Sega
Platform MAC, PC, PS4, PS5, XBO, XBX/S

■ Do you find empire building games too complicated? Amplitude's *Humankind* takes a fresh approach to helping newcomers to the 4X (explore, expand, exploit, exterminate) genre. You start out with a Neolithic tribe, focused on gathering food and hunting animals. Then you need to uncover potential sites for your first city. You can build and develop your civilisation there before expansion begins. There are six further eras to conquer and sixty cultures to choose from, making *Humankind* highly replayable. Another quality feature is the in-game tutorials for every mechanic, making it accessible for even the newest gamer.

Did You Know?
Thirty-one managers have real face scans in Ultimate Team, including relative newcomers Patrick Vieira (Crystal Palace) and Bruno Lage (Wolves).

FIFA 22

Developer EA Canada **Publisher** EA
Platform NS, PC, PS4, PS5, XBO, XBX/S

■ *FIFA 22* is the giant football sim from game studio EA. It's changed in its second year on PS5 and Xbox Series X, but that doesn't mean old features are forgotten. In Career mode, you can create your own club and add them to any league in the world! Plus, there are customisable kits from Nike, Adidas and Hummel. Street football mode Volta also expands with zany online options, such as foot tennis and even dodgeball.

The game also comes with tech updates like HyperMotion. EA used the same technology as Marvel blockbuster movies to copy the moves of real-life footballers. Can you imagine twenty-two professional footballers wearing full motion-capture suits on the pitch? You don't have to, *FIFA 22* has brought those moves straight to your PS5 and Xbox Series X. This data means players work together in tandem to keep their shape or go up for headers in a cluster. It stops the games from being weighted towards one-on-one battles.

Got-Got-Need

Ultimate Team, the game's most popular mode, has made a lot of noise. It lets gamers build a fantasy squad by collecting digital football player cards, then offers the chance to drop real cash on packs. Even if you want to avoid shedding pennies, it's still one of sports gaming's greatest elements. It blends the joy of sticker collecting with rapid end-to-end matchplay.

You can still have some casual 'friendlies' against mates in head-to-head matches, either locally or online.

Feeling sad about how your team is doing in real life? Then take control and oversee their journey to the very top in Career mode.

There's nothing more satisfying than banging a free kick in top bins. Definitely helps when you use highly-ranked footballers like Messi.

Hall of Heroes

Developer EA Canada has introduced new 'heroes' cards – yesteryear favourites who are famed for their games in one league.

Jürgen Kohler

Jürgen Kohler is an ace German centre-back. In the heroes cards, Kohler represents the Bundesliga after 145 appearances during his Dortmund career.

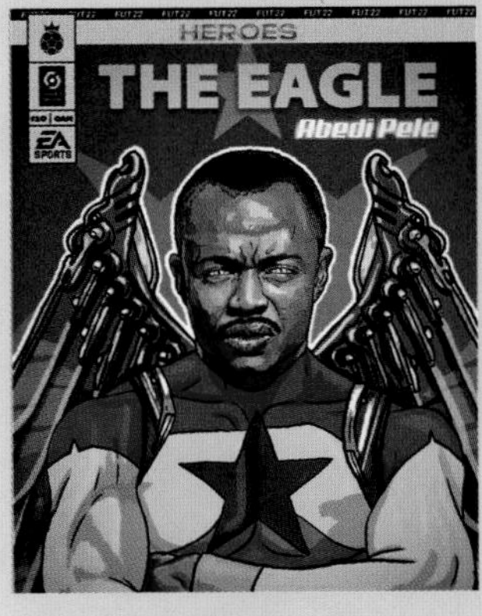

Abedi Pele

Ghana's best ever player gets a Ligue 1 heroes card as a reward for starring at Marseille and Lyon. He's father to Jordan Ayew (Crystal Palace) and Andre Ayew (Al Sadd).

David Ginola

The most popular heroes card marks the flying Frenchman's years at Paris St Germain – which Newcastle and Spurs fans may have something to say about.

Ole Gunnar Solskjær

The ex-Manchester United boss enters the digital turf to mark an Old Trafford career where he amassed a whopping ninety-one goals.

The Ultimate Ultimate Team

11 Unforgettable FIFA 22 Faves

GK: Gigi Donnarumma

96

Paris St Germain won their way to the French championship, and their Italian keeper was a force! This super-powerful card was almost unbeatable. Big ratings included 92 Positioning, 97 Reflexes, and 98 Diving.

DIVING	HANDLING	KICKING	REFLEXES	SPEED	POSITIONING
98	90	90	97	63	92

RB: Achraf Hakimi

93

FIFA players love speed, and Donnarumma's PSG teammate was the first player in *FIFA 22* to earn a maximum Pace rating of 99. Little wonder his card cost 1.3 million coins when released in January.

PACE	SHOOTING	PASSING	DRIBBLING	DEFENDING	PHYSICAL
99	80	88	91	90	90

LB: Marcelo

94

The Brazilian captain's card is even better than previous icons like Roberto Carlos and Ashley Cole. It cost a hefty 1.3 million. But in return for that transfer fee, you scored 93 Pace, 91 Defending, 96 Dribbling and 89 Physicality.

PACE	SHOOTING	PASSING	DRIBBLING	DEFENDING	PHYSICAL
93	86	93	96	91	89

CB: Virgil van Dijk

96

Liverpool's Dutchman was dominant for a third straight year. His 87 Sprint Speed meant few attackers got past him. Then, when close enough, he'd use his 99 Awareness and 99 Standing Tackle to nip the ball away.

PACE	SHOOTING	PASSING	DRIBBLING	DEFENDING	PHYSICAL
87	71	80	81	98	94

CB: Paolo Maldini

95

Legendary defenders in *FIFA 22* included England World Cup winner Bobby Moore. Maldini's 95-rated card eclipsed them all. 99 Defensive Awareness made him almost impossible to escape, plus an 87 Pace rating, just in case.

PACE	SHOOTING	PASSING	DRIBBLING	DEFENDING	PHYSICAL
87	65	77	70	98	85

CDM: N'Golo Kanté

96

Kanté has been *FIFA*'s most meta midfielder for half a decade. But while using him gets you slated on social media, it's also a fast track to Division Rivals wins. This card boasts 99 Balance, Reactions, Interceptions and Stamina. Phew!

LW: Neymar

93

PSG are ridiculous, aren't they? The French giant's fourth player on this list regularly shredded defences. 93 Pace was the initial attraction, but it was 97 Dribbling and Ball Control that did the real damage.

PACE	SHOOTING	PASSING	DRIBBLING	DEFENDING	PHYSICAL
93	87	88	96	39	67

CM: Kevin de Bruyne

96

The perfect attacking teammate to Kanté. 99 Short Passing lets him tear defences open, but backing off isn't an option for opponents – do that and he'd destroy you with 97 Long Shots and Shot Power.

PACE	SHOOTING	PASSING	DRIBBLING	DEFENDING	PHYSICAL
86	92	98	93	80	88

ST: Ronaldo

97

FIFA's most expensive striker just about blocks off Kylian Mbappé and an all-PSG front three. How do you stop 98 Pace, 98 Dribbling, 99 Positioning and 99 Finishing? The answer is simple. You don't.

PACE	SHOOTING	PASSING	DRIBBLING	DEFENDING	PHYSICAL
98	97	83	97	46	79

CAM: Pelé

99

The most powerful card in *FIFA 22*. Brazil's greatest ever player scored the maximum possible rating of 99 in four categories: Vision, Short Passing, Finishing and Heading Accuracy. It cost 13 million (!!!) when first released.

PACE	SHOOTING	PASSING	DRIBBLING	DEFENDING	PHYSICAL
96	97	96	97	62	79

RW: Lionel Messi

98

If you could afford Little Leo, there was only one right-wing option in *FIFA 22*. 99 Dribbling, Ball Control and Composure made him unstoppable on the flank, before cutting inside to curl home with that wand-like left foot.

PACE	SHOOTING	PASSING	DRIBBLING	DEFENDING	PHYSICAL
93	97	98	99	40	76

02

October - December

Catch up on all the games awards, find out about the coolest DLC and read our round-up of next-gen consoles, one year on. Plus, all the biggest and best game releases from the quarter, like the massive *Forza Horizon 5*.

GAMING HIGHLIGHT

Forza Horizon 5

Page 108

Console Catch Up

PlayStation 5 & Xbox Series X/S

DualSense™ Download

Sony added a **free copy of *Astro's Playroom* with every PS5**. The game showcased the new controller tech, like feeling raindrops reverberating or the upward blow of a fan.

■ Catch up on the newest and biggest consoles after their dramatic releases. Xbox Series X/S launched on 10th November 2020, just two days ahead of PlayStation 5 on 12th November. Both consoles were challenging to get hold of in the first twelve months, but for those fortunate enough to snag one they provided many highlights ...

PS5: The First Year

Sony has a history of amazing PlayStation exclusives. It lived up to that in PS5's early months. *Marvel's Spider-Man: Miles Morales* wowed with a massive world for web-slinging. In *Ratchet & Clank: Rift Apart*, players dimension-hopped to platforming perfection. Then the remake of PS3 classic *Demon's Souls* was somehow even more brutal after being rebuilt from the ground up.

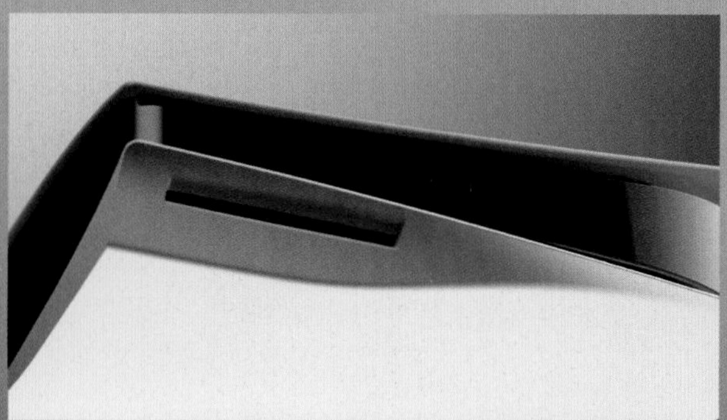

The big PS5 challenge was simply finding one. A whopping 13.4 million consoles were sold in the first year, but a global computer chip shortage meant Sony couldn't produce enough machines to match demand. As a result, many gamers spent months refreshing websites, hoping to snag an in-stock console.

New features added throughout the year included fresh colours for the DualSense™ controller. Plus, support for SSD (solid-state drive) storage, letting you stash even more saves and games. All the launch features still feel incredible too. Loading times are unbelievably swift, and graphics and sound have advanced hugely since PS4.

PS5 Trivia

- PS5 has internal dust catchers hidden behind removable side plates, meaning you can easily vacuum detritus out of the machine.
- The machine comes with *Astro's Playroom* pre-installed – a platformer that shows off the DualSense™ controller's new features.
- PS5's cooling system was deliberately designed to be quieter than PlayStation 4.

Essential PlayStation Exclusives

GHOST OF TSUSHIMA

RATCHET & CLANK: RIFT APART

DEMON'S SOULS

GRAN TURISMO 7

HORIZON: FORBIDDEN WEST

Next-gen Must-play: **Spider-Man: Miles Morales**

Developer Insomniac Games **Publisher** SIE

Miles Morales was the launch title most commonly packaged with PS5 machines. It's the perfect intro into the machine's 60 FPS visuals and gameplay capabilities. Swing across a snowy open-world Manhattan unlocking cool new powers like invisibility and bio-electric blasts. Finally grabbed yourself a Sony console? Then be sure to give this a go.

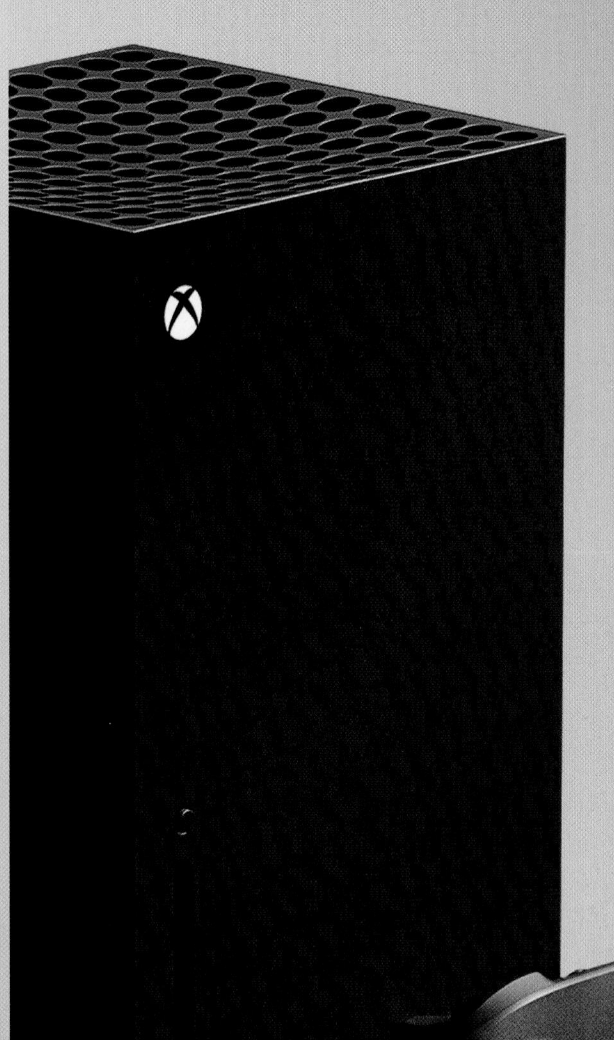

Xbox Series X/S: The First Year

Xbox's first year focused on a huge list of high-quality games. Microsoft isn't big on single-console exclusives, preferring to release games across Xbox Series X/S, Xbox One and PC. This isn't to say it's been short on special releases. Sneaking in just ahead of the one-year anniversary, *Forza Horizon* added racing wow factor to a line-up that already included *Psychonauts 2* and *Microsoft Flight Simulator.*

Xbox has become the machine to beat for backwards compatibility. Every Xbox One game works on Xbox Series X, as do a good number of Xbox 360 and original Xbox games. Plus, Microsoft's Game Pass subscription has more than 400 titles across consoles, PCs and mobile devices.

Like the PS5, 60 FPS and 4K have become the standard for Xbox Series X/S games. Performance is similar to a reasonable gaming PC. New features included a 4K dashboard with increased sharpness and text readability and customisable night mode. Getting your hands on an Xbox Series X has been just as hard as nabbing a PS5, but Xbox Series S is a little more widely available.

Xbox X/S Trivia

- Microsoft's new console pair sold 8 million copies in their first year on sale.
- The machine was known as Project Scarlett for months before its real name was unveiled in December 2020.
- An internet meme comparing the Series X to a refrigerator was so popular that Microsoft made one for Snoop Dogg – then later released official mini-fridges too.

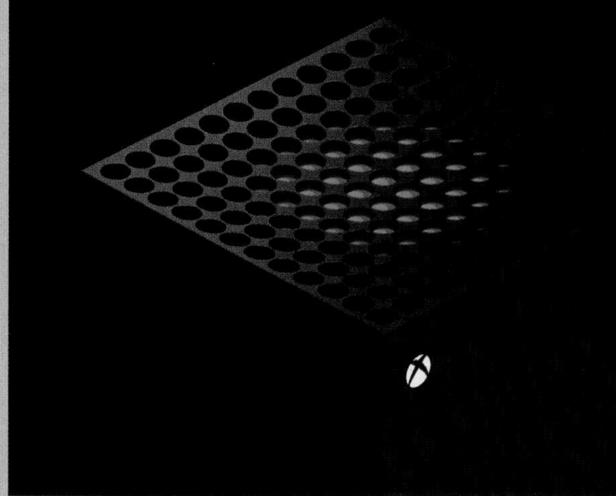

Next-gen Must-play: **Assassin's Creed Valhalla**

Developer Ubisoft Montreal **Publisher** Ubisoft

Valhalla merges together all the best bits of *Assassin's Creed* games in a fresh Viking setting. It's a phenomenon on both PS5 and Xbox Series X. As if the original wasn't colossal enough, 2021 brought two new DLCs in *Wrath of the Druids* and *The Siege of Paris*. Whatever your next-gen machine, it's a raid that can't be resisted.

Next-gen Must-play: Cyberpunk 2077

Developer CD Projekt Red **Publisher** CD Projekt

CD Projekt's futuristic open-worlder dropped on PS5 and Xbox Series X consoles. Explore the metropolis of Night City as a mercenary who goes by V. Brawl, hack and take down foes using bullet time, upgrading as you go. V is fully customisable so you can style your fighter however you like. Listen out for Keanu Reeves as Johnny Silverhand.

X Or S?

Microsoft released two new consoles in 2020. The Xbox Series X tkaes physical game discs, while the Xbox Series S works from downloads – so make sure you've got good WIFI!

Essential Xbox Exclusives

MICROSOFT FLIGHT SIMULATOR

FORZA HORIZON 5

HALO INFINITE

ORI AND THE WILL OF THE WISPS

SEA OF THIEVES

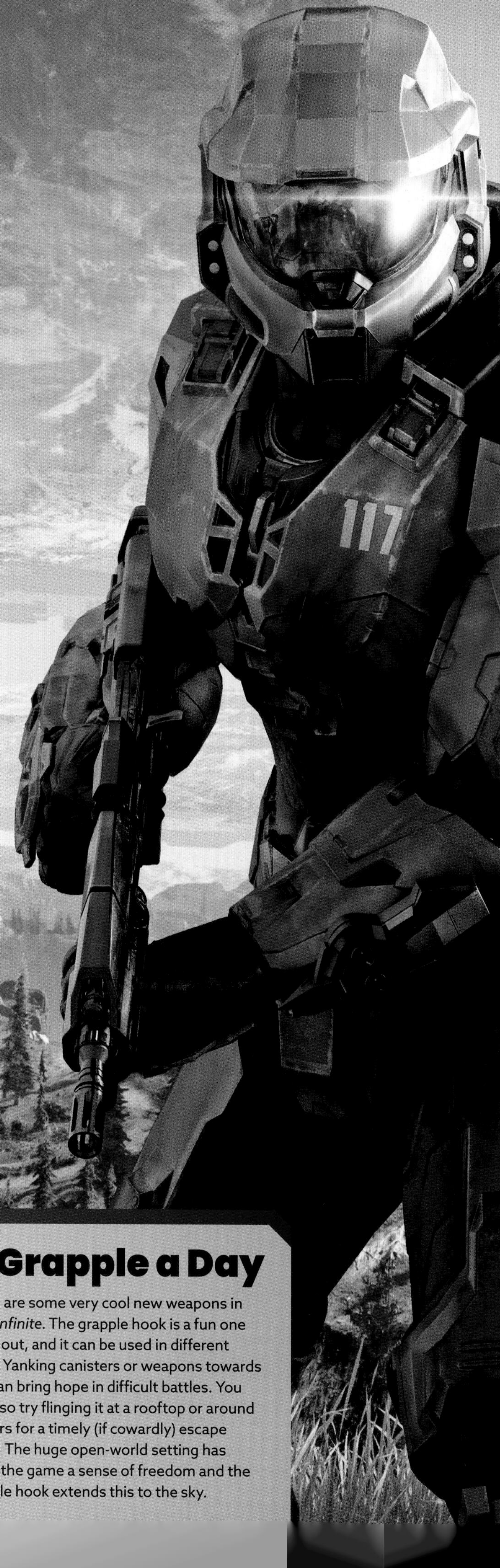

Halo Infinite

Developer 343 Industries
Publisher Xbox Game Studios
Platform PC, XBO, XBX/S

■ The original *Halo* inspired twenty years of shooter games. It's a giant of the genre but even legends find ways to stay fresh. This sixth sequel adds an open-world setting and a brand new AI partner embedded in Master Chief's suit. Plus, there's an especially cool addition to the big guy's guns.

Back to the Future

The game is set in 2560 and based on the ring world Zelta Halo. This futuristic space setting is packed full of bases to clear and capture, and targets to blast into bits. Plus, valour to be turned into cooler weapons and vehicles.

If *Halo*'s multiplayer mode is your thing, then get ready for an even bigger battle royale. Team battle matches have grown from sixteen players to a maximum of twenty-four players. Deathmatch and capture the flag battles are even better with ability pick-ups like dashing and camouflage. Turns out you can teach an old war dog new tricks.

A Grapple a Day

There are some very cool new weapons in *Halo Infinite*. The grapple hook is a fun one to try out, and it can be used in different ways. Yanking canisters or weapons towards you can bring hope in difficult battles. You can also try flinging it at a rooftop or around corners for a timely (if cowardly) escape route. The huge open-world setting has given the game a sense of freedom and the grapple hook extends this to the sky.

The Grunts in Halo Infinite *are more than just cannon fodder, listen for some hilarious dialogue.*

The open-world setting provides gamers with a huge playground to explore.

Behold The Weapon

Master Chief's friendship with new virtual assistant, The Weapon, adds an emotional storyline. She was created as an exact copy of long-time holo-buddy Cortana, and brings humour and tactical info to your rumblings. Watching the growth of her relationship with Master Chief in the second half of the game is as entertaining as any gunfight.

Call Names

Master Chief was nameless for most of *Halo*'s early development, simply being known as 'Future Soldier' as well as 'The Cyborg'.

Did You Know

There are four soft toys to find in the game: Master Chief, Pilot, Arbiter and Grunt.

Sniper scopes help players check out possible enemies from afar.

Halo Infinite *introduces a new pilot, Echo-216, who helps Master Chief.*

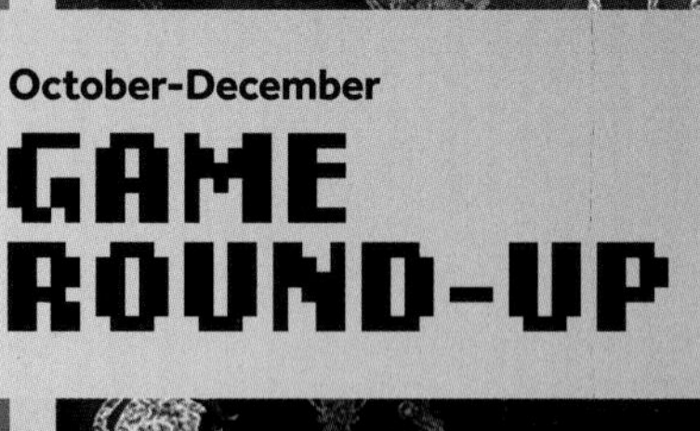

Tetris Effect Connected

Developer Monstars / Resonair **Publisher** Enhance Games
Platform NS, PC PS4, XBO, XBX/S

■ ***Tetris* is officially the second biggest game series in the world. It beats *Call of Duty*, *Fortnite*, *Minecraft* and *Pokémon*. The game has sold almost 500 million copies over the past four decades. *Tetris Effect Connected* takes the classic block-falling gameplay and throws in four new multiplayer modes for super competitive chaos.**

Block Party

Zone battle is the traditional fave, when you complete a line it drops junk on your opponent's board. There's also a cunning twist where you can briefly freeze time to clear your field. It's joined by two versions of score attack, focused on racking up bigger numbers than your foes. Want to make friends rather than enemies? Then co-op mode is the one you need, where you team up with three other puzzlers to take on an AI opponent. Each team member is given a special power like an increased block speed. It's the second most popular game ever, what's not to love?

Connected mode enables up to three players to merge their screens and play as one.

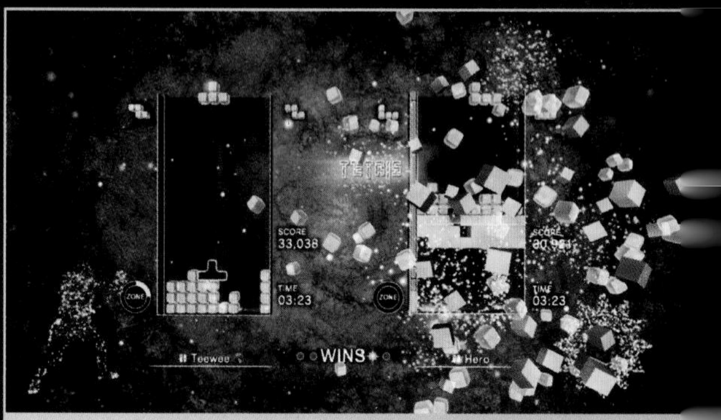

The zone battle mechanic lets players go one-on-one against an opponent, and stop time!

Bestsellers

By 2022, the greatest gaming franchises of all time are:

Mario (772m copies sold)
Tetris (495m sold)
Call of Duty (400m sold)
Pokémon (380m sold)
Grand Theft Auto (355m sold)
FIFA (325m sold)
Minecraft (238m sold)

There are multiple versions of the classic Single Player mode to try out in the new game.

Did You Know

The series started out under a different name – *Championship Manager*, which emerged on PC in 1992.

Football Manager 2022

Developer Sports Interactive **Publisher** Sega
Platform ANROID, IOS, MAC, NS, PC, XBO, XBX/S

■ The latest *Football Manager* game lets players control every aspect of their club. Plus, there are tons of interesting new ways to interact with your team. As always, playing with the transfer market to build your dream squad is one of the best bits. You can also tweak tactics mid-match to turn a 0-1 loss into a late 2-1 victory. A huge player-performance data hub and jazzed up Transfer Deadline Day make this release stand out against its mobile-game rivals.

The Riftbreaker

Developer Exor Studios **Publisher** Exor Studios
Platform ANDROID, NS, PC, PS4, PS5, XBO, XBX/S

■ Stomp around the alien world of Galatea 37 as Ashley, the soldier-scientist wearing a giant mech suit. She follows a blissfully simple motto: "kill it before it kills us." The 'it' being plural. Specifically, a ton of creatures who can be taken out with plasma guns, rocket launchers and nukes. The game involves base-building but the strategic element is light. The combat isn't though – at times you're fighting thousands of enemies in one go. Good luck, soldier.

Top Tip

It's easy to run dry of firepower, so make sure you build an armoury on your base for a constant ammo supply.

Chorus

Developer Fishlabs
Publisher Deep Silver
Platform NS, PC, PS4, PS5, XBO, XBX/S

■ Superpowered Nara has escaped an evil space cult and wants to take down her former masters. Players travel across the galaxy in a spaceship that has a mind of its own. *Forsaken*, your trusty ship, is also a character in this intergalactic openworlder. New star systems unlock as you dodge, stalk and destroy enemy ships. Battles constantly evolve through a mechanic called rites. Rite of the storm removes an enemy's shield, while rite of the hunt lets you teleport behind a foe.

Check Out
The PS5 and Xbox Series X version of *No Man's Sky* has a thirty-two-person multiplayer! It's an alien exploration with even larger bases.

Loop Hero

Developer Four Quarters
Publisher Devolver Digital
Platform MAC, NS, PC

■ Welcome to the apocalypse! But don't worry, you're armed with a deck of cards. Your pixelated hero moves around an endless looping map. Using the cards helps his chances in battle. They also transform the scenery in useful ways, like placing a mountain to give him more HP. The dark world is slowly brought back to its natural beauty, but the boss fights along the way can seem world-ending. Try not to play a card on every loop, as doing so can trigger these before you're ready.

Top Tip
Build watchtowers as early as possible. They back you up with archers who fire at foes while you move.

Did You Know

Cloud Strife has also made guest appearances in *Kingdom Hearts*, *Monster Strike* and *Super Smash Bros.*

Final Fantasy VII Remake Intergrade

Developer Square Enix **Publisher** Square Enix **Platform** PC, PS4, PS5

■ *Final Fantasy* was a game-changer, like *Zelda* or *Minecraft* or *Fortnite*. In the 1990s, *Final Fantasy VII* brought a ground-breaking 3D art style, adorable cast, gripping story and a ton of combat options to the scene. Twenty-five years later, Square Enix have remade the game for PS5 and, boy, does it hold up!

Way of the Ninja

Remake first dropped in 2020. The story and cast stayed the same, but it was rebuilt using new graphics. The fight system had some big changes too, taking place in real-time instead of using pre-selected commands. This PS5 release vamps up the visuals and adds in Intermission, a new adventure with ninja Yuffie Kisaragi at its heart.

Despite the flashy new tech, the magic of the original still shines through. It's the perfect mix of old and new. Favourite cut-scenes have been beautifully reanimated and story twists that didn't occur first time around are what put this remake on another level.

Battles are now fought in real-time, making them more fast-paced than ever before.

Tifa Lockhart performs a whirling uppercut against the sewer beast, Abzu.

Cast List

The key players found in and around the world of Midgar:

CLOUD STRIFE

YUFFIE KISARAGI

SONON KASUKABE

AERITH GAINSBOROUGH

TIFA LOCKHART

BARRET WALLACE

RED III

SEPHIROTH

STUDIO PROFILES
The Teams Behind Your Favourite Games

LEADER OF THE PAC

Bandai Namco Studios

■ The *Tales of Arise* developer sounds relatively new. It opened its doors in Kōtō, Japan in 2012. But its history dates all the way back to 1955. Japanese businessman Masaya Nakamura started a chain making rocking horses. Its name, Namco, was short for Nakamura Seisakusho Co (Nakamura Manufacturing). Two decades later, it found fame thanks to *Pac-Man* and merged with toy maker Bandai. As well as *Tales*, it's home to flight sim *Ace Combat* and legendary fighter *Tekken*.

Have You Played?

Tales of Arise

Scarlet Nexus

Ace Combat 7: Skies Unknown

Soulcalibur VI

Biggest Series: Pac-Man

Introduced in 1980, Bandai Namco's ghost-gobbling mascot rivals *Mario* and *Sonic* as a digital icon. If you're looking for a first foray into his world, try *Pac-Man Championship Edition 2* – it's available on PS4, Switch and Xbox One.

RACING KINGS

Codemasters

■ No British studio has a rep for racing games like Leamington-based Codies. But your mum, dad or computer-loving uncle will know them for something completely different. Dizzy was one of the 1980s' most celebrated adventure series. You rolled a live egg through levels packed with obstacles and enemies. As well as *Micro Machines*, *F1*, *Dirt* and *Grid*, it's made sports fans happy with *Brian Lara Cricket*, *Jonah Lomu Rugby* and *LMA Manager*.

Biggest Series: Dirt

It's tempting to put *F1* in this spot, but *Dirt*'s illustrious history can't be ignored. Between 1998 and 2004, it transformed point-to-point racing with the *Colin McRae Rally* games. They were based around real World Championship Rally seasons and then expanded to include more unconventional events from *Colin McRae Dirt* (2007) onwards. The fast, colourful *Dirt 5* sees the series still going strong on PS5 and Xbox Series X.

Have You Played?

F1 2021

Grid Legends

Dirt 5

F1 Race Stars

NEWS FLASH

Netflix Streams Games Now?

Find Out All About Netflix's Gaming News

Play Your Fave Shows

As well as the games currently available on the app, Netflix has announced it plans to create new ones based on some of its hit shows, like *The Queen's Gambit* and *Shadow and Bone.*

■ Netflix's huge catalogue of bingeable TV series and movies has made it an entertainment sensation. The service stepped it up another gear in 2021 by launching its own brand of video games. Five titles were available at launch, with two of them focused on one of its biggest shows: 1980s-set sci-fi horror *Stranger Things*.

The games are available on both iOS and Android and there's no hidden cost such as in-app purchases. All you need to play are a Netflix account and mobile phone or tablet. They're available on multiple profiles, although aren't available on kid profiles. You'll need to have an adult profile or ask your parents if you want to play.

By early 2022, nine more games were added, like tenpin simulation *Bowling Ballers* and quirky hand-drawn webcomic *Krispee Street*. They're all worth trying if you already have a Netflix account and can tear yourself away from *Cobra Kai* for the occasional half-hour. Check out the five launch games here!

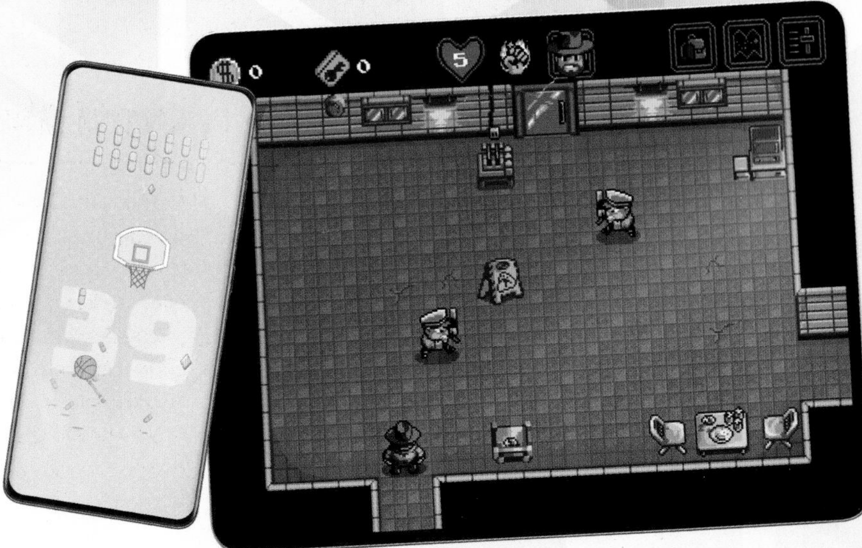

Stranger Things 3: The Game

The official companion game to the third series has playable events from the *Stranger Things* along with fresh quests. You can play as twelve different characters from the show, all with special attacks and moves. Nancy downs enemies using surgical shears, and Mike offs them with a baseball bat.

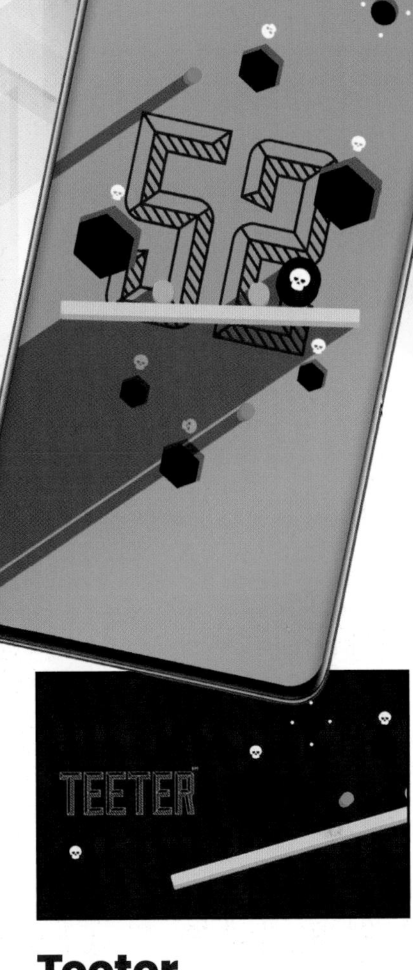

Teeter

Physics are the focus in this simple but frustrating game. You move a horizontal platform up a screen to get a ball into a hole – without it falling off the edge or into a different hole marked with a skull. It's easy to begin with but grows seriously tough over 150 levels.

Shooting Hoops

Basketball with a difference. You use a dart gun to fire the balls! There's a selection of different balls to unlock, all with different weights and effects. As well as the very unique balls, there are some seriously crazy physics at play here. *Shooting Hoops* has created a unique way to land baskets.

Card Blast

Netflix has given poker a fun arcade twist. Players grab cards from a conveyer belt to form a winning hand. If you fail, the end is a little explosive! Abilities include being able to freeze or boost your way to victory. You can play *Card Blast* against the AI or invite other humans to join in.

Stranger Things: 1984

Welcome to Hawkins! This pixelated, retro-styled adventure lets you explore the town, including areas that never appeared in the show. Unique character abilities help you solve puzzles, and collecting Eggos and gnomes unlocks secret treats.

Check Out
If you love mini-games but want something even weirder, try *Warioware* for some brilliantly bonkers fun!

Mario Party Superstars

Developer NDCube **Publisher** Nintendo **Platform** NS

■ ***Mario Party Superstars* is packed with greatest hits. It brings together all the best games from the first ten *Mario Party* titles on Gamecube and Nintendo 64. There's a whopping 100 kooky challenges to entertain and enrage your family and friends.**

Chorus of Boos

Superstars has a few tweaks on the original games. One of those changes is King Boo replacing Big Boo in the haunted forest of Horror Land. *Super Mario Party* fans should know that custom dice blocks and buddies are also absent.

Having so many past collections to pick from means the choice is filled with hits. As always, it's best played against three other people. The elite mini-games mix competitiveness with humour. In Pushy Penguins, you try to survive on a block of ice as boisterous birds charge at you from all directions. Monty's Revenge is basically Whack-A-Mole in reverse: you switch between holes in the ground to avoid being thunked by Monty's massive mallet.

Boulder Roll is a mini-game where one player faces off against three rivals.

Retro Warnings
Some mini-games feature a warning not to rotate the analogue stick with the palm of your hand, due to injuries caused on the original Nintendo 64 *Mario Party.*

Toad Stalled

There is one big surprise in *Mario Party Superstars*. Nintendo chose not to add some popular plumbers, princesses or fire-breathing Koopas to its list of playable characters. There's no way to control Bowser, or Toad, or Shy Guy. But pink dino-lady Birdo returns for the first time since 2012's *Mario Party 9*. Plus, there's always Luigi, Peach and Wario to play a round of games with, and they're a blast! You'll have so much fun dodging obstacles and rotating platforms in Dungeon Duos, or freezing your cartoon toes off in Bobsled Run, or munching melted cheese as fast as you can in Eatsa Pizza. Or, or, or ...

Mini-game Insanity

Speed Hockey

Table football meets puck-smacking madness, where the first team to score three times wins.

Revers-a-bomb

Press the buttons that light up to send Bob-ombs at your rivals. Ten successful strikes earn victory.

Dizzy Dancing

The vinyl revolution continues, as clefs hover above a record while it spins. Grab the most clefs for the W.

Chip-shot Challenge

Mario Golf in miniature. You only get one shot, and whoever's ball lands nearest the hole takes the spoils.

Mushroom Mix-Up mini-game: Bounce from mushroom to mushroom and stay out of the water to win.

Did You Know
The Hinokami Chronicles sold 1.32 million copies by the end of 2021.

Demon Slayer: Kimetsu no Yaiba – The Hinokami Chronicles

Developer CyberConnect 2 **Publisher** Sega
Platform NS, PC, PS4, PS5, XBO, XBX/S

■ The Japanese anime series *Demon Slayer* is absolutely massive. It's expanded into TV shows, movies and games. The Hinokami Chronicles delves into the story of blade-wielding Tanjiro Kamado. His family was murdered by demons and his sister was turned into one, so he's searching for a cure. It's packed with gorgeous manga cutscenes and boss battles against a ginormous green slab with multiple hands, or a red-eyed humanoid with drums (yes, drums) attached to his shoulders, hips and chest.

Combo Deal

If it sounds ludicrous that's because it is ludicrous. The tale is linear and is filled with collectible memory fragments, earned by completing objectives or taking a few moments to search your surroundings. These tell Tanjiro's back story and give players a break from all the action, which is visually extreme. There's also a standalone-versus mode that gives you the chance to play against a friend. But don't forget to unlock characters for it in the main campaign!

Enmu, a demon who works for the Twelve Kizuki, takes out Tanjiro with a tentacle attack. Enmu was added in a DLC update.

Akaza is another of the many demons affiliated with the Twelve Kizuki, and Kyojuro Rengoku's battle with him is intense.

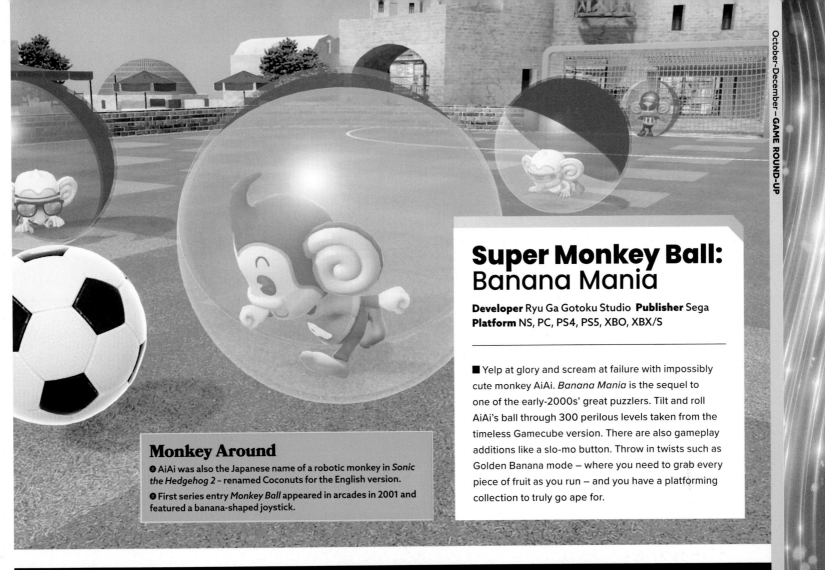

Super Monkey Ball: Banana Mania

Developer Ryu Ga Gotoku Studio **Publisher** Sega
Platform NS, PC, PS4, PS5, XBO, XBX/S

■ Yelp at glory and scream at failure with impossibly cute monkey AiAi. *Banana Mania* is the sequel to one of the early-2000s' great puzzlers. Tilt and roll AiAi's ball through 300 perilous levels taken from the timeless Gamecube version. There are also gameplay additions like a slo-mo button. Throw in twists such as Golden Banana mode – where you need to grab every piece of fruit as you run – and you have a platforming collection to truly go ape for.

Monkey Around

- AiAi was also the Japanese name of a robotic monkey in *Sonic the Hedgehog 2* – renamed Coconuts for the English version.
- First series entry *Monkey Ball* appeared in arcades in 2001 and featured a banana-shaped joystick.

Inscryption

Developer Daniel Mullins Games
Publisher Devolver Digital **Platform** PC

■ Fancy playing a spooky card game? Go head-to-head with an AI opponent by playing creature cards against their hand. If the corresponding card is a creature, you inflict damage. If it's unopposed, you're hurt instead. Get up from the table and your surroundings switch to an escape room vibe, full of riddles offering rewards that help you in matches as well as objects from past fights bleeding into the room. Dark yet impossible to stop playing.

Check Out

The same developer made hilarious puzzler *Pony Island*, set in a spooky broken arcade machine.

Did You Know?
Cordona is fictional but inspired by real history, with Venetian elements on the north side, and Ottoman influences in the east.

Sherlock Holmes: Chapter One

Developer Frogwares **Publisher** Frogwares
Platform PC, PS4, PS5, XBO, XBX/S

■ Forget Benedict Cumberbatch. Forget Watson, too. This origin story follows a dapper twenty-one-year-old Holmes returning to his childhood home on the Mediterranean isle of Cordona. It's loosely open-world along the lines of *LA Noire. Sherlock Holmes: Chapter One* is packed with five mysteries, twenty-five side cases and numerous disguises to try on. Holmes does still have a sidekick to riff off – but is childhood 'best friend' Jon exactly what he seems?

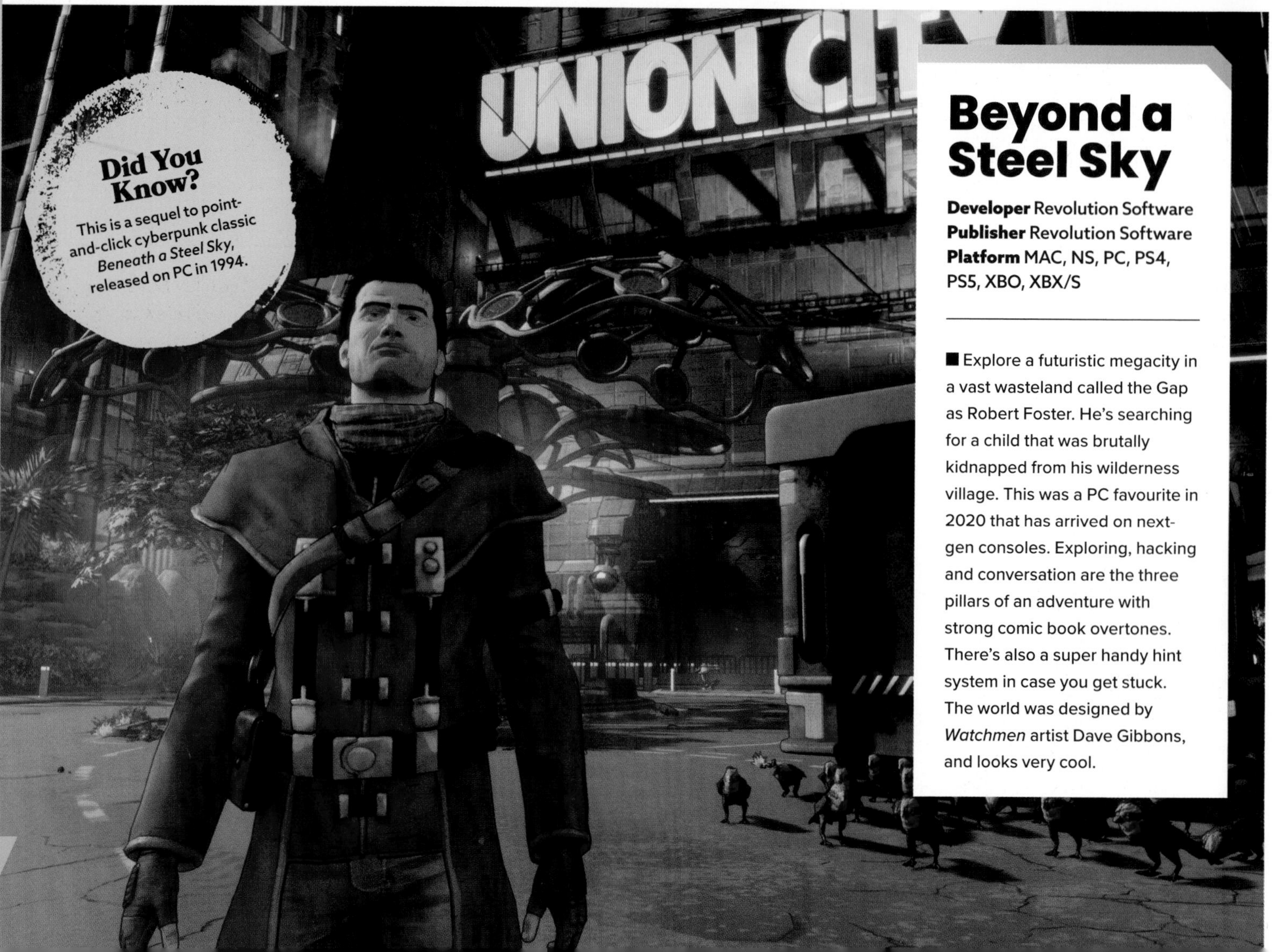

Did You Know?
This is a sequel to point-and-click cyberpunk classic *Beneath a Steel Sky*, released on PC in 1994.

Beyond a Steel Sky

Developer Revolution Software
Publisher Revolution Software
Platform MAC, NS, PC, PS4, PS5, XBO, XBX/S

■ Explore a futuristic megacity in a vast wasteland called the Gap as Robert Foster. He's searching for a child that was brutally kidnapped from his wilderness village. This was a PC favourite in 2020 that has arrived on next-gen consoles. Exploring, hacking and conversation are the three pillars of an adventure with strong comic book overtones. There's also a super handy hint system in case you get stuck. The world was designed by *Watchmen* artist Dave Gibbons, and looks very cool.

Exo One

Developer Exbleative
Publisher Future Friends Games
Platform PC, PS4, PS5, XBO, XBX/S

■ Roll, guide and fly your tiny alien ship across purple clouds and over roiling seas in this breathtaking journey through a fictional solar system. As you travel through the skies, you're searching for a light on the horizon that will shoot the spacecraft on to the next place to explore. Soothing electric guitars and a blissful lack of onscreen clutter combine for the most calming experience on next-gen consoles.

Top Tip
If you want to maximise your speed, stay as low to the ground as possible, and don't worry about glide power-ups.

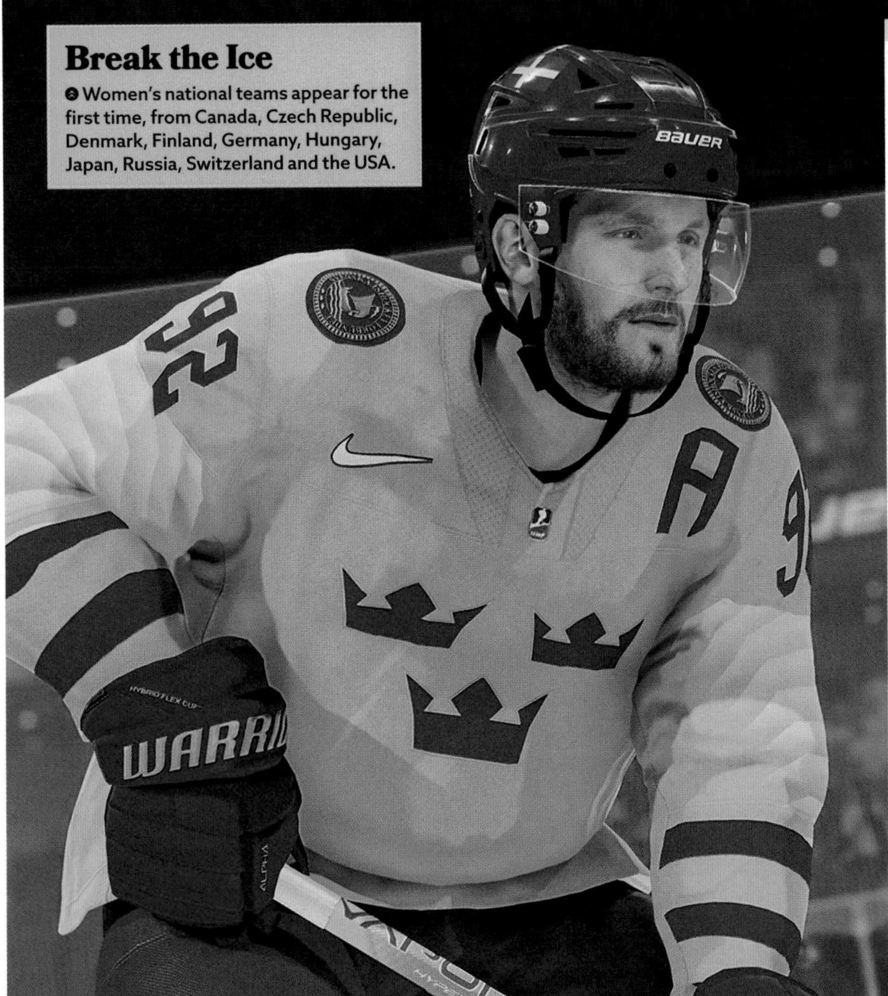

Break the Ice
● Women's national teams appear for the first time, from Canada, Czech Republic, Denmark, Finland, Germany, Hungary, Japan, Russia, Switzerland and the USA.

NHL 22

Developer EA Canada **Publisher** EA
Platform PS4, PS5, XBO, XBX/S

■ EA have taken *NHL 22* off ice. The thirty-first edition in EA's ice hockey series has a new engine, switching from Ignite to Frostbite. *Madden NFL*'s superstar x-factor mechanic has been added, so players with the 'One Tee' ability can fire off faultless first-time shots. There's also an expansion draft for new team Seattle Kraken. The developer has now added the ability to share roster files to the game too, after a lot of requests from fans!

Forza Horizon 5

Developer Playground Games **Publisher** Xbox Game Studios
Platform PC, XBO, XBX/S

■ The newest release in the champion of all racing games is every bit as exhilarating as you'd hope. The game is set in an open-world recreation of Mexico. You zoom past ancient temples and an active volcano in an incredibly wide range of weather conditions, from glorious sunshine to tropical storms. *Forza 5* is a breathtaking drive in both feel and beauty.

As with previous games, the massive map is littered with stuff to do. There are race events or more off-beat challenges, and victories in these unlock money and new vehicles. You race a monster truck down a mountain. You race against jet-skis, and trains and a cargo plane. Wait! Actually, it's a cargo plane *dropping dirt bikes*. It's beyond bonkers and all the more thrilling for it.

Let's Waste Time, Chasing Cards

The best new feature is a custom race creator called EventLabs, where you can dream up your own race or download those made by others – expanding the ton of options in an already massive game. Even *FIFA* Ultimate Team fans are unexpectedly catered for, with the game's full set of cars available in collectible-card form.

The Car's the Star

Forza Horizon 5 gives you more than 500 cars to choose from, with every major brand name represented: Ford, Dodge, Ferrari, Chevrolet, Honda, Porsche and so many more. Like your vehicles to be contemporary? Hop into the 2020 Koenigsegg Jesko. Prefer a vintage ride? The 1959 Jaguar Mk II 3.8 awaits. The choice feels endless and, while you quickly find favourites, there's little chance you'll ever manage to drive them all. But you'll have fun trying.

Fancy the chance to sit in the driving seat of the most elite cars in existence? You got this.

The range of biomes doesn't just add variety to the scenery, they also come with new challenges, such as driving through tight streets in the urban setting.

DLC

Playground Games are constantly releasing new cars and challenges through **Forza Horizon 5 Festival Playlist**. There are also plans for paid DLC with heftier content, but no release date yet.

Arcade Distractions

Racing excellence is par for the course in *Forza*, but a more casual alternative is Horizon Arcade. This series of multiplayer mini-games adds loopy twists such as Piñata Pop, where you have to burst piñatas within a time limit as they're dropped from a plane above you, or Bullseye, where you launch yourself off ramps to hit floating targets.

Stat Attack

More than 4.5 million people played *Forza Horizon 5* in the first twenty-four hours after launch.

DLC FTW

More DLC

If you've tried all of these and want more DLC, some other great options from the last year are *Final Fantasy 7 Remake: INTERmission*, *Outer Wilds: Echoes of the Eye* and *Super Mario 3D World: Bowser's Fury*.

How Four of the Biggest Games Got Even Bigger

■ Downloadable content for the win! There have been tons of exciting new games, especially on next-gen. But some old favourites were determined to keep you playing. Check out four memorable add-ons from the last year.

Destiny 2: The Witch Queen

Arguably the DLC that outdid them all, *Destiny 2* first appeared in 2017 and *The Witch Queen* is the sixth expansion. At seven to twelve hours' playtime, it's bigger than many standalone games. The evil regent of the story is Savathûn, and the adventure is set in her swamp-like Throne World. She uses the power of light to control her servants, the Lucent Brood. They are grey, spike-skinned enemies who can raise the dead. Helping players take them down is a new weapon archetype called The Glaive. It can stab enemies, fire projectiles and act as a shield. Cool! Once the campaign's done there's also a new raid called Vow of the Disciple, set in a sunken pyramid, and six-player challenge The Wellspring. Incredibly, there's still more to come in *Destiny 2: Lightfall* (2023) and *The Final Shape* (2024).

Marvel's Avengers: Black Panther – War for Wakanda

Black Panther comes to Crystal Dynamics' superhero action adventure game, taking its playable character list to nine. The pack adds seven missions based in and around the Wakandan Jungle and introduces villain Ulysses Klaue. T'Challa's unique abilities, such as pouncing cat-like at enemies or throwing kimono beads, make this essential for fans of the standalone game.

Animal Crossing New Horizons: Happy Home Paradise

Switch's cutesy community simulation serves up a whole new beach holiday. Join the paradise planning team to help clients live their vacation home dreams on a new group of islands. The homes need to be built, customised and shared on the internet via the Happy Home Network app. Fan favourite past characters can also be invited to the islands using Amiibo™ figures and cards.

Assassin's Creed Valhalla: Dawn of Ragnarök

If *Destiny 2* had the year's best DLC then *Assassin's Creed Valhalla* came a very close second. *Dawn of Ragnarök* takes the already epic Norse adventure into the breathtaking yet deadly lands of Svartalfheim. The main character Odin gets truly god-like powers such as resurrecting dead enemies or shape-shifting into a raven.

What in the Weird?

Wild and Weird Gaming Stories From Across the World

World's Biggest eSports Stadium

Toronto eSports Stadium looks like a huge spaceship ready to take off. Just like eSports has across the world. The arena cost a whopping $500 million to build and will be the planet's biggest purpose-built eSports arena. It will seat 7,000 people. That's 1,500 people more than the current largest eSports stadium. It's in China, if you were wondering. The stadium will serve as the home for *Call of Duty* franchise Toronto Ultra and *Overwatch* super-team Toronto Defiant when it opens in 2025 and will also host concerts and plays.

New Zephyr Mouse Keeps Things Cool

Do you find your palms get sweaty during a long session of *Fortnite* or *Minecraft*? Mindshunter has crafted the Zephyr mouse to put an end to any sweaty slip-ups. It has a heavily perforated outer body that kicks out air from a built-in fan, keeping gamers' hands cool as they play. After easily crushing a Kickstarter funding campaign in 2020, the mouse went on sale in August with an entry level price tag of $59/£42.55. It isn't wireless, but at a weight of just 69 grams you barely notice anyway.

Google Maps Comes to NES

In 2012, Google pulled an obscure April Fools' Day joke. They announced a plan to port Google Maps to the original NES console. Nine years later, YouTuber ciciplusplus brought the idea to life for real. His custom cart contains the innards of a RaspberryPi minicomputer. It uses Google's mapping service to turn the real world into something that looks more like 1986's *The Legend Of Zelda* and place names take on NES's unmistakeable font. Now you can go around the world in (something like) eighty button-presses.

Resident Evil's Anniversary Bath Salts

Resident Evil turned twenty-five last year and creator Capcom found a unique way to celebrate the survival horror king's big birthday. Bath salts! Wait, what? Mixing red and green herbs found in and around Raccoon City is a way to heal yourself in-game. The Japanese publisher produced red and green bath salts in sachets bearing the Umbrella Corp logo, to enhance your next soak in the tub.

October-December

GAME SPOTLIGHT

Metroid Dread

Stat Attack
Samus has appeared in more than twenty other games, including Super Smash Bros and Animal Crossing: City Folk.

Developer MercurySteam **Publisher** Nintendo **Platform** NS

■ Explore complex, side-scrolling levels on the planet ZDR as bounty hunter Samus Aran. Try to evade capture by EMMI robots and – when that fails – down enemies with the right arm of your cybernetic power suit. It was originally conceived as a sequel to Nintendo DS game *Metroid Fusion* from 2002. *Metroid Dread* is a 2D sci-fi adventure that hugely benefits from the larger console.

Cavern Club

Putting plasma blasts to good use never grows old, but Samus has skills far beyond simple kill-shots. Her magnetic ability lets her hang on to and scale blue walls, and she can become temporarily invisible using a phantom cloak. By placing all this together you rattle along – and up – tight corridors and oppressive cave systems. As you explore, her suit upgrades, giving you better protection against boss characters and some familiar faces!

Greatest Bits

While *Metroid Dread* is technically a sequel to a twenty-year-old game, Nintendo has still been releasing games in the series over those two decades. A lot of the best elements from those games have been used in *Metroid Dread*. New features from 2017's *Metroid: Samus Returns* on 3DS carry over, such as melee counters and the main character's ability to free fire at any angle. The melee counters see you parry enemy attacks by pressing X just before a charging foe makes contact.

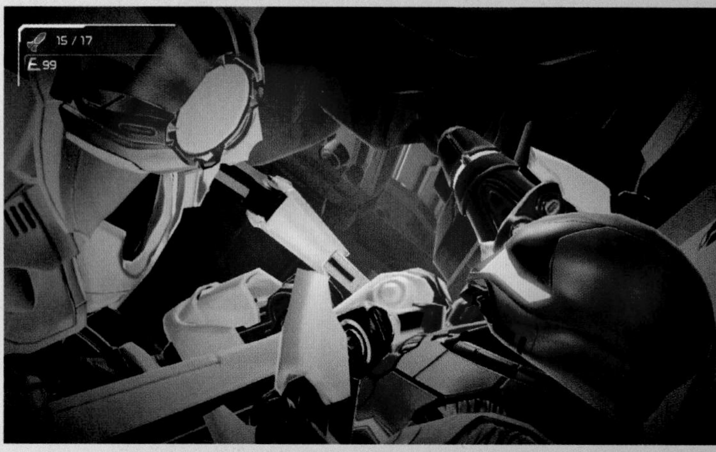

The wide beam upgrade can be used to attack enemies and unlock three dot doors.

There are nine areas in Metroid Dread *where you'll encounter a variety of different enemies and boss battles.*

Map it Out

Level designs really make *Metroid Dread* feel special. There are nine maps in total, each with unique obstacles and threats. Robots roam the former biological research institute of Dairon, where areas can be plunged into darkness by power outages. Half of Burenia is submerged in water and it's filled with some very unusual marine life, such as squid creatures that emit a blue light when you get too close.

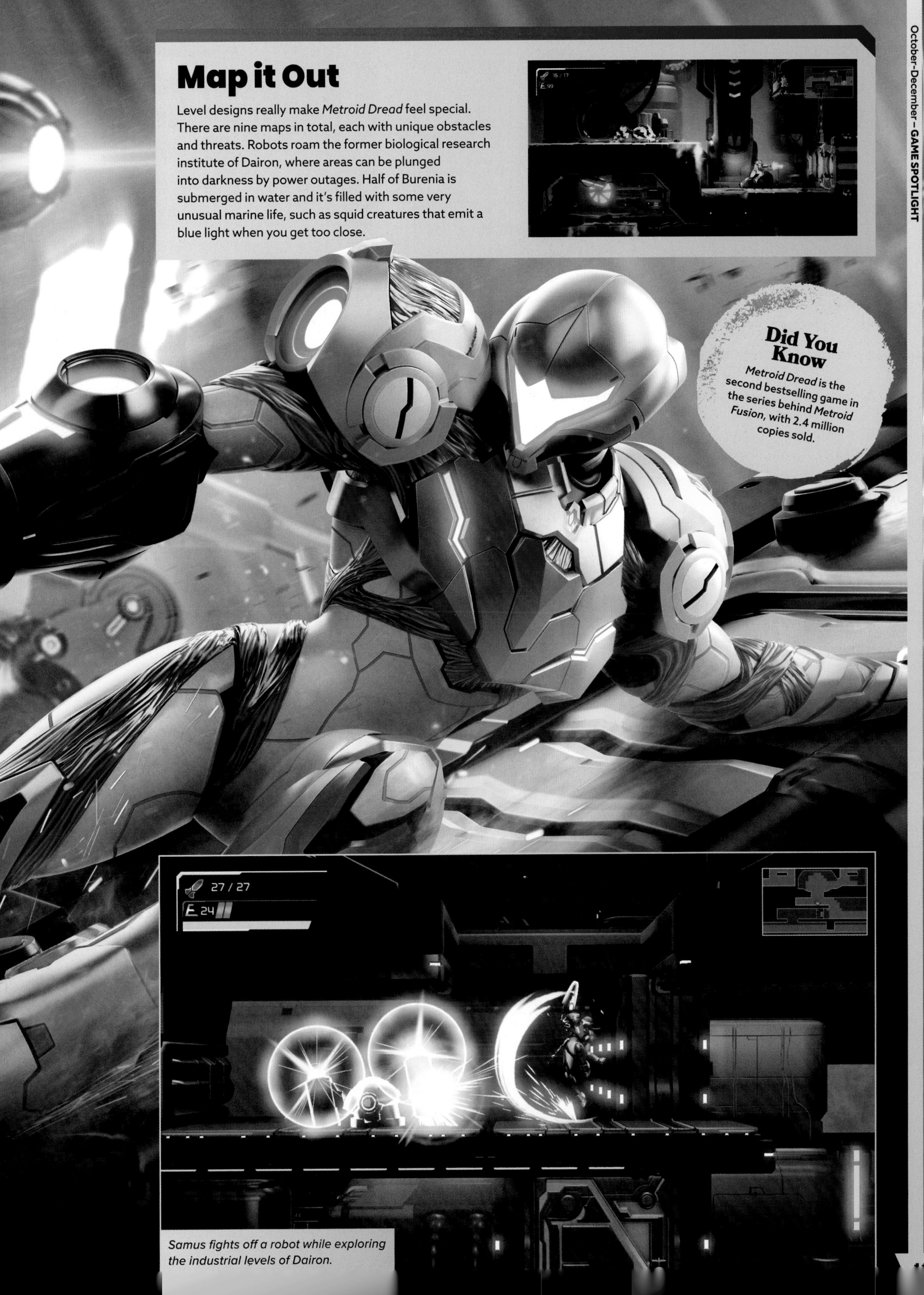

Did You Know

Metroid Dread is the second bestselling game in the series behind *Metroid Fusion*, with 2.4 million copies sold.

Samus fights off a robot while exploring the industrial levels of Dairon.

Jurassic World Evolution 2

Developer Frontier Developments **Publisher** Frontier Developments
Platform PC, PS4, PS5, XBO, XBX/S

■ Imagine *RollerCoaster Tycoon* or *SimCity* with dinosaurs! Construct enclosures and aviaries for deadly dinosaurs in this theme park builder based around the *Jurassic World* movies. There are seventy-five species in total and all your favourites from the films are here: T-Rex, velociraptor, Pteranodon. You need to constantly manage the pens where they're all kept. The game has a dynamic territory system, where the dinos compete for resources, with boundaries changing as a result.

Tricky Customers

It's not only the dinosaurs you need to pacify. Scientists must be hired and kept happy, and those who aren't like to cause mischief by letting animals escape. The success of your park also comes down to ensuring guests are content by building gift shops and restaurants, and catering to their dino preferences – like nature lovers wanting to see herbivores.

Watch out for those teeth! As you would expect from a Jurassic World game, the dinosaurs are likely to escape.

The iconic Jurassic Park entrance gate, still standing in one piece as you start the game.

Jurassic Park Evolution 2 *isn't just for the chaos lovers, calm herbivores such as Stegosaurus can be played too.*

Check Out

Planet Coaster offers traditional theme park building without the threat of a Megalosaurus on the loose.

Cricket 22

Developer Big Ant Studios
Publisher Nacon
Platform NS, PC, PS4, PS5, XBO, XBX/S

■ After a decade as gaming's forgotten sport, virtual six-smacking made a comeback with the excellent *Don Bradman Cricket* in 2014 – and *Cricket 22* is the latest simulation from the same Australian developer. Batting is the highlight, with an array of shots available by moving the right stick, but there's impressive variety in bowling too. England and Australia are both licensed, and while most other national teams aren't, it's easy to get real names and kits using the community sharing feature.

Top Tip
Fielding is the toughest part of the game – switch it to 'Auto' to just enjoy swatting fours and clattering the stumps.

Gloomhaven

Developer Flaming Fowl Studios
Publisher Asmodee Digital **Platform** PC

■ *Gloomhaven* was originally a super popular tabletop board game. Playing it as a video game makes it much easier and quicker! You'll quest through caves, forests and dungeons to take down a mix of monsters. Players drop cards to initiate combat and level up their band of adventurers. Up to four people can join in, but even alone it's great fun. There are also plenty of video guides explaining its many rules for you to watch before you play.

Did You Know
The *Gloomhaven* board game rule book is eighty-two pages long, and this version largely stays true to it. Hardcore.

Shin Megami Tensei V

Developer Atlus **Publisher** Nintendo **Platform** NS

■ Adventure through a crumbling alternative version of Tokyo in *Shin Megami Tensei V*. The latest game in this huge Japanese RPG series lets you battle absurd beasts and take on school bullies. For turn-based battles, your party is made up of three demons. You can then fuse two or more monstrous squad-mates together into an even bigger, more terrifying one to help your team get further in the game.

Hand to Hand

Shin Megami Tensei V was developed as a Switch exclusive as producer Kazuyuki Yamai wanted it to have both HD visuals and portability.

Echo Generation

Developer Cococucumber **Publisher** Cococucumber **Platform** PC, XBO, XBX/S

■ Welcome to Maple Town! This quaint and spooky village is packed with nostalgic references, making it the perfect game for any *Stranger Things* fan. A group of kids investigate supernatural occurrences in this pixelated adventure. Sound familiar? Find out if the local repair shop owner really was murdered by a giant clown. Chatting with the townsfolk will help you to complete the quests. And pet companions all have strange skills – like the family cat Meowsy being able to lick you better.

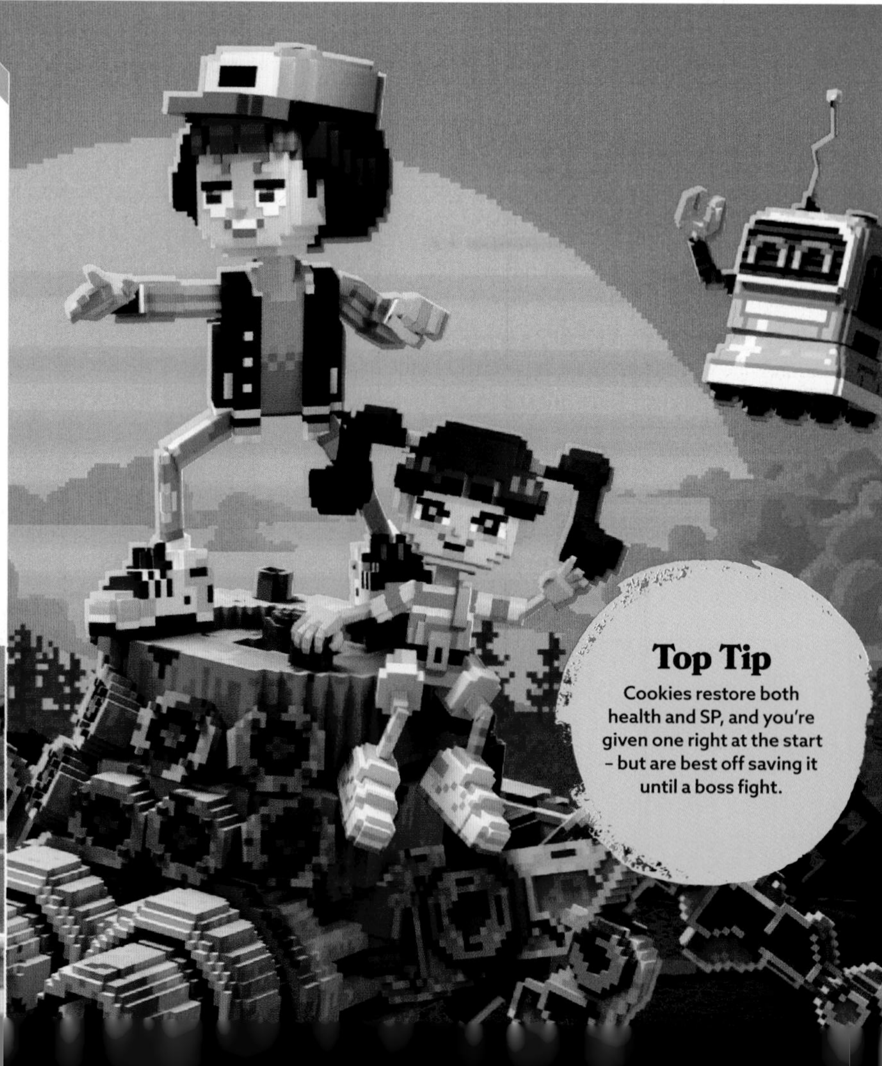

Top Tip

Cookies restore both health and SP, and you're given one right at the start – but are best off saving it until a boss fight.

Pokémon Brilliant Diamond & Pokémon Shining Pearl

Developer ILCA **Publisher** Nintendo **Platform** NS

■ **One beloved game, two unique options. The biggest decision you'll face on this one comes before you've even bought it, as each edition has creatures exclusive to that version. Do you go with *Brilliant Diamond* for access to Arcanine, Caterpie and Electabuzz, or will Sandshrew, Vulpix and Magmar sway you towards *Shining Pearl*? Perfectionist players who love to complete games will want to collect the entire set. It is possible but you may need to engage in some pretty hard bargaining with your fellow trainers.**

Ready to Train

The base gameplay is identical in both editions of the game. Explore the fictional Japanese region of Sinnoh to hunt wild Pokémon, then pitch yours into battle. Win fights to capture defeated beasts, and earn XP that eventually evolves your Pokémon into new species. Newer fans are likely to be surprised to find recent favourites such as Toxtricity missing. The roster is faithful to the original 2007 DS games – but that 'gotta catch 'em all' mantra still inspires you to keep on hunting.

Ramanas Park is a new area that offers a chance to collect legendary Pokémon.

Electric Pokémon Pachirisu can be found in both Brilliant Diamond *and* Shining Pearl.

Early Choices

You get one of three super-cute buddies to choose from as your first partner Pokémon.

Turtwig (Grass)

Chimchar (Fire)

Piplup (Water)

Did You Know

Together this pair formed Switch's second best-selling launch title of 2021, after *FIFA 22*.

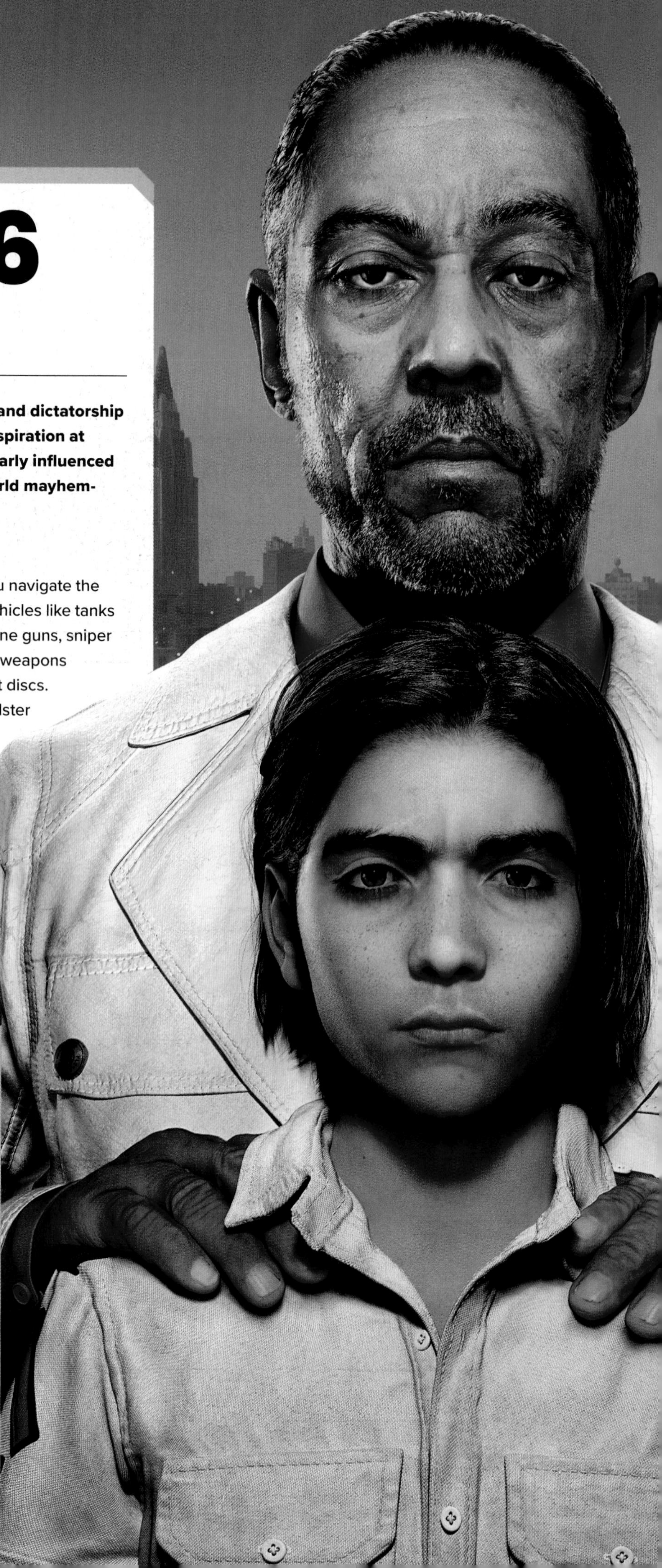

Far Cry 6

Developer Ubisoft Toronto **Publisher** Ubisoft
Platform NS, PC, PS4, PS5, XBO, XBX/S

■ ***Far Cry 6*** **takes players to the Caribbean. The island dictatorship of Yara is fictional, but there's plenty of real-life inspiration at play in the storyline. Ubisoft Toronto were particularly influenced by the 1950s' revolution in Cuba for their open-world mayhem-causing game.**

You Sound Horse

Guerrilla fighter Dani Rojas is your main character. You navigate the adventure's seven regions on foot, horseback or in vehicles like tanks and helicopters. As well as the expected mix of machine guns, sniper rifles and grenade launchers, *Far Cry 6* adds resolver weapons with bizarre perks – like a projectile that fires compact discs. Shootouts can be avoided using the new option to holster your gun. It's a peaceful statement which means enemy characters don't immediately attack you on sight and you can try out stealthier moves.

In a smart throwback move, three DLC packs reintroduce former series bosses as playable characters: Vaas Montenegro from *Far Cry 3*, Pagan Min from *Far Cry 4* and *Far Cry 5*'s Joseph Seed.

Combative Catalyst

Yara President Anton Castillo channels real-life fascist dictators. *Far Cry 6* focuses on his obsession with delivering stability across the island on his terms, using a new cancer drug developed from tobacco. *His* tobacco. A draft lottery enslaves citizens to work his fields, and the country's army round up the poor people of capital city Esperanza – it's a failed attempt to escape that triggers Dani Rojas into going after the big bad guy.

One of the more unusual resolvers in the game, el susurro, a silent nail gun.

DLC

Ever wanted to control an enemy? Now you can with three paid DLCs: **Insanity**, **Control** and **Collapse**. Ubisoft also released three free crossover missions, featuring Dani Trejo and Rambo!

The tostador flamethrower resolver makes for a very dramatic weapon.

Series History

Six main series games and two highlights.

FAR CRY (2004)

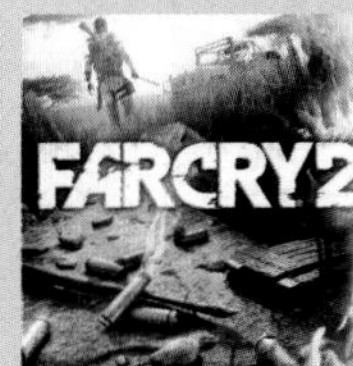

FAR CRY 2 (2008)

FAR CRY 3 (2012)

FAR CRY 4 (2014)

FAR CRY PRIMAL (2016)

FAR CRY 5 (2018)

FAR CRY NEW DAWN (2019)

FAR CRY 6 (2021)

A New Decision

Similar to *Assassin's Creed Valhalla*, Dani can be either male or female. Shortly after the intro scene, you're presented with two passports and get to be either a brunette woman or a bearded man. There's no gameplay difference, but's it's still a welcome option to have in place. Nisa Gundez voices the badass female Dani, while Dani-with-Adam's-apple is voiced by Sean Ray.

The Game Awards

The Game Awards is like the Oscars for the game industry. It's an annual celebration of all the best games of the previous year. Major global artists, like Imagine Dragons and Sting, played at this year's ceremony with songs from *Bastion* and smash hit show *Arcane*, based on *League of Legends*. While huge names in film, Guillermo del Toro and Ming-Na Wen presented awards. There were thirty-two awards in total, and here we celebrate ten of the big winners.

Best Fighting Game
Guilty Gear Strive

Virtual Fighter 5: Ultimate Showdown and *Demon Slayer: The Hinokami Chronicles* were strong nominees here, but the seventh main *Guilty Gear* game pounded them down for a KO. It largely stays faithful to the always-robust 2D predecessors, while introducing two new characters: vampire samurai Nagoriyuki and special ops officer Giovanna.

Best Ongoing Game
Final Fantasy XIV

Final Fantasy XIV was released worldwide nearly a decade ago and is still breaking records. By the end of 2021, players had reached 24 million. It's officially the most profitable *Final Fantasy* ever. Square Enix's colossal MMORPG (massively multiplayer online role-playing game) keeps old players hooked and brings in newcomers with expansions like *Endwalker.*

Best Indie Game
Kena: Bridge of Spirits

Bridge of Spirits charmed its way to both this award and Best Debut Indie game. Not surprising, with art inspired by Japan and Bali, and the heartwarming story of main character Kena helping spirits cross to the afterlife. Also nominated in the debut category were kitsch musical adventure *The Artful Escape* and Roman Empire themed mystery *The Forgotten City.*

Best Sports/Racing Game
Forza Horizon 5

Xbox Game Studios' dreamy drive was this year's joint-most successful game. It matched *It Takes Two*'s haul of three wins. As well as this award, it snagged Best Audio Design and Innovation in Accessibility. Defeated finalists in this particular category included *F1 2021*, *FIFA 22*, *Riders Republic* and *Hot Wheels Unleashed*.

Gaming for All *Horizon 5* also took home the Best Audio and Innovation in Accessibility Award. The latter recognises software that pushes the medium forward by adding features which help games be played and enjoyed by a wider audience. This includes the implementation of American and British Sign Language options during cutscenes in the game.

Complete List of Winners

Game of the Year: It Takes Two

Best Game Direction: Deathloop

Best Narrative: Guardians of the Galaxy

Best Art Direction: Deathloop

Best Score: NieR Replicant ver.1.22474487139

Best Audio: Forza Horizon 5

Best Performance: Maggie Robertson in Resident Evil Village

Games of Impact: Life Is Strange: True Colors

Best Ongoing Game: Final Fantasy XIV

Best Independent Game: Kena: Bridge of Spirits

Best Mobile Game: Genshin Impact

Best Community Support: Final Fantasy XIV

Best VR/AR Game: Resident Evil 4

Innovation in Accessibility: Forza Horizon 5

Best Action Game: Returnal

Best Action Adventure Game: Metroid Dread

Most Anticipated Game
Elden Ring

This category packed in five incredible-looking games, although many felt *Returnal* and *Forza Horizon 5* were unlucky to miss out on nominations. *Elden Ring* won the prize ahead of Aloy's comeback in *Horizon: Forbidden West*, Kratos sequel *God of War: Ragnarok*, space-themed RPG *Starfield* and Nintendo's *Legend of Zelda: Breath of the Wild* sequel.

Best Game Direction
Deathloop

We've seen plenty of games on these pages that tinker with time, but one stands above them all. Action shooter *Deathloop* has a masterful day-to-night cycle and a throwback 1960s setting. *Deathloop* also managed to score more nominations than any other game, with nine.

Best VR Game
Resident Evil 4

Resident Evil 4 scored a second life with its release in VR form for Oculus Rift. It was already thought to be one of the best PS2 games ever made and is now more zombie-fied than ever in virtual reality. Classic features such as combat and inventory management were reworked for first-person play, helping it to beat *Hitman 3* and *Lone Echo II* to grab this award.

Best Esports Game
League of Legends

A phenomenon so huge that 'game' doesn't quite do it justice. *League of Legends* has been going since 2009 and is the world's largest eSport, so picking up this award for the third year running was hardly a surprise. *Call of Duty, Counter-Strike: Global Offensive, Dota 2* and *Valorant* were the other nominees.

Best Narrative
Guardians of the Galaxy

Guardians of the Galaxy's brilliantly told story makes it a winner. Even though it exists outside of the MCU! There are loads of recognisable characters and pretty hilarious team-based banter. It beat *Ratchet & Clank: Rift Apart* to this award. The losing game ended up with 'unluckiest' status – PS5's pretty platformer scored six nominations, but no wins.

Complete List of Winners

Best Role-Playing Game: Tales of Arise

Best Fighting Game: Guilty Gear Strive

Best Family Game: It Takes Two

Best Sports/Racing Game: Forza Horizon 5

Best Sim/Strategy Game: Age of Empires IV

Best Multiplayer Game: It Takes Two

Best Debut Indie Game: Kena: Bridge of Spirits

Most Anticipated Game: Elden Ring

Players' Voice: Halo Infinite

Best Esports Game: League of Legends

Best Esports Player: s1mple (Oleksandr Kostyliev)

Best Esports Team: Natus Vincere

Best Esports Coach: kkOma (Kim Jeong-gyun)

Best Esports Event: 2021 League of Legends World Championship

Content Creator of the Year: Dream

Global Gaming Citizens: The Drag Stream Community / Kahlief Adams / Anisa Sanusi

Game of the Year
It Takes Two

With their marriage on the rocks, Cody and May become trapped inside dolls' bodies and are forced to work together to become human again. Part platformer, part action-adventure, players must pick a partner to go on this minimised adventure with them. Hazelight Studios wowed the world in this co-operative classic. The constantly changing gameplay and beautiful attention to detail are a lot of fun to play.

Previous Game of the Year winners *The Last of Us Part II* (2020), *Sekiro: Shadows Die Twice* (2019), *God of War* (2018), *The Legend of Zelda: Breath of the Wild* (2017), *Overwatch* (2016), *The Witcher 3: Wild Hunt* (2015) and *Dragon Age: Inquisition* (2014)

Top Tip
All the characters can be upgraded, but spending skill points on them means fewer boosts for Quill. Pick your upgrades carefully.

Marvel's Guardians of the Galaxy

Developer Eidos-Montréal **Publisher** Square Enix **Platform** NS, PC, PS4, PS5, XBO, XBX/S

■ This Marvel shootout is just as big and bursting with explosions as any blockbuster movie. All the Guardians of the Galaxy are here: Peter Quill, Groot, Drax, Gamora, Rocket and Nebula. They're blasting their way through an all-action adventure that also has its sweet moments. You play as Quill (AKA Star-Lord) with his jet boots and snazzy guns but you also have access to the other characters' special abilities. As you would expect, it's big on banter with funny one-liners and hilarious dialogue choices.

Line of Duty

Open-world, right? Nope. *Guardians of the Galaxy* is a linear game, and that's a good thing. Its story is on par with what you're used to from the films. There's an evil cult-like church that the Guardians must stop from brainwashing entire planets. There's only one ending, but any trip through the universe is about the journey as much as the destination. Dodge-rolling other ships in the *Milano* or playing a flashback of the day Peter's mum died are just two of many moments that pull you in.

Did You Know

There are tons of Easter eggs from the movies. Did you notice the reference to Baby Groot?

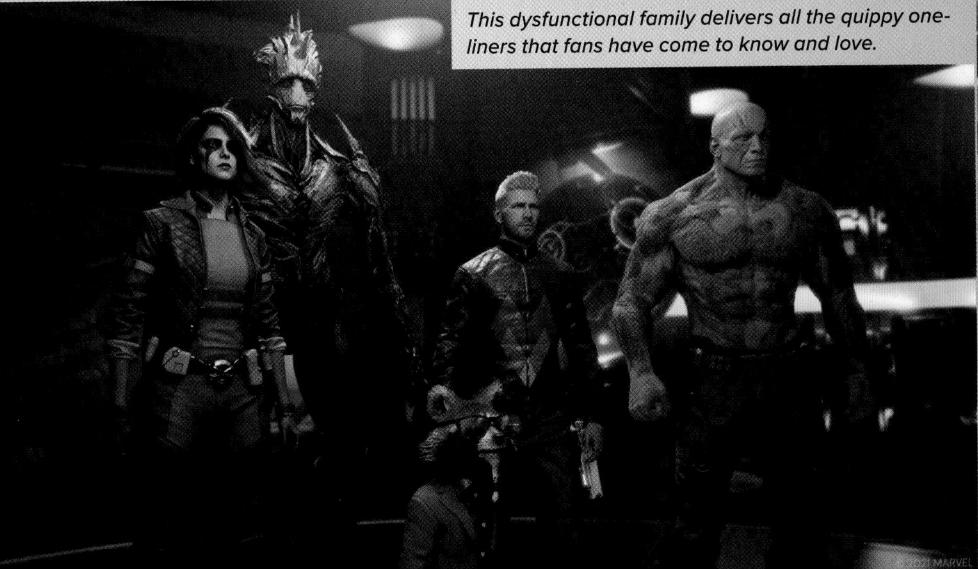

This dysfunctional family delivers all the quippy one-liners that fans have come to know and love.

Turn Around, Bright Eyes

The neon 1980s vibe of the *Guardians* movies was iconic, and it shows up in the game too. You get *a-ha*, Tears for Fears and Bonnie Tyler on the soundtrack and in-game nods to *Tron* and *Pac-Man*. The cast's wise-cracking also makes it into the game. It's pretty classic *Guardians of the Galaxy*, with Quill coming in for relentless stick when siding with one teammate over another.

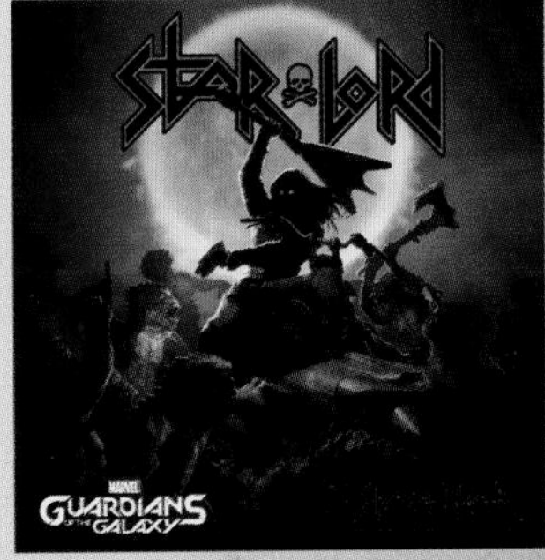

As players progress through the game, new armour and outfits are unlocked, including the Gold Guardians set.

Each Guardian has their own special powers that can come in handy during attacks.

Cast List

Peter Quill is the only playable character, but the team's strengths still have a major role in shootouts. Groot's powers are defensive, he can pull up roots to restrain enemies and help you to move in for the kill. While Gamora's powers are the opposite, she can drop precise strikes that unleash major damage against the team's enemies.

STAR-LORD

GROOT

NEBULA

GAMORA

DRAX

ROCKET

Evil Genius 2: World Domination

Developer Rebellion Developments **Publisher** Rebellion Developments **Platform** PC, PS4, PS5, XBO, XBX/S

■ So, you think you're an evil genius? Pick one of four masterminds and plot to build a doomsday device in this joyously devious RTS. Just like a Bond villain, you construct your lair on a tropical island. A casino is used to front dastardly operations like training minions and planning a criminal network. Standing in the way are the Forces of Justice, who dispatch agents to put a stop to your plans.

Blessed Voices

The game is great to replay too, as each genius has unique missions and devices. There's also a celebrity flavour to the cast. Former henchman Red Ivan can project an aura around him to rally minions ... and unleash a rocket launcher! He's voiced by the booming tones of Brian Blessed. Ex-spymaster Emma has minions who can see through agent disguises. She's portrayed by Samantha Bond, who played Miss Moneypenny in four Bond movies. As funny as it is replayable, *Evil Genius 2* was nominated for Best Sim/Strategy in the Game Awards.

All evil geniuses need a super-secret science lab to test out their dastardly new gadgets. Boom!

All evil geniuses need an island hideout. Lay low and plot your next world takeover with an ocean breeze and your very own helipad.

Delayed Genius

This sequel was first planned way back in 2004, but original developer Elixir closed down. *Sniper Elite* studio Rebellion took up the reins in 2017.

Farming Simulator 22

Developer GIANTS Software
Publisher GIANTS Software
Platform MAC, NS, PC, PS4, PS5, XBO, XBX/S

■ *Farming Simulator 22* is the ultimate crop-growing, livestock-rearing sim. Four hundred machines and tools are on offer from real-life manufacturers. Players can choose between three environments and will farm across all four seasons. Raise pigs, cows, sheep and even bees, then earn the tasty rewards. And yes, you get a trusty hound to keep you company too.

We All Farm Together

Farming Simulator 22 supports cross-play across consoles and PC, with up to 16 people able to share a map and build together.

Did You Know?

The studio's biggest challenge was having the entire team working from home, given the pandemic restrictions in place across Melbourne.

Heavenly Bodies

Developer 2pt Interactive
Publisher 2pt Interactive
Platform PC, PS4, PS5

■ Become a puppet master in *Heavenly Bodies*. It's a tactile puzzler where each part of the PlayStation controller matches up with an astronaut's body. The left stick for his left arm, R2 for right fingers, L1 and R1 for his feet. Got it? Don't worry! You pick it up very quickly. Use these controls to fix antennae and transport cargo while drifting in zero gravity. It's short and sweet at seven levels, but highly original and wonderfully simple. The game is even more fun if you add a mate for co-op space hi-jinks.

STATE OF PLAY

Heroes of the Year

Gaming's Biggest Superstars

Rivet

Game Ratchet & Clank: Rift Apart
First Appearance Ratchet & Clank: Rift Apart
Occupation Resistance Fighter
Height Unknown **Age** Unknown
Hair Colour White **Eye Colour** Light Blue
Home Sargasso **Voiced by** Jennifer Hale

Ratchet & Clank's first major addition in years is a female version of our lombax hero. She teams up with Clank after Dr Nefarious destroys the Dimensionator. Rivet is single-minded, funny and determined. She even built her own robot arm after losing the limb on a past mission. Her hammer is a brilliant weapon, too.

Commanding Voiceover

Rivet was voiced by Jennifer Hale, who's also played Commander Sarah Palmer in the **Halo** series, Maria Hill in **Marvel's Avengers** and Commander Shepard in the **Mass Effect** games.

Alex Chen

Game Life is Strange: True Colors
First Appearance Life is Strange: True Colors
Occupation Unemployed
Height 162 cm **Age** 21
Hair Colour Black
Eye Colour Brown
Home Haven Springs
Voiced by Erika Mori

True Colors' hero is clever and funny. She's also sensitive, to the point of being able to see people's emotions physically. This comes in useful while solving the mystery of her brother's death but it can have rough side effects. Although she's dealing with a lot, she's still open to making friends and is one of the most likeable characters of the year.

Mario

Game Mario Party Superstars
First Appearance Donkey Kong
Occupation Plumber **Height** 156 cm
Age 25 (approx) **Hair Colour** Brown
Eye Colour Blue **Home** Mushroom Kingdom
Voiced by Charles Martinet

Think you've learned all there is to know about Nintendo's moustachioed plumber? Californian actor Charles Martinet has voiced the company mascot since the 1992 classic *Super Mario Bros*. If you've ever wondered why Luigi, Wario and Waluigi sound similar, it's because those guys are played by Martinez, too.

Razputin Aquato

Game Psychonauts 2 **First Appearance** Psychonauts
Occupation Junior Psychonaut **Height** 132 cm **Age** 10
Hair Colour Burgundy **Eye Colour** Green
Home Aquato Family Circus **Voiced by** Richard Steven Horvitz

Psychonauts' mini mastermind serves up some awesome powers. We're talking clairvoyance, levitation, time slowing and pyrokinesis. That last one enables him to make objects or other creatures burst into flames. He's the perfect blend of cool and geeky, even if his dress sense is never going to lead to any struts down the catwalk.

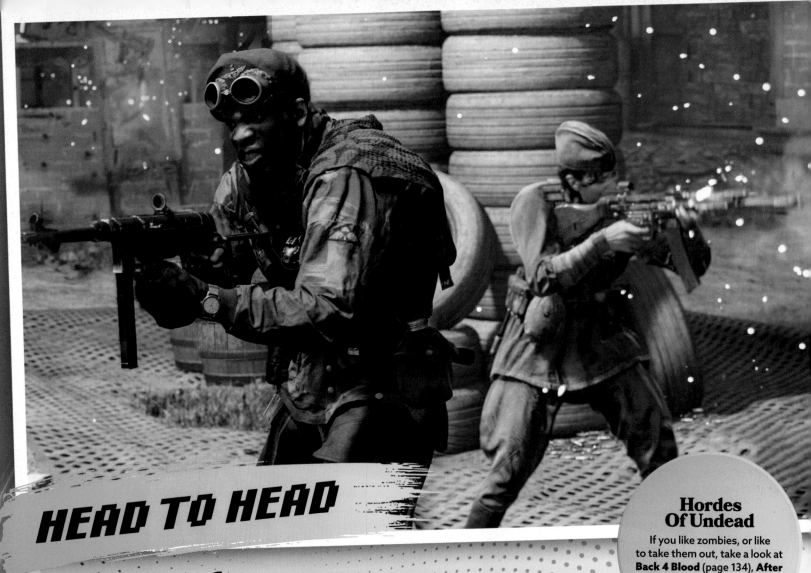

HEAD TO HEAD

Call of Duty: Vanguard

Hordes Of Undead

If you like zombies, or like to take them out, take a look at **Back 4 Blood** (page 134), **After the Fall** and **Resident Evil Village** (page 65).

Developer Sledgehammer Games **Publisher** Activision **Platform** PC, PS4, PS5, XBO, XBX/S

Trivia

A tie-in comic book series was released through the official *Vanguard* website in November 2021. This is the eighteenth *Call of Duty* overall. The studio's co-founders previously created the scary shooter *Dead Space*.

Background | The bestselling shooter series of all time has sold over 400 million copies. It started out in 2003 with a focus on World War II and expanded to include the Cold War, Middle East and even the future. Oh, and zombies. In one of its most famous levels, in *Call of Duty 4: Modern Warfare*, you explore Chernobyl.

Features | *Call of Duty: Vanguard*'s campaign takes the series back to World War II. It's mainly based in 1945 but also has flashbacks to the preceding four years. Zombies return! Plus, there's a new feature called the Altar of Covenants that lets you purchase buffs between rounds. Standard multiplayer has also expanded with Champion Hill, where you fight to remain the last soldier standing.

Gameplay | *Vanguard* is the *Call of Duty* you love in a familiar-yet-fresh setting. Characters are inspired by real-life World War II soldiers. It's not all about blasting on foot though, you also get to pilot a plane through the Battle of Midway.

Play as a World War II soldier taking on the added global (and totally historical) threat of the undead!

Ever wanted to fly a 1940s fighter plane through an ongoing war? Now you can!

Trivia

American actor Michael K Williams, known for *12 Years A Slave* and *The Wire*, returns as US marine Kimble 'Irish' Graves from *Battlefield 4*. It was one of his final performances before passing away, aged just 54. EA released a standalone short movie called *Exodus* that expanded on the game's story as a tribute to the actor.

Battlefield 2042

Developer DICE **Publisher** EA
Platform PC, PS4, PS5, XBO, XBX/S

Background | The first game, *Battlefield 1942,* was released on PC back in 2002, making DICE's shooter series slightly older than *Call of Duty*. This series also initially focused on World War II, before taking in conflicts set in places such as Vietnam, Azerbaijan, the United States and many more. The new game is set in the near-future, which is where the 2042 part of the title comes from.

Features | The storyline is told through multiplayer. There's a global blackout in 2040 that escalates to war between the USA and Russia. All-Out Warfare Mode can support up to 128 players on PS5 and Xbox Series X/S. There's also the highly-customisable Battlefield Portal and co-op based Hazard Zone Modes.

Gameplay | After some early bugs, the developers brought in patches to make improvements. *Battlefield 2042*'s big plus points are fun, futuristic weapons. Plus, you're able to commandeer monstrous vehicles like an M1A5 tank and Apache Warchief helicopter.

Each specialist has a trait and Pyotr 'Boris' Guskovsky's is being a sentry operator – when he's near the SG-36, its efficiency is boosted.

Check out the range of giant tanks and vehicles you can drive in Battlefield 2042, *like this EBAA Wildcat.*

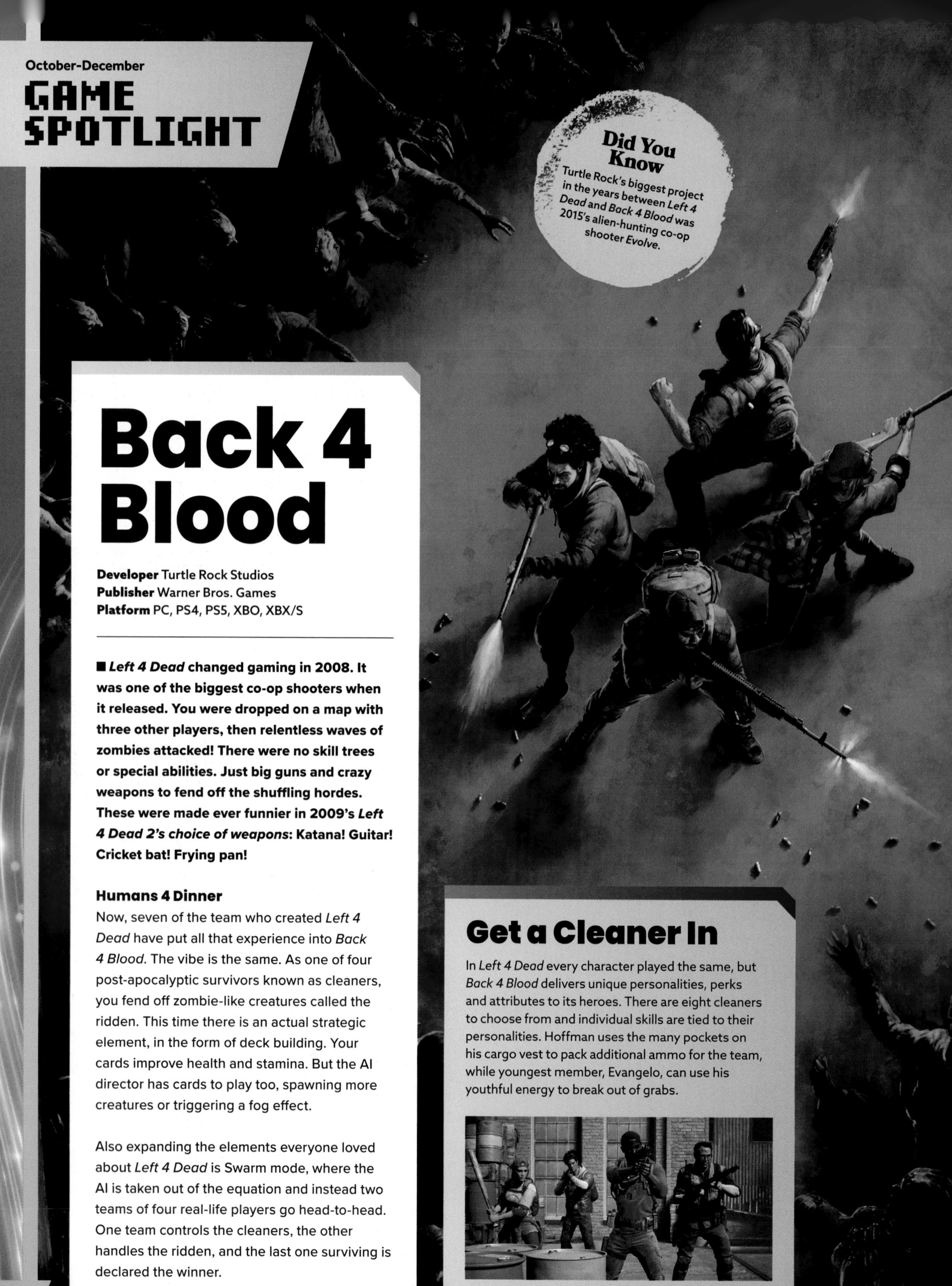

Did You Know
Turtle Rock's biggest project in the years between *Left 4 Dead* and *Back 4 Blood* was 2015's alien-hunting co-op shooter *Evolve*.

Back 4 Blood

Developer Turtle Rock Studios
Publisher Warner Bros. Games
Platform PC, PS4, PS5, XBO, XBX/S

■ ***Left 4 Dead* changed gaming in 2008. It was one of the biggest co-op shooters when it released. You were dropped on a map with three other players, then relentless waves of zombies attacked! There were no skill trees or special abilities. Just big guns and crazy weapons to fend off the shuffling hordes. These were made ever funnier in 2009's *Left 4 Dead 2's choice of weapons*: Katana! Guitar! Cricket bat! Frying pan!**

Humans 4 Dinner

Now, seven of the team who created *Left 4 Dead* have put all that experience into *Back 4 Blood*. The vibe is the same. As one of four post-apocalyptic survivors known as cleaners, you fend off zombie-like creatures called the ridden. This time there is an actual strategic element, in the form of deck building. Your cards improve health and stamina. But the AI director has cards to play too, spawning more creatures or triggering a fog effect.

Also expanding the elements everyone loved about *Left 4 Dead* is Swarm mode, where the AI is taken out of the equation and instead two teams of four real-life players go head-to-head. One team controls the cleaners, the other handles the ridden, and the last one surviving is declared the winner.

Get a Cleaner In

In *Left 4 Dead* every character played the same, but *Back 4 Blood* delivers unique personalities, perks and attributes to its heroes. There are eight cleaners to choose from and individual skills are tied to their personalities. Hoffman uses the many pockets on his cargo vest to pack additional ammo for the team, while youngest member, Evangelo, can use his youthful energy to break out of grabs.

Knife to a Gunfight

Turtle Rock tones down the crazy weapons in *Back 4 Blood*. Although melee combat still brings options like a baseball bat, machete and fire axe. They've also ramped up the firepower, with close to thirty guns available. If you need an assault rifle, go for the M4 Carbine. Prefer picking enemies off from a safe distance? Then grab the M1A sniper rifle, which reloads speedily yet still does significant damage.

Shredders, far-reaching and hard-to-kill monsters, are one of three new warped ridden that were introduced in the Tunnels of Terror DLC.

DLC

Back 4 Blood's paid expansion pack **Tunnels of Terror** added two new cleaners and three different types of creature to take down. Plus a bunch of new levels to explore or hide in!

Pick your players carefully as each comes with their own bonus skills.

When a swarm of ridden spawn attacks, the cleaners must work together to stay alive.

Evangelo, Jim, Hoffman and Holly prepare to take down one of the monstrous shredders as it begins to charge.

Dusk

Developer David Szymanski
Publisher New Blood Interactive **Platform** MAC, NS, PC

■ Kill the intruder! This old-school shooter made the swap from PC to Nintendo Switch, and it's worth the wait. You speed through otherworldly levels packed with ugly enemies. And it is pretty speedy. Despite the retro vibe, it's one of the fastest shooters around.

The Foothills Are Alive

The spooky tale is told in three episodes, each with a slightly different theme. The Foothills is set in farmland where evil scarecrows and toxic rats await. The Facilities pulls you through a corrupt military world. Then you're off to a parallel dimension in the final episode, The Nameless City. Running through all of them is one consistent theme: shoot everything that moves.

Tools for all this carnage range from shotguns and assault rifles to crossbows and mortars. Plus, every level has a single soap bar in it that deals 1,000,000,000 damage when it strikes an enemy. Ha! Cool features on this new Switch version include 60 FPS, HD rumble and full gyro support.

Drawn to Dusk

Dusk **composer Andrew Hulshult also penned the scores for *Quake Champions* and *Doom Eternal.***

Exploring The Facilities can take you to some rather realistic rooms – toilet break, anyone?

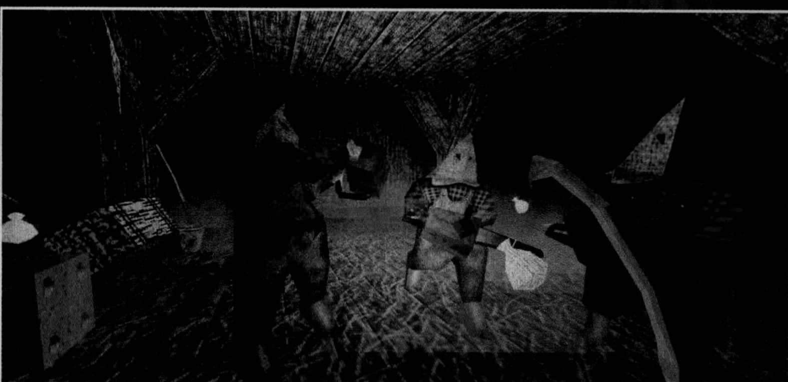

The game kicks off with your character hanging upside down and you have to work out how to get free.

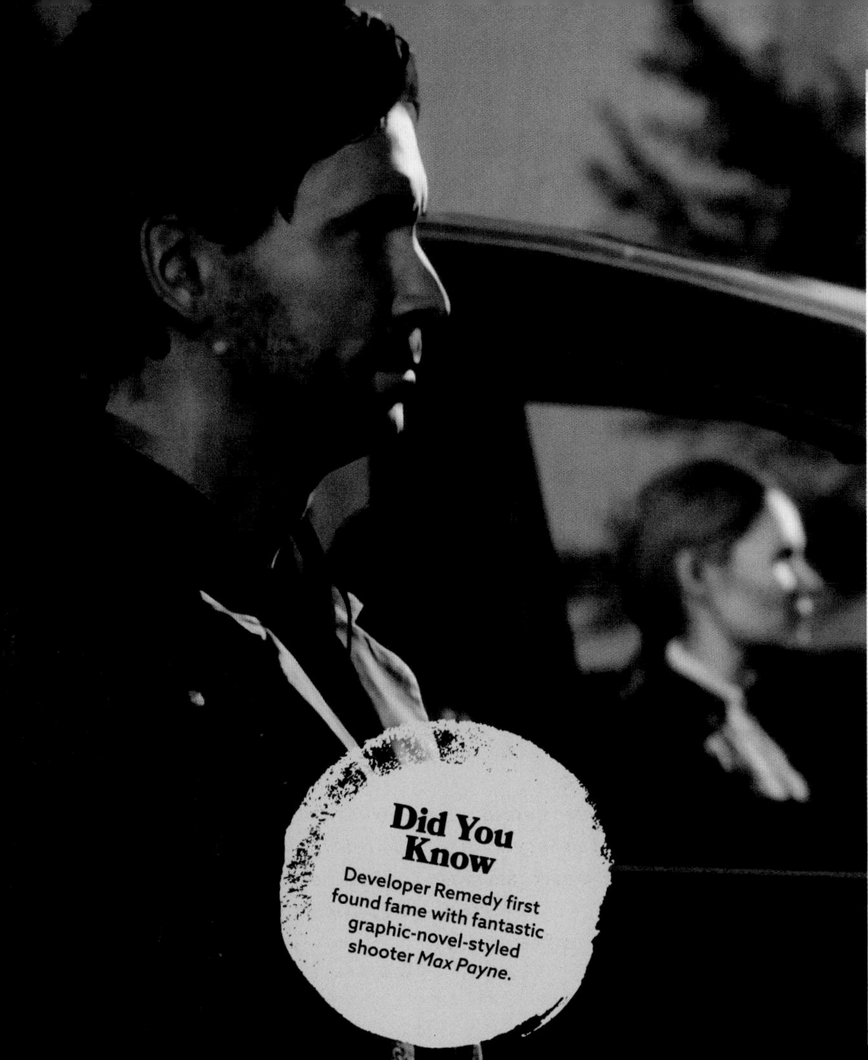

Alan Wake Remastered

Developer Remedy Entertainment
Publisher Epic Games
Platform PC, PS4, PS5, XBO, XBX/S

■ Crime author Alan Wake's wife has gone missing. The only clues towards finding her are sections of a horror book he can't remember writing. Spooky! Take a torchlit journey through the creepy town of Bright Springs and pick off enemies with whatever comes to hand. The rewarding mix of combat and scares make this well worth a try on PS5 or Xbox Series X.

Did You Know

Developer Remedy first found fame with fantastic graphic-novel-styled shooter *Max Payne*.

Moonglow Bay

Developer Bunnyhug Ltd
Publisher Coatsink Software Ltd
Platform PC, XBO, XBX/S

■ Take a weekend trip to the sea! *Moonglow Bay* takes that holiday destination, adds *Animal Crossing*-style visuals and launches you into a career as a fisherman. Reeling in your catch of the day is as chilled as it sounds. But there are complications: the town is in ruin and all the villagers are afraid of the water. It's a relaxing indie RPG with a cute community.

Save As Houses

Moonglow Bay launched without a way to automatically back up progress, but a patch means it now auto-saves while you sleep.

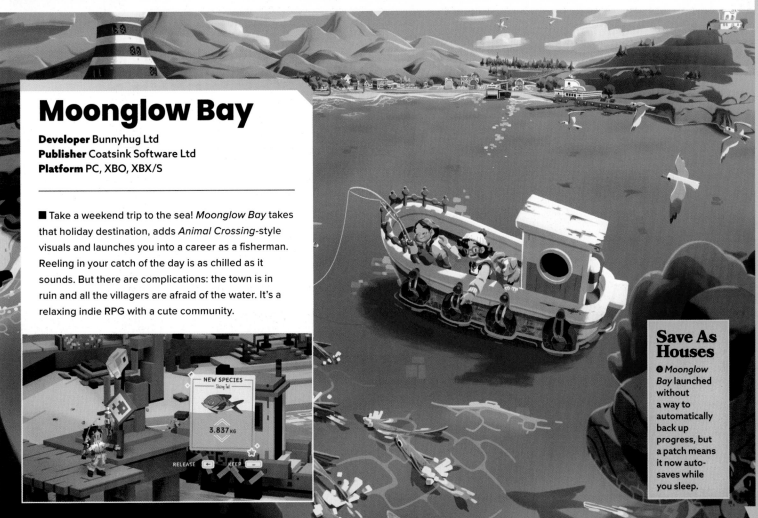

Top Tip
Spells only require a couple of ingredients, whereas regents need a variety of properties – so pick up every single item you can.

Wytchwood

Developer Alientrap **Publisher** Whitethorn Games
Platform MAC, NS, PC, PS4, PS5, XBO, XBX

■ If you go down to the woods today ... a demon-possessed goat (yes, goat!) will send you on soul-gathering errands. *Wytchwood* is a gentle crafting adventure that doubles as a dark fairy tale, full of wacky characters. You play as a witch able to mix potions and create new items – mostly using bits of animals and monsters you've just killed. It sounds gross but looks lovely.

Check Out
Australian studio Prideful Sloth also made lovely PS4 island explorer *Yonder: The Cloud Catcher Chronicles*.

Grow: Song of the Evertree

Developer Prideful Sloth **Publisher** 505 Games
Platform NS, PC, PS4, PS5, XBO, XBX/S

■ The decaying lands of Alaria need your help. You start off by planting seeds and tending to crops. But the greater mission is to find fragments of a song and return them to your Evertree's heart chamber. Each one makes your neighbours a little happier and lets you expand a little further. This peacefully paced world-builder is a cute escape from real life.

Check Out

For more serious swinging, *PGA Tour 2K21* has a very authentic round.

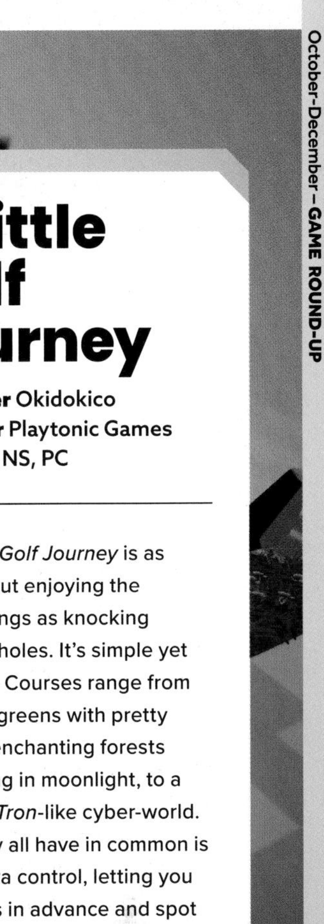

A Little Golf Journey

Developer Okidokico
Publisher Playtonic Games
Platform NS, PC

■ *A Little Golf Journey* is as much about enjoying the surroundings as knocking balls into holes. It's simple yet eccentric! Courses range from standard greens with pretty trees, to enchanting forests glimmering in moonlight, to a futuristic *Tron*-like cyber-world. What they all have in common is full camera control, letting you plan putts in advance and spot collectibles. Its soundtrack is super chilled, too.

Time Loader

Developer Flazm **Publisher** META Publisher
Platform NS, PC, PS4, PS5, XBO, XBX/S

■ Adam Wright builds a time-travelling robot to go back to the 1990s and change his past. What could go wrong? He's been haunted for decades by the memory of a tragic treehouse accident. Players solve puzzles based in his childhood home and learn more about the family's past. The game has a fun, domestic theme filled with weird but cute moments, like scaring a cat from Adam's bedroom with a balloon and toy dart. VHS tapes, a fax machine and a 1995 calendar all nail the flashback vibe.

Did You Know?

It's set in 1995 when the Super NES was the world's biggest-selling console and *Dragon Quest VI* was the bestselling game.

Did You Know?
The Curator, an NPC from previous games in the series, makes lots of mysterious appearances in background scenes.

The Dark Pictures Anthology: House of Ashes

Developer Supermassive Games **Publisher** Bandai Namco
Platform PC, PS4, PS5, XBO, XBX/S

■ Remember Sharpay from *High School Musical*? American actress Ashley Tisdale has brilliantly reinvented herself from the Disney movie character to a CIA field officer. In *House of Ashes*, Tisdale's character Rachel King is trying to escape a temple infested with vampire-like monsters.

Killer Decisions

Rachel is one of five playable characters. Joining her are Rachel's separated husband Eric, her new boyfriend Nick (awks!), US military lieutenant Jason and Iraqi Republican Guard soldier Salim. All these characters need to work together to fend off the bigger threat. But love-triangle distrust and Jason and Salim's natural animosity adds tension. The choices that players make can affect the outcome of the story, and it's in a drastic way! Every single one of the characters can die, transforming the story's very unpredictable path.

Events mostly unfold as an interactive drama. The player's role is to perform QTEs (AKA button-matching events) to steer gunfights or evade enemies. The five-strong squad are looking for weapons of mass destruction. So there are lots of claustrophobic journeys through dark tunnels and potential for leap-behind-the-sofa horrors.

Vamp It Up

House of Ashes merges real-life history with the supernatural. The prologue takes place in Akkad, the former capital of Mesopotamia. It's 2231BC and vampiric creatures are slaughtering two warring human armies during a solar eclipse. After hibernating for thousands of years, the monsters are at large again. They're causing chaos in an Akkadian Temple while the US-Iraq war unfolds outside. Cue shootouts, secrets and scares.

Five Alive

There are three different ways to play *House of Ashes*. You can go solo, team up with one friend to share the story or have four mates join in on a single controller and each of you can control one character.

Celebrity Connections

Ashley Tisdale isn't the first big name signed up to this series. *House of Ashes* is the third entry in *The Dark Pictures Anthology*, which Supermassive Games plans to run for at least eight games. Experienced British actor Pip Torrens, AKA Colonel Kaplan from *Star Wars: The Force Awakens*, narrates *Man of Medan*'s ghost-ship tale. Then, in the demon-evading storyline of *Little Hope*, Will Poulter (*We're the Millers*, *Guardians of the Galaxy Vol 3*) plays the main character.

US Marine Nick and Iraqi Republican Guard Salim form a truce to work together against the undead creatures.

Ashley Tisdale's Rachel delves deeper into the creepy cave of monsters.

As the team explores more of the underground cave, they discover caverns filled with bones and more creatures than you can dream of – actually, it's the stuff of nightmares! The sacrificial room is made even scarier by the monstrous vampire statue.

Top of the Crofts

The Pop-Culture Sensation Has Been Raiding Tombs For Over Two Decades

■ The first *Tomb Raider* game was released on Sega Saturn in 1996. Since then, the treasure-hunting action-adventure spawned sequels, movies and a ton of copycat games. The franchise has made Lara Croft the most famous female character in gaming.

Croft's Cookbook

Square Enix has been busy celebrating their heroine's success, and they got creative. The publisher uploaded top-secret design documents to the *Tomb Raider* website and launched *Tomb Raider: The Official Cookbook and Travel Guide*, with recipes and tour tips from locations visited by Lara. Plus, Square Enix donated £25,000 to the International Rescue Committee charity in honour of all who'd worked on the series.

The publisher also created a special video of all the Lara Crofts from the last twenty-five years. The huge number of talented actors and models who've played the iconic archaeologist chatted about their time defeating foes in the artefact-hoarding, bad-guy-bashing role. Natalie Cook, the original model from the 90s was joined by Nell McAndrew, Keeley Hawes, Camilla Luddington and Rhona Mitra.

Trivia

- Lara Croft has appeared on over 1,000 magazine covers – more than any real-life model.
- Rhona Mitra recorded two albums in-character as Lara Croft: *Come Alive* in 1998 and *Female Icon* in 1999.
- The rebooted games revealed that Lara celebrates her birthday on Valentine's Day.

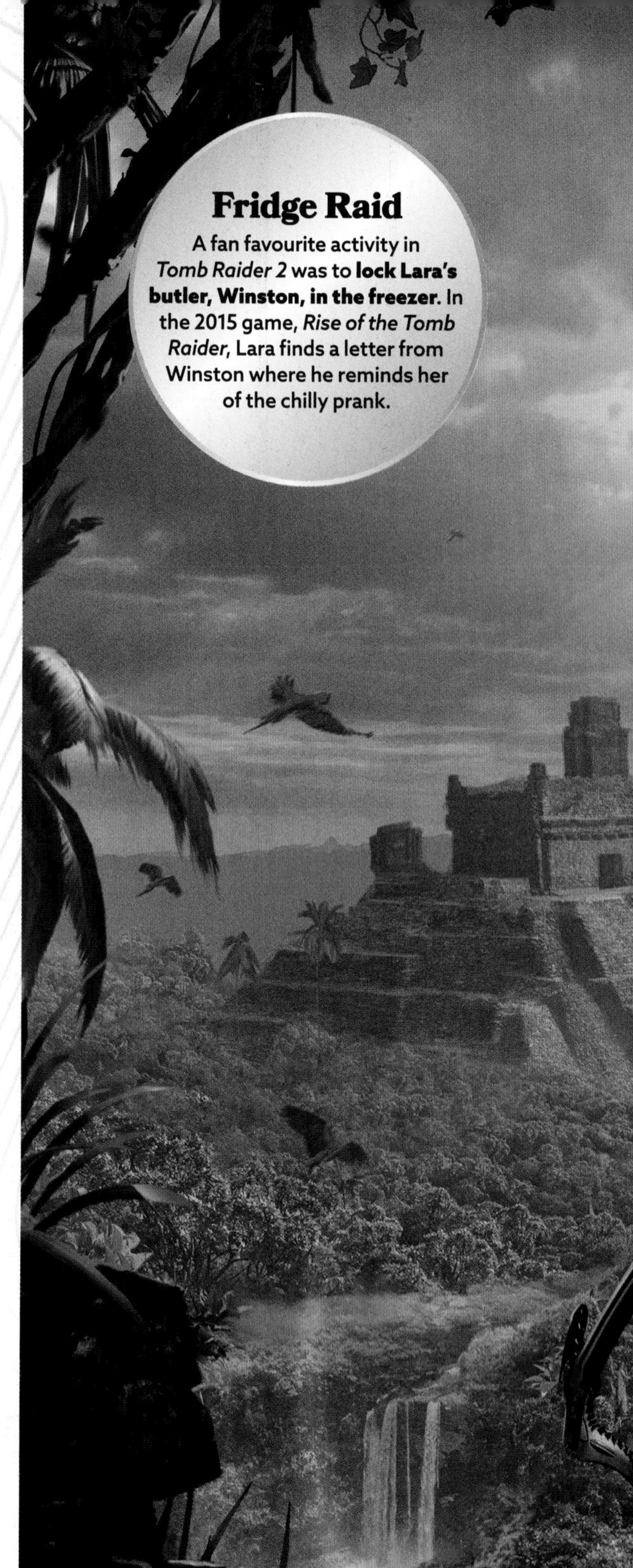

Fridge Raid

A fan favourite activity in *Tomb Raider 2* was to **lock Lara's butler, Winston, in the freezer.** In the 2015 game, *Rise of the Tomb Raider*, Lara finds a letter from Winston where he reminds her of the chilly prank.

Lara Decade-by-Decade

Check out Tomb Raider's twenty-five years of adventure-hunting history.

The 1990s

In 1994, game studio Core Design begins work on a tomb and pyramid exploration game. They start out with a male Indiana Jones-style character then turn him female and rename him Laura Cruz, then Lara Croft. *Tomb Raider* is released in 1996 and three sequels follow. Croft becomes an instant pop culture phenomenon.

The 2000s

After being presumed dead in *Tomb Raider: The Last Revelation*, Lara springs back to life for 2000's *Tomb Raider Chronicles*. A year later, the first movie arrives with Angelina Jolie in the lead role. Three more games are released during the decade: *The Angel of Darkness*, *Legend* and *Underworld* (pictured).

The 2010s

In 2013 there's a reboot to the series with the survival-focused *Tomb Raider*. New actress Camilla Luddington and the game both receive rave reviews. It goes on to sell 14.5 million copies, the most in the game's history. Two sequels follow, along with a fresh film starring Alicia Vikander. Lara is officially massive again.

The 2020s

The original game turns twenty-five. Crystal Dynamics teases future adventures that will merge together Lara's two different realities from before and after the 2013 reboot. An animated Netflix show is also confirmed, with Hayley Atwell – AKA Agent Carter in the MCU – cast as the new voice of Croft.

EAT, PREY, LOVE

Arkane Studios

■ Back in the 1990s, EA employee Raphaël Colantonio became fed up with the company's focus on sports games. He persuaded ten other investors and Arkane was born. Its first game, *Arx Fatalis*, offered a mix of cave exploring and spell casting. In 2006, the studio opened its Texas branch. Since then, it's become super-famous for *Prey*, *Dishonored* and *Deathloop*. In 2017, Colantonio departed to create a new developer, called WolfEye Studios.

Biggest Series: Dishonored

In *Dishonored*, you explore the plague-ridden city of Dunwall as assassin Corvo. Its sense of freedom was ground-breaking when released in 2013, with loads of ways to pick off enemies and complete missions. The city's dark vibe, inspired by 19th-Century London and Edinburgh, oozed intrigue. Its voice cast was special too. Carrie Fisher (*Star Wars*' Princess Leia) and Lena Headey (Cersei from *Game of Thrones*) were among the big names.

Have You Played?

Dishonored 2

Prey

Wolfenstein: Youngblood

Deathloop

SPACEFARING SHOOTER

343 Industries

■ *Halo* was originally created by legendary Washington studio Bungie. When those guys split from Microsoft, the Xbox publisher needed someone new to make its splendid shooter. It created 343 Studios, named after in-game character 343 Guilty Spark. The company has made 11 *Halo* games in total and also teamed up with Mega Bloks to create brick-based toys of Master Chief and co. It's based in Redmond, near Seattle, and has around 450 employees.

Have You Played?

Halo 4

Halo 5: Guardians

Halo Wars 2

Halo Infinite

Biggest Series: Halo

Halo isn't merely 343's biggest series – it's the only one. It started out with *Halo: Combat Evolved Anniversary* in 2011 and most recently released *Halo Infinite*, which you can find elsewhere in this book. It also made a seven-part collection of short films called *Halo Legends*. Original developer Bungie didn't do too badly after letting *Halo* go. It's the studio behind *Destiny* and *Destiny 2*.

Age of Empires IV

Developer Relic Entertainment/World's Edge
Publisher Xbox Game Studios **Platform** PC

Go power mad and destroy your enemies. Become a kind leader and forge allies. The choice is up to you. The fourth game in this real-time strategy series gives players four definitive chunks of history to visit and transform based on their instincts. Head back to 1066 to take part in the Norman conquest of England. Or go to battle in the Hundred Years' War. Perhaps overseeing the massive Mongol Empire is your jam – or will you relive the Late Middle Ages rise of Moscow?

Siege Mentality

Player choice is everything. Armies can be tailored to a specific play style, with a huge variety of tactics on offer. Do you wade in with battering rams? Quietly position soldiers on walls? Try to balance aggression with stout defence? The choices quickly become second nature as you work through the decades and upgrade your tech.

If you're new to the game then Skirmish Mode is a great place to start. Select a civilisation, collect some resources and ready your infantry. Then go to war with a single win condition: destroy all enemy landmarks, control all sacred sites or build and defend a wonder. These one-off missions are super fun on their own and are also easy intros to the main campaigns.

Historial Arty Facts

- *Age of Empires IV* snagged the prize for Best Sim/Strategy Game at The Game Awards.
- *Age of Empires* debuted on PC in 1997 and was widely labelled as *Civilisation* meets *Warcraft*.
- This is Relic's first *Age of Empires* game, although it has lots of RTS experience – such as the 7-million selling *Warhammer 40,000: Dawn of War*.

The UI gives a detailed overview of how well your kingdom is doing and has all the building and development options in easy access.

Wall or Nothing

Age of Empires IV lets you relive defining moments and battles in history, from the Early Middle Ages onwards. Breach China's Great Wall in the Mongol Empire campaign or take part in the famous Battle of Hastings through the Norman storyline and become a piece of the 230-foot-long Bayeux Tapestry. You'll also get to be involved in the dramatic Fall of Bayeux in a later mission.

Did You Know?

RTS (or real-time strategy) is different from other tactical game genres because every team moves at the same time.

Try your hand at being a peaceful leader! When a neighbouring kingdom comes knocking, you can always choose to talk instead of waging war.

Figure of Eight

You can pick between eight civilisations in *Age of Empires IV*, each with unique traits. The English are a defensive powerhouse with sturdy castles and deadly archers, while the Mongols are able to expand their army at a rapid rate. Also playable are the Rus, Chinese, Holy Roman Empire, Delhi Sultanate, French and Abbasid Dynasty.

Fancy taking to the seas? Age of Empires IV *gives players the chance to build up their navy and take down their rivals in a seafaring battle.*

Unpacking

Developer Witch Beam **Publisher** Humble Bundle
Platform MAC, NS, PC, PS4, PS5, XBO

■ Packing for a house move sucks. But unpacking in a new space rules, and that's exactly what happens here. You help the narrator unpack boxes in each new home as she moves from childhood house to university halls to boyfriend's apartment. The items you remove from boxes give clues to the life of the owner. What's she studying? How does she feel about her ex? Charmingly, some belongings stay with her through the entire journey from her first bedroom in 1997 to a family house in 2018.

Numbers Unboxed

● *Unpacking* features eight stages with a total of thirty-five rooms – and more than 14,000 special sound effects.

Happy Game

Developer Amanita Design **Publisher** Amanita Design **Platform** NS, PC

■ Don't be fooled by the cheery title. *Happy Game* is a psychedelic horror. It's full of smiling faces but they're worn by monsters haunting a little boy's dreams. Play through three thought-provoking nightmares as each one serves up vibrant levels that hide unnerving twists. It's one of the very few Switch games that takes real bravery to play after dark while home alone.

A Reason to be Happy

● Czech designer Jaromír Plachý loves a creative point-and-click – he also designed excellent mobile games *Botanicula* and *Chuchel*.

Riders Republic

Developer Ubisoft Annecy **Publisher** Ubisoft
Platform PC, PS4, PS5, XBO, XBX/S

■ You've heard of open-world shooters, open-world racers and open-world RPGs, but *sports*? The idea raised some eyebrows when it was first announced. *Riders Republic* came through on that bold target. There are four main sports: mountain biking, skiing, snowboarding and wingsuit flying. As great as those options are, you can just as easily lose yourself exploring Yosemite national park on two wheels or peering over the peaks of Mammoth Mountain.

Steep Inspirations

Make the most of those quiet sight-seeing moments because this is a breathless experience. Races are packed with leaps and obstacles. Stunt contests require snazzy tricks and twitchy reflexes. Wingsuit challenges test your willingness to play chicken with the environment around you. There's an insane amount to do and all of it unlocks new goodies, bearing brands such as Red Bull, Burton and Rossignol. If you liked previous Ubisoft games *Steep* or *The Crew*, you'll love this. It's is a perfect mix of that pair.

What is wingsuit flying? Exactly what it sounds like! Put on a suit with wings fitted and jump off something tall. Arghhh!

If jumping out of a plane isn't your thing, you could explore beautiful parks without leaving your room.

Ubi Softplay

Ubisoft's sporting CV is stellar. Just don't mention *Pure Football*.

ACTION SOCCER (1995)

ROCKY LEGENDS (2004)

SPORTS PARTY (2008)

NITROBIKE (2008)

SHAUN WHITE SNOWBOARDING (2008)

SHAUN WHITE SKATEBOARDING (2008)

STEEP (2016)

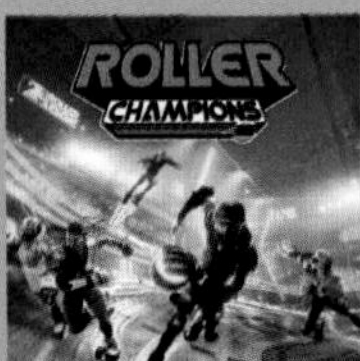

ROLLER CHAMPIONS (2022)

Did You Know?
Endwalker was so popular upon release that Square Enix had to disable the game's trial version for two months to stop the server from breaking.

Final Fantasy XIV: Endwalker

Developer Square Enix **Publisher** Square Enix
Platform MAC, PC, PS4, PS5

■ *Final Fantasy* games from the past, present and future can be a minefield to keep track of, so here's the backstory on *Endwalker*. There are callbacks to past games in this one, but it's not linked to the *Final Fantasy VII* remake featured earlier on these pages. *Endwalker* is the fourth expansion pack for MMORPG *Final Fantasy XIV* – which first emerged back in 2013. It's also the first of those expansions to arrive on PS5.

Signs of the Zodiark

Endwalker's main goal is to put an end to the war between angelic goddess Hydaelyn – also known as the Mothercrystal – and dragon-like supernatural Zodiark. This long-spanning battle has waged across all the previous games. There's definitely a dramatic climax to the war in *Endwalker*, but the joy is in the journey. The game takes you through the bustling city of Old Sharlayan, the trading hub of Radz-at-Han and ultimately beyond the moon.

The tale is packed with engaging quests, charismatic friends and charming foes. The cutscenes wouldn't look out of place in a movie. In case that isn't enough, raids and side quests add even more to the story, which is super helpful if you've not played previous spin-offs.
It's a brilliant ending for a story ten years in the making, with twists and turns that even the most dedicated fan won't see coming. Oof!

New patches for the game came with alliance raids. Quests for you to complete to win coins, gear and even more loot.

Out of the Shadows

Endwalker works as a standalone adventure, but the creators were determined to add a ton of goodies for returning players from the previous expansion *Shadowbringers*. There are two new classes, Sage and Reaper, and the level cap is increased to ninety. Eight new dungeons are added, along with a 240-player alliance raid series called Myths of the Realm. It obviously also looks incredible on PS5.

The player character leads a group of fighters and gamers get to choose between a warrior of light or warrior of darkness.

The PvP mode in Final Fantasy XIV: Endwalker *is called Crystalline Conflict and it puts players into teams of five.*

History Rewritten

Final Fantasy first launched on PC in 2010 but feedback was so critical that the PS3 version was cancelled and its development team replaced. Square Enix then relaunched the game as *Final Fantasy XIV: A Realm Reborn* with the original setting and story, built new from the ground up. The original *Final Fantasy XIV* is the only game that is unplayable on any format.

Final Fantasy XIV: Endwalker *builds on the lore and story of the earlier games. You meet Vrtra, one of the first brood. Vrtra is the child of Midgardsormr, a dragon boss from previous games.*

Get ready for some super dramatic battles. As warrior of light (or darkness), you get to unleash some awesome powers against enemies. And they're pretty powerful too!

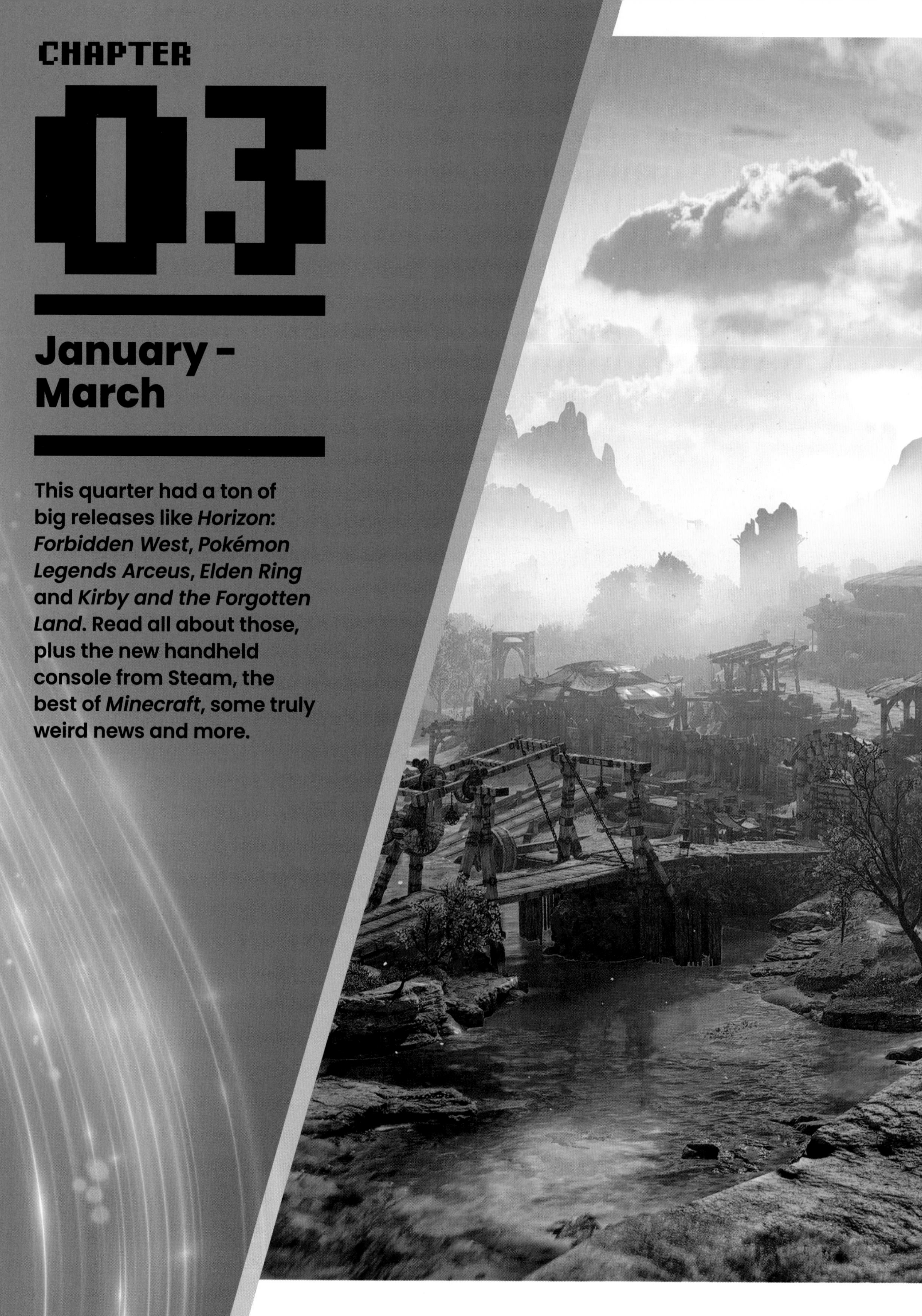

CHAPTER

03

January - March

This quarter had a ton of big releases like *Horizon*: *Forbidden West*, *Pokémon Legends Arceus*, *Elden Ring* and *Kirby and the Forgotten Land*. Read all about those, plus the new handheld console from Steam, the best of *Minecraft*, some truly weird news and more.

GAMING HIGHLIGHT

Horizon Forbidden West

Page 172

Steam Decks the Handheld Competition

Our Guide to the Newest Handheld

■ PC gaming on the go? In 2022 this dream became reality. Steam makers Valve released its own handheld console. It's called the Steam Deck and is very different to past faves like the Nintendo DS or PSP. Two sticks and four face buttons feel familiar. But you can also use Linux apps to turn it into a mini-PC and even install other operating systems like Windows. So how does it compare to Switch, and what are its best games?

Running on Steam

The Steam Deck runs off your Steam account, so any games you have there will be available. But there's also a slot for an SSD card. Handy!

01 D-pad **02** View **03** Thumbsticks **04** Mic **05** 7" Touchscreen **06** Menu **07** ABXY **08** Trackpad **09** Quick Access **10** Right Speaker **11** Left Speaker **12** Steam

Steam Deck Essentials

Sonic Mania

Steam Deck can play thousands of games from the Steam Store, and Sonic's 2017 comeback is perfect for handheld. It's inspired by the 1990s Mega Drive games. To the point that one of its most beloved levels is a remix of the original Green Hill Zone. It's mostly side-scrolling, but giant rings open up 3D special stages like those on *Sonic CD*. Trusty favourites Tails and Knuckles are playable, too.

Cuphead

Five years after it came out, everyone still loves this cartoon run-and-gunner. It steals its style from simple animated movies of the 1930s. Cuphead and his brother Mugman have to collect souls to undo a deal with a devil. Dark as it sounds, it's loads of fun. Boss battles are a highlight, like fighting Captain Brineybeard – who has a ship that fires giant pink lasers!

Elden Ring

FromSoftware's colossus never came to Switch. But with Steam Deck you can play it on a plane or train or toilet! Everything you love about the vast adventure is the same, including crafting, horse-riding and combat. All your progress transfers back and forth to the PC version through Cloud Saves. Just make sure to cap the frame rate at 30 FPS for the smoothest experience.

Gran Turismo 7

Developer Polyphony Digital **Publisher** Sony **Platform** PS4, PS5

DLC

Sony released some free new content that included exciting new rides: **Subaru BRZ GT300 '21, Subaru BRZ S '21** and **Suzuki Cappuccino (EA11R) '91**. Plus a new track layout at **Spa-Francorchamps**.

■ **For nearly two decades, Xbox and Sony fans have argued over the king of driving games. Now players get to decide which deserves top spot on the podium. *Gran Turismo 7* followed *Forza Horizon 5* into living rooms around the world this year.**

Gran Designs

Gran Turismo 7 is a simulation-style game, though it's just as stylish as any other racer out there. Developer Polyphony Digital calls it 'the real driving simulator', which means that tuning your vehicle is almost as important as driving it. Transmission, brakes, tyres and suspension are all customisable. You can even wash your car before events to give it extra sheen.

Wheel rims, bumpers and spoilers can also be fiddled with, and the game's detailed livery editor even lets you truly make any vehicle your own. Don't worry if you just want to drive, though. With more than 400 cars and ninety-four tracks, there's plenty to keep you hooked, even if you have no interest in popping the bonnet or pimping your ride.

Stat Attack

With 85 million all-time sales, *Gran Turismo* is the third biggest-selling race series ever, behind *Mario Kart* and *Need for Speed*.

Try out Gran Turismo 7*'s Music Rally mode and race to the end of a song.*

Check the oil, give the windows a clean, fine tune the engine ... you can act as mechanic and driver in GT7.

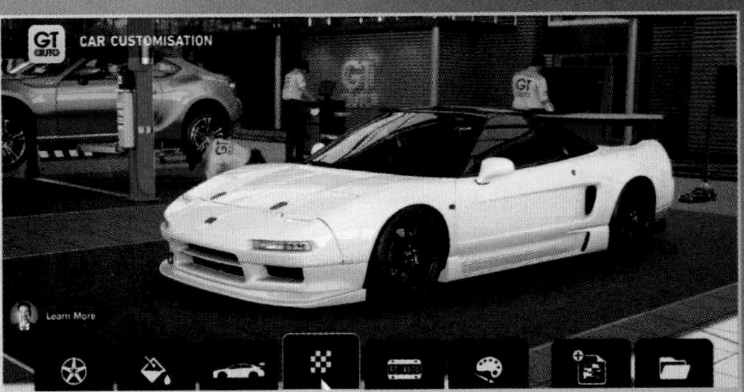

Fancy making some changes to your car? Gran Turismo 7 *gives you so much control over everything.*

Audi You Do

For some, playing a racing game is all about the brand name cars. *Gran Turismo 7 has* hundreds of vehicles to choose from. The game launched with more than a dozen BMW models, over twenty Ferraris and ten swish motors from Jaguar. Lexus, Lamborghini, Nissan, Peugeot and Audi also offer up a huge selection for you to test drive.

Find out all about your opponents as you get ready to leave them in the dust.

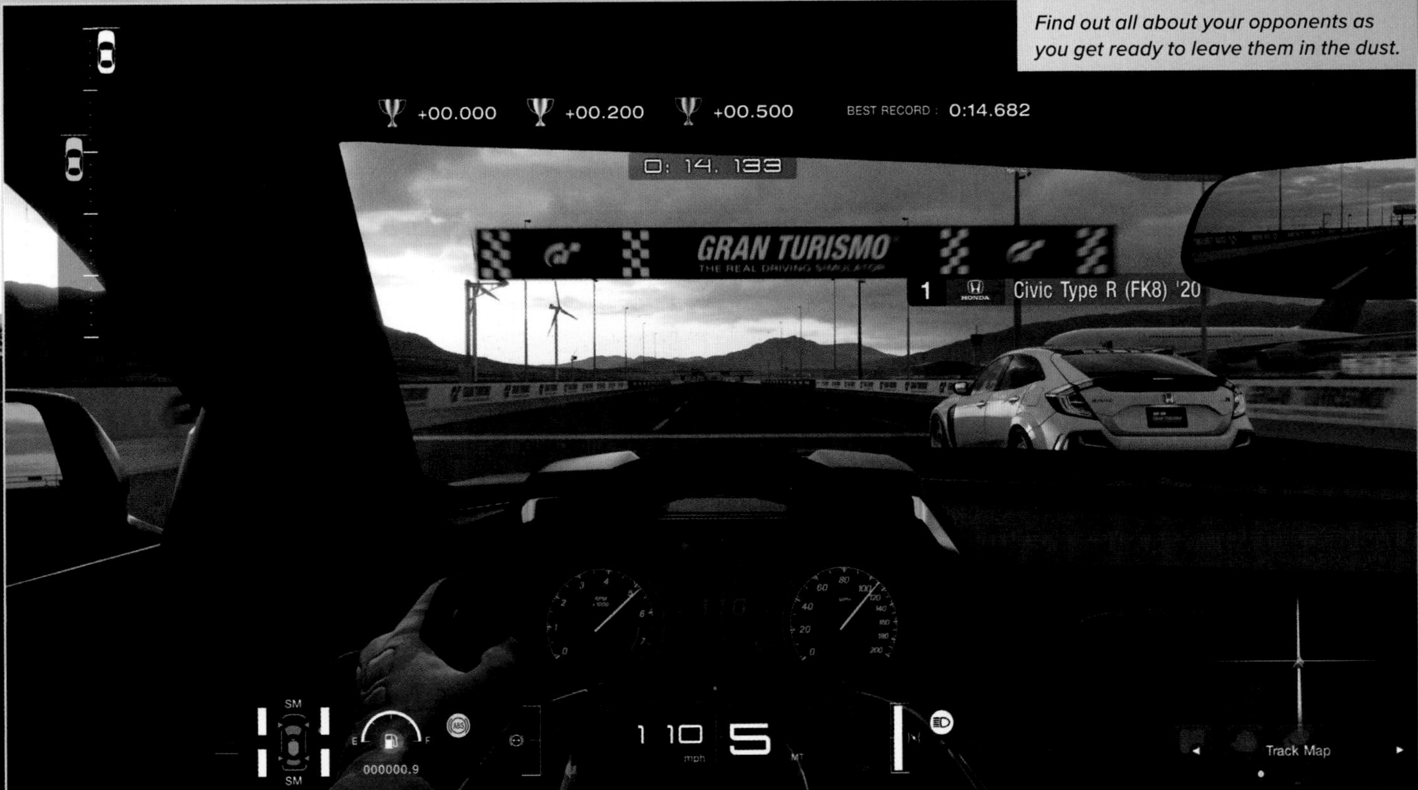

Tracking All Over the World

Gran Turismo 7's ninety-four launch tracks are spread over thirty-four locations. There are plenty of fictional and real circuits to choose from. Some of the real-life tracks are Germany's Nürburgring, England's Goodwood and Brands Hatch, Daytona in the United States and Tsukuba Circuit in the developer's home nation of Japan.

GT By Numbers

- Despite the seven in the title, this is actually the eighth main series game – with 2017's *Gran Turismo Sport* messing up the naming conventions. Doh!
- *Gran Turismo 3: A-Spec* is the series' bestselling entry. It came out in 2001 and shifted 14.8 million copies on PS2.

Check Out

Fancy taking on the Empire? Try *Star Wars: Republic Commando Remaster* for an intergalactic team-up.

Rainbow Six Extraction

Developer Ubisoft Montreal **Publisher** Ubisoft
Platform PC, PS4, PS5, XBO, XBX/S

■ ***Rainbow Six Extraction* is the online spin-off to 2015's *Six Siege*. Drop into alien-infested areas with two teammates to hoover up samples and find intel. Oh, and shoot the snot out of enemies called Archaeans. There are different types of Archaean, like rooters, who can slow you down, and spikers, who shoot sharp objects that sting more than a paper cut.**

Call the Operator

Before each mission you choose an operator from eighteen options, each with unique abilities. Helicopter pilot Jäger can deploy an automated turret that handily intercepts attacks, while cumbersome Rook is still worth choosing despite his lack of speed as he drops protective armour plates.

Nailing the make-up of your three-man team is the secret to progression through the thirteen missions and twelve maps – set in New York, San Francisco, Alaska and Truth or Consequences.

Rainbow Six Extraction *has an online co-op system that lets you play with two friends, making your chance of success against the aliens even better.*

Another type of Archaean is the smasher. They're the tankiest of the enemies you'll face in the game and like to charge at full force. But they've got a weak spot on their backs so try to aim as they run past you.

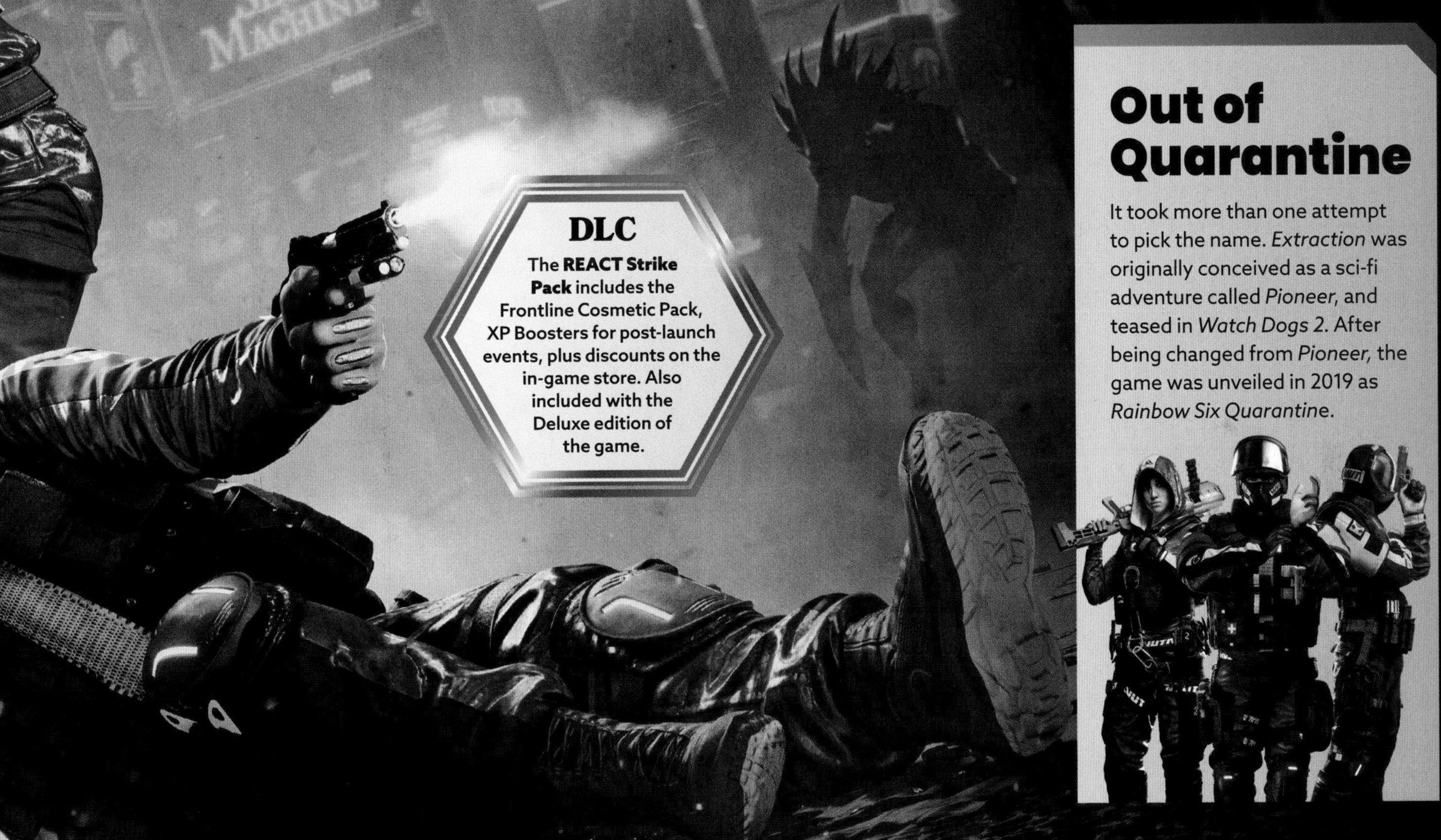

DLC

The **REACT Strike Pack** includes the Frontline Cosmetic Pack, XP Boosters for post-launch events, plus discounts on the in-game store. Also included with the Deluxe edition of the game.

Out of Quarantine

It took more than one attempt to pick the name. *Extraction* was originally conceived as a sci-fi adventure called *Pioneer*, and teased in *Watch Dogs 2*. After being changed from *Pioneer*, the game was unveiled in 2019 as *Rainbow Six Quarantine*.

As you play, you'll learn how to take out the Archaeans, different moves work for different types.

Watch out for the nests! Giant birthing pods filled with new aliens, you'll want to destroy them before they hatch.

A Cause for Celebration

Feel-Good Gaming Stories

Zeldathon

Do you love **The Legend of Zelda** and helping others? Check out the live-streamed **Zelda** marathon that takes place every year. It raises money for Special Effect, a charity aimed at making games playable for everyone.

Nintendo Brings Gaming to Hospitals

The world loves Nintendo, and Nintendo loves the world. The Japanese publisher proved this when they installed gaming stations in hospitals across America. The idea was to bring joy to poorly children. They're called Starlight Nintendo Switch Gaming Stations and have more than twenty-five games. *Super Mario Party* and *The Legend of Zelda: Breath of the Wild* are two of the biggest. The Starlight Stations come on wheels so they can be taken to the patients.

Post-pandemic Pals

The pandemic changed how people make friends. The average American adult made five new friends during lockdown, thanks to video games. *World of Warships* did some research. They discovered over a third of people they asked had expanded their online friendships since the pandemic began. These new mates were so ace, the average gamer would invite four of them to their wedding. Two-thirds said that games made them less lonely and connected them to other people.

The Bionic Babe

Twenty-one-year-old Laiken Olive is an American gamer who was born without a hand. Their new $11,000 'Venom Snake' bionic arm has changed their life. It was named after the main character in *Metal Gear Solid* and the colours match his red-and-black arm. The limb uses special sensors to read muscular outputs. These are then converted into bionic hand movements. As thebionicbabe, Olive has racked up more than a million views on TikTok.

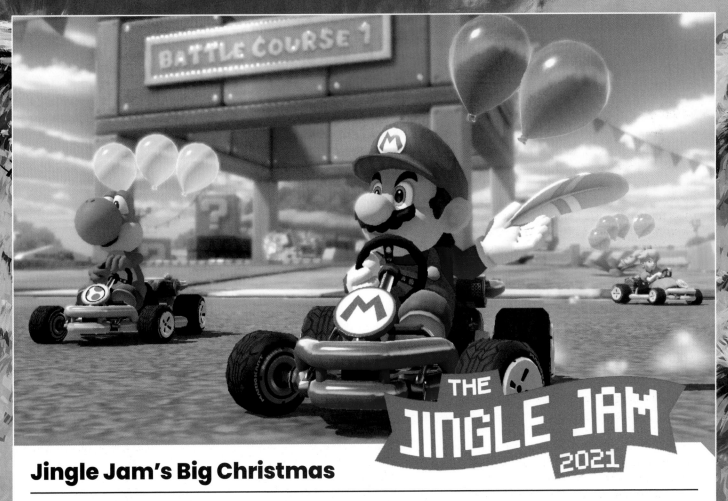

Jingle Jam's Big Christmas

Gaming's biggest charity event celebrated its 11th consecutive year. Gamers across the globe raised funds for fourteen different causes through Jingle Jam. These included disabled access to gaming and sport, structural racism and LGBTQ+ causes. Event organisers Yogscast hosted four streams per day featuring the likes of *Pokémon*, *Minecraft* and *Mario Kart*. Supporters got rewards like Steam keys to fifty-five games and the event raised over $4.4 million.

STATE OF PLAY

Heroes of the Year

Gaming's Biggest Superstars

Rey Mysterio

Game WWE 2K22 **First Appearance** WWE Smackdown! Here Comes The Pain **Occupation** Wrestler **Height** 168 cm **Age** 47 **Hair Colour** Bald **Eye Colour** Brown **Home** San Diego **Voiced by** Óscar Gutiérrez

WWE 2K22's cover star has the distinction of being the only real person on the heroes shortlist. But colourful masks and a history of high-flying moves mean Mysterio feels like a real-life video game character. The popular wrestler is the star of Showcase mode, in the *WWE*'s first official sim in more than two years.

Dani Rojas

Game Far Cry 6
First Appearance Far Cry 6
Occupation Guerrilla Fighter
Height 173 cm (approx)
Age 25 **Hair Colour** Brown
Eye Colour Green
Home Esperanza
Voiced by Sean Ray / Nisa Gundez

Far Cry 6's main character has an extra edge over the others on this shortlist: Dani can be either male or female. Whatever their gender, the character is passionate and emotional. Skills-wise, they are adept with a grapple hook, and deadly with a gun. And a shock candidate for James Corden's Carpool Karaoke too – happily belting out 'Livin' La Vida Loca' as they motor across Esperanza.

Behind the Voice

Laura Bailey is the voice of Nadine Ross. She's also played Black Widow in **Marvel's Avengers**, Abby in **The Last of Us Part II** and Vex'ahlia in the hugely popular **Dungeons & Dragons** series **Critical Role**, plus the spin-off **The Legend of Vox Machina**.

Nadine Ross

Game Uncharted: Legacy of Thieves Collection **First Appearance** Uncharted 4: A Thief's End **Occupation** Mercenary / Treasure Hunter **Height** 165 cm **Age** Early 30s **Hair Colour** Brown **Eye Colour** Brown **Home** South Africa **Voiced by** Laura Bailey

You get to see both sides of the badass yet brilliant Nadine in *Uncharted: Legacy of Thieves Collection*. In *Uncharted 4: A Thief's End* she helps shady businessman Rafe Adler search for a mystical pirate colony. And in *Uncharted: The Lost Legacy* Nadine uses her cool attitude, martial arts expertise and killer instincts for good alongside Chloe Frazer.

Chloe Frazer

Game Uncharted: Legacy of Thieves Collection **First Appearance** Uncharted 2: Among Thieves **Occupation** Treasure Hunter **Height** 173 cm **Age** 38 **Hair Colour** Black **Eye Colour** Blue **Home** Australia **Voiced by** Claudia Black

Chloe was introduced as a potential Nathan Drake love interest. By *The Lost Legacy* she had taken over as *Uncharted*'s lead. The Aussie is an independent thinker, masterful driver and skilled fighter. She's a cunning manipulator too, ingenious at using her looks and sharp wit to charm and disarm. Particularly when dealing with Drake.

January-March
GAME SPOTLIGHT

Did You Know
You can buy merch phone cases that make it look like you have your very own Arc phone.

Pokémon Legends: Arceus

Developer Game Freak **Publisher** Nintendo / The Pokémon Company **Platform** NS

■ *Pokémon* fans had a year of sweet treats. *Arceus* dropped on Switch not long after the *Brilliant Diamond* and *Shining Pearl* remakes. This game is a prequel to that pair, heading back to a time when Sinnoh was instead known as Hisui. Much of the setting is based on the real-life Japanese island of Ezo – which 700 years later is better known as Hokkaido.

While roaming vast plains and stomping up beautiful mountains, players find Pokémon who need to be added to your Pokédex. So far, so familiar. Except the Pokédex is a paper notebook, and the cute critters are treated as wild animals, rather than companions. Along the way, you also come across noble Pokémon who've turned berserk and you need to fight them to calm them down. A curious method, but it works.

Something Smells Fishy

The biggest surprise here is the story. There's plenty of cuddliness in the game, but *Arceus* has a serious and sometimes dark side too. Anyone lucky enough to play the game before it was released was actually banned from saying too much, in case it leaked online. No spoilers! But it features the Diamond and Pearl clans squabbling over their choice of god. There are also some rather spooky character features – such as Basculegion, a ghostly fish-like Pokémon who is possessed by the souls of the dead.

Battles against other Pokémon take place exactly where you find them, instead of transporting you to another screen – and making you wait while it loads.

Arceus Explained

The name of *Pokémon Legends: Arceus* relates to the god of Pokémon. Arceus is white and centaur-like with four-pointed feet that are tipped with gold hooves. Legend states that Arceus shaped the Pokémon universe using its 1,000 arms and continues to watch over the world right through to the modern day. However, in this adventure, Arceus is a villain, not a hero.

You'll find some exciting Pokémon of all levels in Hisui. Like this Garchomp, a Dragon-and Ground-type Pokémon.

Walk in the Wild

There might be a darker tone to *Arceus*, but the Hisui region is a wonder to explore. Its centre point is the breathtaking Mount Coronet, then the surrounding areas have their own distinct features, ecosystems and Pokémon. The Obsidian Fieldlands are filled with lush plant life so are home to Pokémon who like meadows and forests.

Wander through the beautiful hills and fields in this open world adventure. You'll come across wild Pokémon like this adorable Bidoof. Watch out though, some of them might attack!

New Faces

Basculegion isn't the only new Pokémon introduced in *Arceus*. Wrydeer is one of the forest-loving Pokémon found in the Obsidian Fieldlands. It has gold antlers and is loved by the people of Hisui for its warm, protective fur. Bug-Rock hybrid Kleavor is the final form of Scyther and has powerful arms that can chop down trees. Enamorus is a pink-horned genie who can turn into a mix of turtle and snake. Oh, and can also unleash mini cyclones. Tread carefully ...

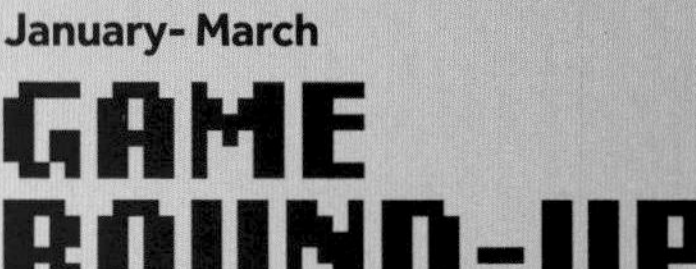

Top Tips

You can change your settings so that your items can be used quickly. Set the quests radial menu to access important items, like potions and bombs.

Monster Hunter Rise

Developer Capcom **Publisher** Capcom
Platform NS, PC

■ *Monster Hunter World* was originally a niche Japanese favourite. But after a successful Switch launch, the beast-bashing series scored worldwide acclaim. This sequel has now come to PC so even more people can KO the creatures. You start out against dino-like monsters before working up to dragons and wyverns. Use swords, hammers and horns for maximum monster-downing mayhem. It's super tough but super rewarding too.

If you saw two giant monsters having an airborne battle, would you get involved or keep running?

Join up with friends online and take down explosive monsters like this Magnamalo spouting Hellfire.

Two sets of teeth might sound terrifying but ... no wait, that's pretty scary. Luckily, there are a ton of different weapons available to help you stay alive.

Hounding Enemies

❸ *Rise* is another game that gives you a canine companion, there are dog-like Paramules helping you navigate the map without losing stamina.

King of Fighters XV

Developer SNK **Publisher** Koch Media **Platform** PC, PS4, PS5, XBO, XBX/S

■ *Street Fighter's* more serious rival game returns. Teams of three warriors go head-to-head in a tournament set up by a rookie commissioner, Anastasia. A one-button, combo-launching 'Rush' command opens the series up for new players. Enjoy thirty-nine characters such as the Hero Team of Shun'ei, Meitenkun and Benimaru, or the Bogard brothers and Joe Higashi from *Fatal Fury*.

Check Out

Sad this isn't on Switch? Give the all-female *SNK Heroines: Tag Team Frenzy* a try instead.

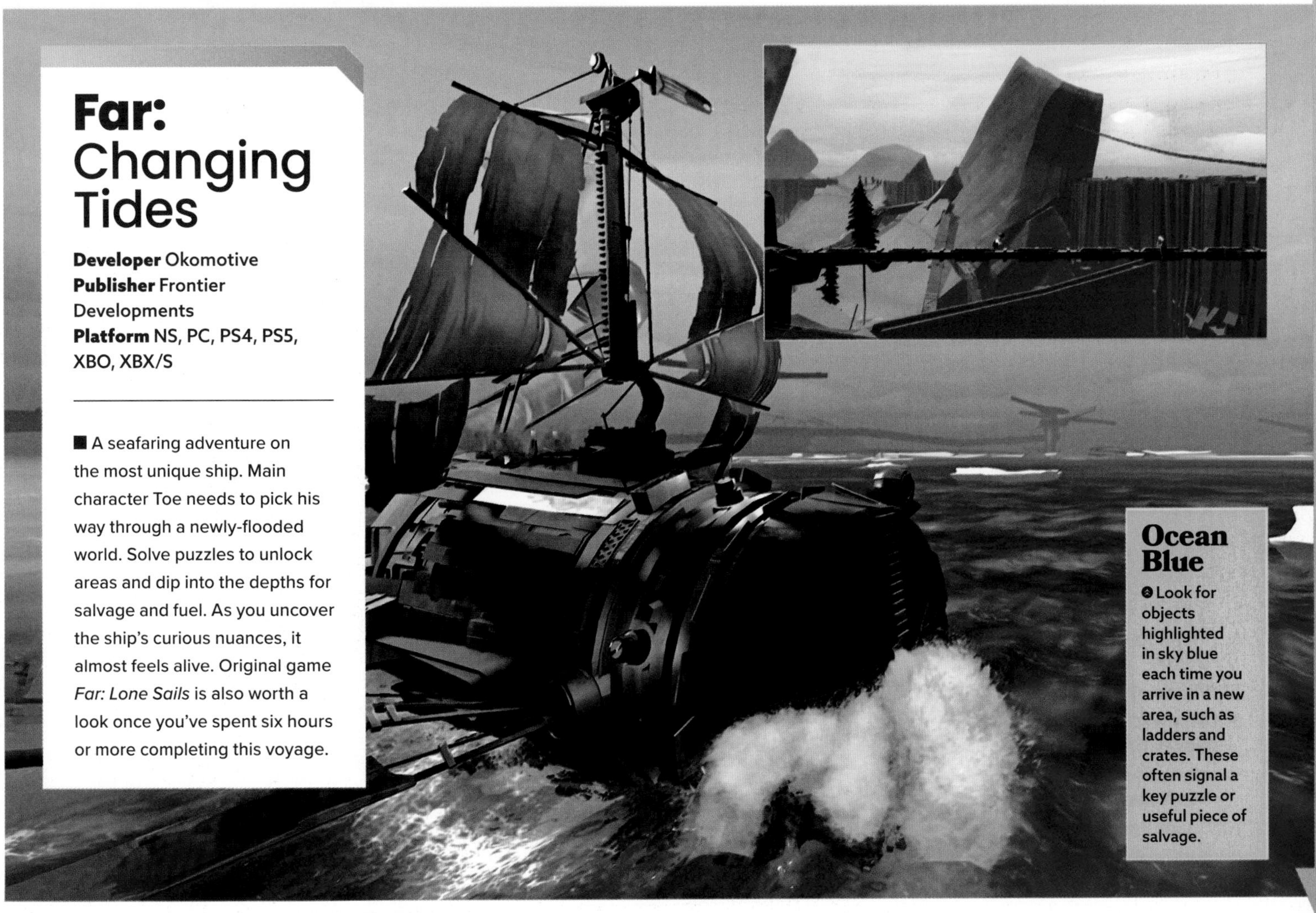

Far: Changing Tides

Developer Okomotive **Publisher** Frontier Developments **Platform** NS, PC, PS4, PS5, XBO, XBX/S

■ A seafaring adventure on the most unique ship. Main character Toe needs to pick his way through a newly-flooded world. Solve puzzles to unlock areas and dip into the depths for salvage and fuel. As you uncover the ship's curious nuances, it almost feels alive. Original game *Far: Lone Sails* is also worth a look once you've spent six hours or more completing this voyage.

Ocean Blue

Look for objects highlighted in sky blue each time you arrive in a new area, such as ladders and crates. These often signal a key puzzle or useful piece of salvage.

STATE OF PLAY

The Bestselling Games of the Year

How Many Have You Played?

Mario Charts

Despite coming out in 2014, **Mario Kart 8** is still hitting the top ten in all three major game charts. The paid DLC **Booster Course** pass has added even more tracks and obstacles to keep players racing.

Japan

1. Monster Hunter Rise
2. Pokémon Brilliant Diamond/Shining Pearl
3. Momotaro Dentetsu: Showa, Heisei, Reiwa mo Teiban!
4. Super Mario 3D World + Bowser's Fury
5. Ring Fit Adventure
6. Mario Kart 8 Deluxe
7. Minecraft
8. Animal Crossing: New Horizons
9. Mario Party Superstars
10. Super Smash Bros. Ultimate

USA

1. Call of Duty: Vanguard
2. Call of Duty Black Ops: Cold War
3. Madden NFL 22
4. Pokémon Brilliant Diamond/ Shining Pearl
5. Battlefield 2042
6. Spider-Man: Miles Morales
7. Mario Kart 8 Deluxe
8. Resident Evil Village
9. MLB The Show 21
10. Super Mario 3D World + Bowser's Fury

Europe

1. FIFA 22
2. Grand Theft Auto 5
3. FIFA 21
4. Call of Duty: Vanguard
5. Mario Kart 8 Deluxe
6. Red Dead Redemption 2
7. Super Mario 3D World + Bowser's Fury
8. Call of Duty Black Ops: Cold War
9. Assassin's Creed Valhalla
10. Spider-Man: Miles Morales

Narrowly missing out on the charts are ***F1 2021*** (number eleven in Europe), ***Far Cry 6*** (number eleven in USA) and ***Pokémon Sword/Shield*** (number eleven in Japan).

Call of Duty is still hitting the top of Western sales charts. ***Black Ops: Cold War*** was released in 2020 but it outsold every single new USA release of 2021. It's now the third-biggest gaming series ever, after *Mario* and *Tetris*.

Never heard of this one? ***Momotaro Dentetsu*** plays like a virtual board game, where players roll dice to move trains around Japan's railway network. Like *Monopoly*, you need to rack up more wealth than your rivals to win. Also like the house-buying game, a single play can go on for hours!

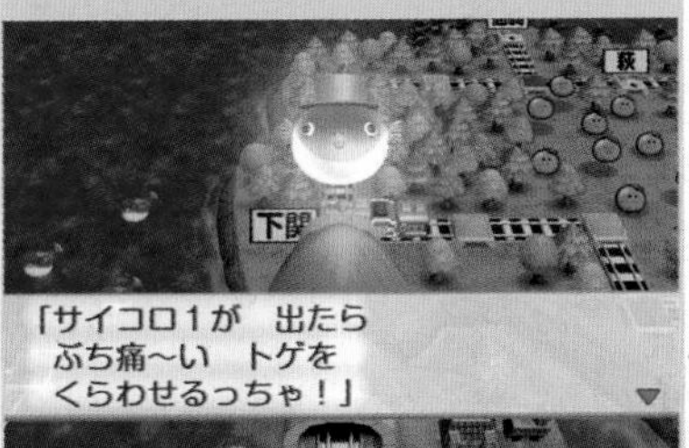

Mario Kart 8 Deluxe is one of only two games on all three charts, along with *Super Mario 3D World*. It's pretty incredible as the racer first came out on Wii U back in 2014. Across Wii and Switch, it has sold a staggering 51 million copies. Woah!

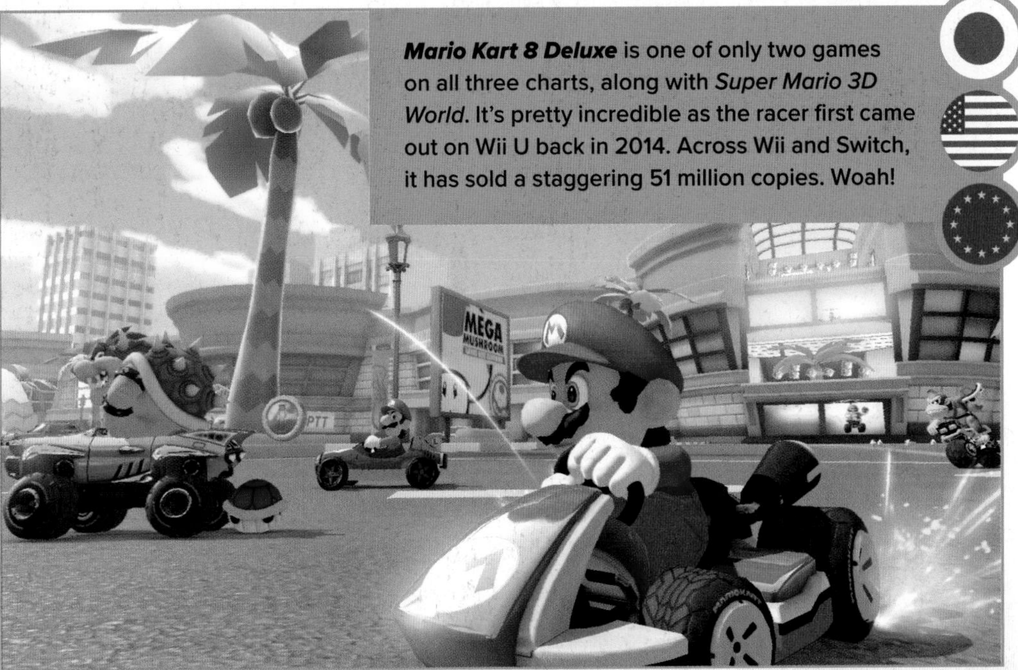

The entire Japanese chart is made up of Nintendo Switch games. The bestselling non-Switch game was ***Tales of Arise*** on PS4 – all the way down at number twenty-two.

The success of ***Brilliant Diamond*** and ***Shining Pearl*** made this *Pokémon*'s biggest year since 2000. Now imagine if *Pokémon Legends Arceus* had also come out in the same period ...

What in the Weird?

Wild and Weird Gaming Stories From Across the World

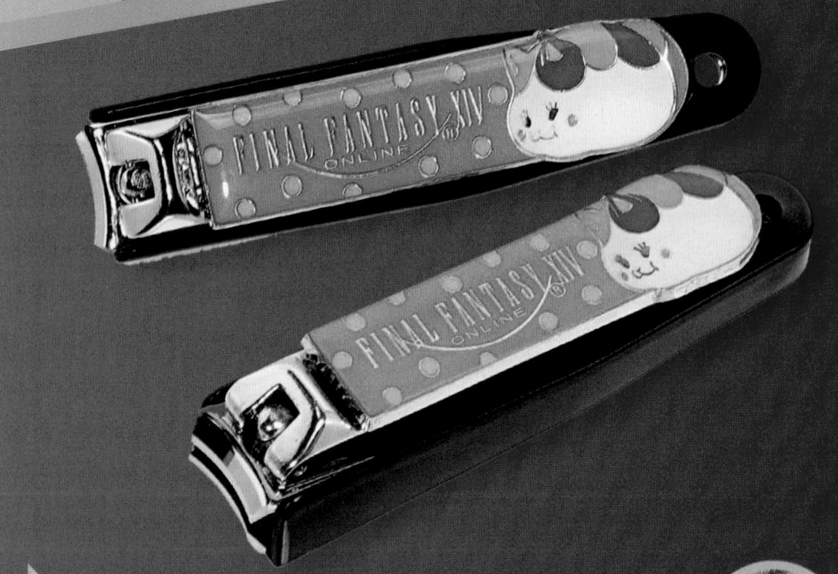

Final Fantasy Gets Cuticle

Final Fantasy has been around since 1987. You'd think that creator Square Enix had dreamed up every possible merch idea since then. T-shirts? Check. Figures? Check. Cuddly toys? Check. But the Japanese publisher released something unheard of: *Final Fantasy XIV* nail clippers. There are two different types. The orange set comes with an image of Fat Cat on them and the black ones show the game's meteor logo. Now you can keep your fingers and toes looking trim in between sessions of *Endwalker*.

Police vs Pokémon

An insane *Pokémon Go* tale has been revealed. Back in 2017, two Los Angeles policemen were called to a robbery at a local mall. Many of their colleagues attended the scene, but the pair never showed up. Instead, they'd gone searching nearby in *Pokémon Go*. The first officer noted that, "Snorlax just popped up ... at 46th and Leimart." They spent twenty minutes apparently hunting more creatures for their Pokédex, with the same officer noticing, "a Togetic just popped up." Both were sacked.

Guitar Hero Dis-chord

Guitar Hero was one of the coolest games of the 2010s. It introduced the world to the joys of a plastic axe. That led to its best players earning minor-celebrity status on YouTube. One of those gods of pretend rock recently revealed that his top-scoring videos were fake. Schmooey had found a way to slow down the game's songs. He then recorded himself playing them perfectly at the gentler pace, and sped them up before uploading to YouTube. Viewers spotted an error in one video and he was forced into confessing his mischief. Oops.

Farewell for Now, E3

E3 is the summer trade show where all the big guns show off their new games. In 2022, gamers were in for a huge shock when its organisers, the ESA, cancelled the event. It had also disappeared off the calendar in 2020 due to the pandemic, and the 2021 version was digital-only. ESA promised the cancellation will make E3 2023 even better. Fingers crossed for next year!

Horizon: Forbidden West

Developer Guerrilla Games **Publisher** Sony **Platform** PS4, PS5

■ From death follows new life. Five years after Aloy wowed the world on PS4, she's back to do the same on PS5. The first game was great and this outshines it in every way. Cut-scenes are well-acted and to-the-point, while side quests feel less important but you'll still want to do them all anyway.

Aloy Old Friend

Forbidden West picks up six months after the end of *Horizon: Zero Dawn*. Aloy and her friend Varl are trying to unearth a back-up for super-powerful artificial intelligence GAIA. The quest takes her to ruined versions of Las Vegas and San Francisco. You'll explore every backdrop imaginable, from snow-capped mountains to tropical beaches and claustrophobic-yet-essential underwater areas.

PS5's DualSense™ controller enhances the feel of combat. Every bow or catapult has a specific sensation when wielded. If you decide not to unleash a shot, the relaxing of your weapon comes through in the trigger buttons. There's motion aiming too, for anyone who wants to live their best life as *Forbidden West*'s hero.

Rise of the Machines

Forbidden West features forty-three different types of machine for Aloy to take down. More than twenty of those are new. Plowhorns are triceratops-like monsters who sew fertiliser and seeds, leaving clouds of dust - perfect for you to hide behind. Sneaky! The tideripper is a robotic Loch Ness monster, capable of downing Aloy with water cannon blasts and tail whips. But as the saying goes: the bigger they are ...

Sharp Cutlery

Feel like your archery skills aren't up to it? Once you unlock the stronger weapons, that won't be a problem. Spike throwers are powerful javelins that need charging before you unleash, but deal colossal damage to enemy machines. Boltblasters can punch through armour and cause extra hurt to whatever is underneath. The shredder gauntlet slices enemies up with a serrated disc. Also handy for cutting pizza. Probably.

The pullcaster is one of the first new tools that you discover. You can use it to bring items closer or climb tall structures.

There are over twenty new machines for you and Aloy to track, battle and destroy in Horizon Forbidden West.

Aloy and her Nora friend Varl voyage into the Forbidden West. The red blight has infected the plantlife here, it's up to them to stop it.

Did You Know?

Guerrilla has a history of making unmissable PlayStation games. They also masterminded five entries in the *Killzone* series across PS2, PS3 and PS4.

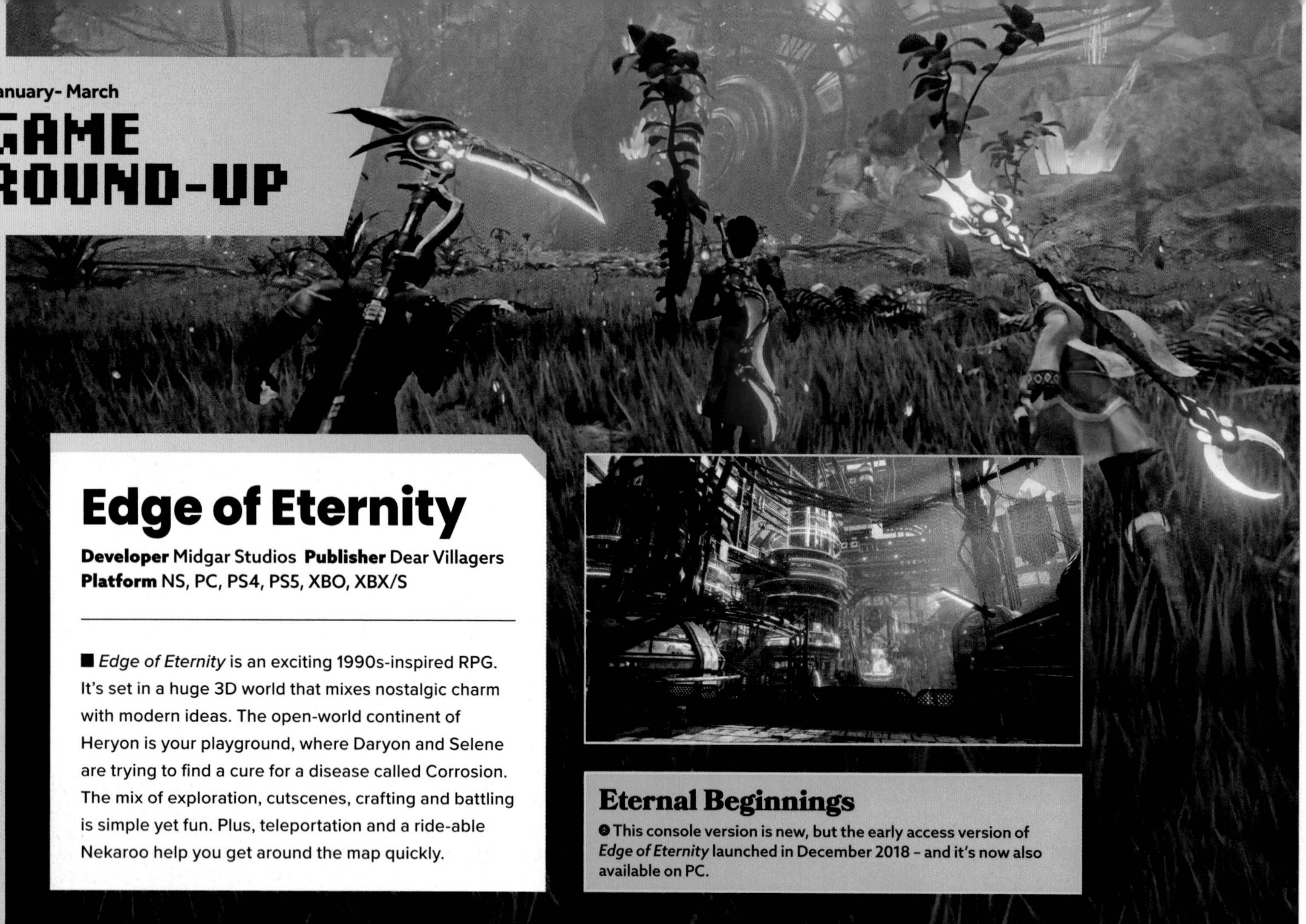

Edge of Eternity

Developer Midgar Studios **Publisher** Dear Villagers **Platform** NS, PC, PS4, PS5, XBO, XBX/S

■ *Edge of Eternity* is an exciting 1990s-inspired RPG. It's set in a huge 3D world that mixes nostalgic charm with modern ideas. The open-world continent of Heryon is your playground, where Daryon and Selene are trying to find a cure for a disease called Corrosion. The mix of exploration, cutscenes, crafting and battling is simple yet fun. Plus, teleportation and a ride-able Nekaroo help you get around the map quickly.

Eternal Beginnings

This console version is new, but the early access version of *Edge of Eternity* launched in December 2018 – and it's now also available on PC.

In Nightmare

Developer Beijing Magic Fish Technology **Publisher** Maximum Games **Platform** PS4, PS5

■ Your freakiest dreams come alive in this troubling yet moreish horror adventure. A young boy called Bill solves puzzles while dodging sinister spiders, stealthy witches and gross lumps with too many eyes. He has an imaginary friend called the Dream Spirit, who can detect invisible pathways and items and warn you about threats that lie ahead.

Number One Fan

Chinese creator Fan Yu combined his own childhood experiences with research on family trauma to create *In Nightmare*'s fearful themes.

Windjammers 2

Developer Dotemu **Publisher** Dotemu
Platform NS, PC, PS4, XBO

■ Frisbee is officially cool again ... or is it for the first time? It's all thanks to *Windjammers 2*. Like *FIFA* with a circular disc, you score points for getting the frisbee into your opponents' goal. Your team's special powers help that aim: the powerful Costa can sling the disc in a zig-zag motion and Raposa's magic throw rides the wall before curling towards goal. They're just two of eleven larger-than-life characters in a sporting sequel that was worth waiting twenty-eight years for.

A Cast You Know

Six characters return from the original Neo Geo *Windjammers*: Mita, Miller, Costa, Biaggi, Scott and super-powerful sunglasses-wearing Klaus Wessel.

Summer in Mara

Developer Chibig **Publisher** Chibig
Platform NS, PC, PS4, XBO

■ This gorgeous single-player farming sim was a cult hit when released digitally. Publisher Chibig have finally dropped a physical edition in 2022 and what a treat it is, too. As well as crafting and exploring across tropical islands, you get an art book, poster, acrylic diorama and sticker sheet. Even without those goodies, this is a dreamy summer holiday in the comfort of your living room.

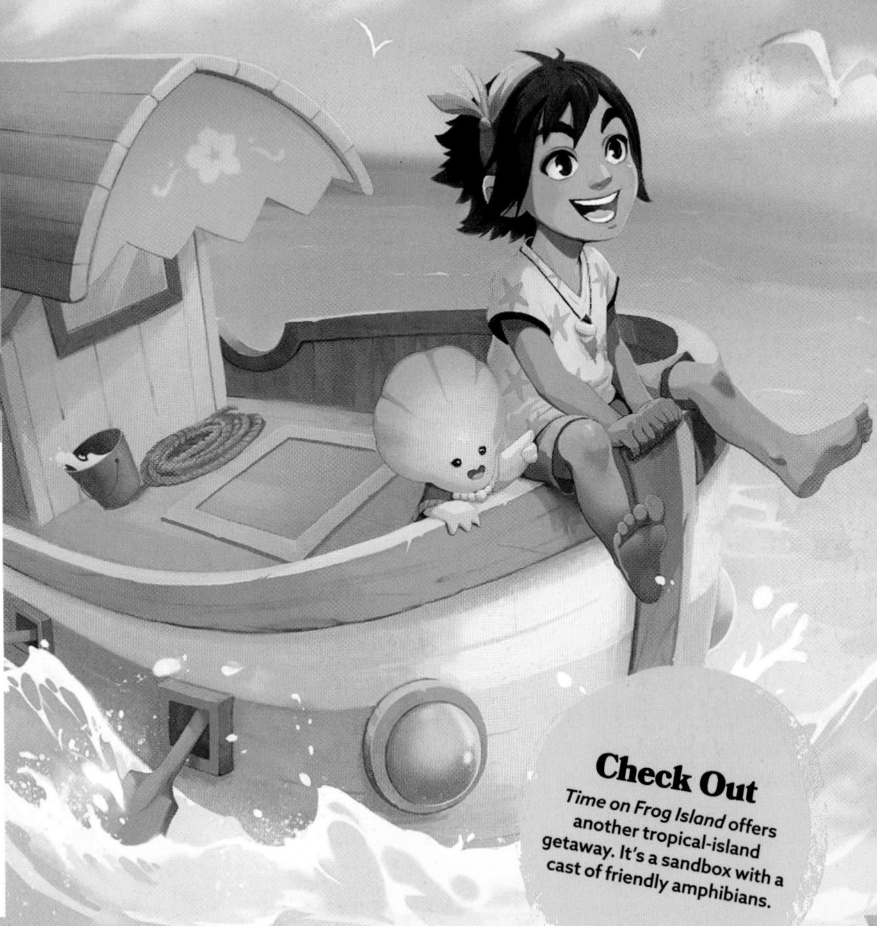

Check Out

Time on Frog Island offers another tropical-island getaway. It's a sandbox with a cast of friendly amphibians.

Uncharted Territory

Nathan Drake's Exploring New Lands

Record Sales

The *Uncharted* movie, starring Tom Holland, made over $100 million on its opening weekend. It's now the fourth most successful gaming movie, after *Rampage*, *Pokémon: Detective Pikachu* and *Sonic the Hedgehog 2*.

Nate's Cast and Crew

Nathan Drake

Uncharted's modern Indiana Jones returns in *A Thief's End*, drawn back into action by a cry for help from the brother he assumed was dead.

Chloe Frazer

Chloe was adored by fans after her banter-filled debut in *Uncharted 2: Among Thieves*. In *The Lost Legacy*, she teams up with Nadine to hunt the Golden Tusk.

Nadine Ross

Chloe's unlikely ally arrives as an enemy in *Uncharted 4*. When she returns in *The Lost Legacy*, the pair team up across the south-west Indian coastline.

Elena Fisher

The original heroine of the *Uncharted* series. Elena and Drake's will-they-won't-they storyline ended in their marriage between the second and third games.

■ When it first came out on PS3, *Uncharted* changed the game for action-adventures. Now even more gamers can get a taster with the *Legacy Of Thieves Collection,* plus a huge Hollywood movie. The game is a mix of *Tomb Raider* and *Indiana Jones*. It perfectly blends humble-yet-feisty characters, rewarding puzzles, snappy combat and barely believable locations. *Uncharted* is a franchise that's as engaging on your tenth play as your first.

An Incredible Legacy

Legacy Of Thieves Collection pairs together 2016's *Uncharted 4: A Thief's End* and the 2017 game *Uncharted: The Lost Legacy*. Wisecracking treasure hunter Nathan Drake is the main character in the first game and fearless Aussie sidekick Chloe Frazer is upgraded to top billing in the second. Not forgetting the beloved series favourites Sully and Ellie.

The PS5 brings faster load times and even more gorgeous visuals, plus lots of clever controller play. DualSense™'s dynamic triggers let you feel the tension in rope swings, while haptic feedback also comes through in punches and driving vehicles. Once you've completed these adventures, consider the PS4 release *The Nathan Drake Collection*. It contains those original classics and runs well on PS5.

Series History

Every *Uncharted* console game and spin-off, in one place.

UNCHARTED: DRAKE'S FORTUNE (2007)

UNCHARTED 2: AMONG THIEVES (2009)

UNCHARTED 3: DRAKE'S DECEPTION (2011)

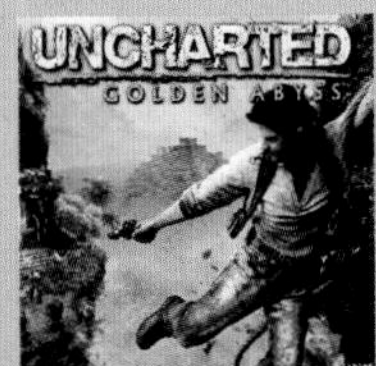

UNCHARTED: GOLDEN ABYSS (2011)

UNCHARTED: FIGHT FOR FORTUNE (2012)

UNCHARTED 4: A THIEF'S END (2016)

UNCHARTED: THE LOST LEGACY (2017)

THE INSIDER TAKE

Developers Share Highlights from a Memorable Year

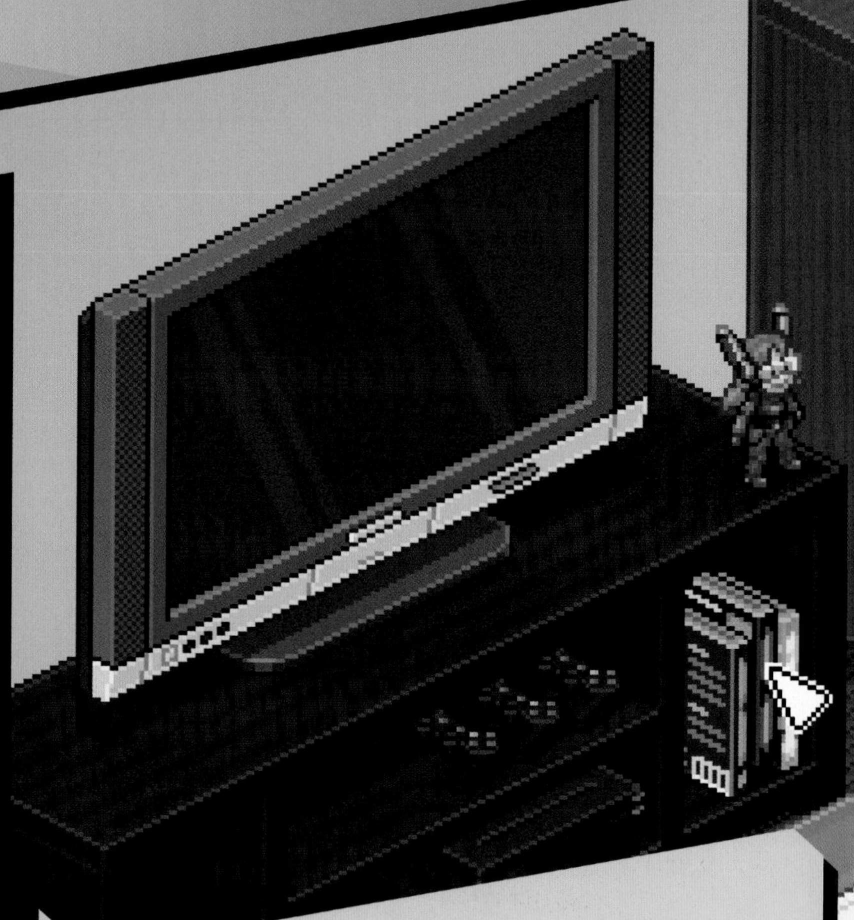

Nick Pearce
Creator of The Forgotten City

What's the best thing you played in the last year?
I replayed *Portal* and *Portal 2*, both of which are masterpieces. The way Valve took a novel gameplay mechanic, built fun puzzles around it, then wrapped it up with a hilarious narrative is ingenious.

What element of The Forgotten City are you most proud of?
Having created a game which is gripping and exciting without relying on combat. It's not easy, but I think it shows that grappling with a mystery, and even fundamental philosophical questions, can be wonderfully engaging!

What game are you most looking forward to?
Starfield! As is my custom whenever a Bethesda game is released, I'll be shirking all my responsibilities for a week so I can lose myself in the world they've created.

Wren Brier
Creative Director of Unpacking

What's the best thing you played in the last year?
Bugsnax! Figuring out how to catch them is a delight. All the characters have a surprising amount of depth and I love the spooky elements, too. Like *Pokémon*, but make it body horror.

What element of Unpacking are you most proud of?
Definitely the storytelling. It was the biggest risk we took – we actually weren't sure if people would get it until about a year into development, when we had the first two levels of the game playable. Thankfully they did!

What game are you most looking forward to?
Cult of the Lamb! It looks like a cross between *Don't Starve* and *Animal Crossing*, with some *Binding of Isaac* vibes. I can't wait to start my own cult of adorable animals.

Mike Mahar
Senior producer on Madden NFL 22

What's the best thing you played in the last year?
I play *FIFA 22* and *Fortnite* with my sons, and the game I enjoy when they're in bed is *Ghost of Tsushima*. I could not get enough of that and 100%-ed it.

What element of Madden NFL 22 are you most proud of?
Our dynamic gameday feature. It added variety and fun depending on which stadium you played in, and how you played on the field. And it represented how our gameplay and presentation and audio and rendering teams work together as one.

What game are you most looking forward to?
Probably *EA Sports FC*, what with *FIFA 23* being the last year of EA's partnership. My son sees me as a cool dad for being able to get the game before it comes out!

Lynell Jinks
Creative Director of WWE 2K22

What's the best thing you played in the last year?
Besides *WWE 2K22*, I would have to say that *Half Life Alyx*. I'm a big fan of VR, and it shows the potential of that platform.

What element of WWE 2K22 are you most proud of?
We changed the gameplay completely and made it way more fun and accessible, which was really challenging. If we created a game that wasn't fun, it wouldn't matter what features we added or how pretty it is. Gameplay is king.

What game are you most looking forward to?
The Quarry. Games like *Heavy Rain*, *Become Human* and *Until Dawn* are my jam. I love the fact that my choices and actions can change the story and ultimately the outcome of the game.

Did You Know?
Techland also made the brilliant *Dead Island*, where you fend off zombies on the paradise of Banoi.

Dying Light 2: Stay Human

Developer Techland **Publisher** Techland
Platform NS, PC, PS4, PS5, XBO, XBX/S

■ If a zombie apocalypse unfolded tomorrow, how would your parkour skills hold up? Don't start trying to clamber across roofs in order to find out. *Dying Light 2* tests your abilities without the threat of an ambulance ride. You play as Aiden Campbell, a masterful wall runner and ledge climber who's also handy with a grapple hook and paraglider.

Dying Light emerged in 2015, and the sequel is set twenty-two years later. The first game's Middle Eastern setting of Harran has been wiped out so the action has moved to Europe, and the city of Villedor. This walled sandbox is four times bigger than Harran and contains masses to do, in addition to downing the undead. Scrap can be scavenged and turned into new weapons, inhibitors upgrade Aiden's health and stamina, and activating windmills attracts merchants and survivors to build settlements.

Out of Reach

Those roof-clambering skills are incredibly useful, too. Exposure to the sun means your enemies are slow in the daytime, but way more hostile in darkness, so staying up high offers the best chance at staying safe. There are seven different regions to explore and there's four-way co-op multiplayer in case your mates wish to team up for some zombie-hammering chaos.

As you gain levels, your weapons become more powerful. You can also win new ones after completing missions.

As you explore, you'll come across safes. They're usually hiding important mission items so try breaking into them.

Can You Kick It?

Crossbows, shotguns and spears can all be put to use in *Stay Human*, but this is mostly a melee-focused action-RPG. Aiden's feet are more creative than a Premier League footballer's. His dropkicks and head stomps are a pretty effective way of felling zombies, plus brass knuckles and machetes dish out some brutal blows. Deploy your new-found tools wisely, though. The more you use a weapon, the more it degrades.

Not all zombies are slow movers. The infected walk and run at different speeds. If you're cornered by a group of slow infected, keep an eye out in case you're about to get attacked by something swift!

DLC

The **Ultimate Upgrade** pack includes the 'Legendary' outfit, paraglider skin and renewable weapons. You will also get access to two new story DLCs that will become available later on in the year.

Subway for Lunch

Despite its fictional background, Villedor feels like an authentic, once-great city housing the last few survivors on earth. The story dates it to around 930 AD and places it on the banks of the Turzawa river. It's broken up into twelve districts – seven of these need to be captured – and boasts nine metro stations. They act as fast travel points later in the game, so try to unlock them all as soon as you can.

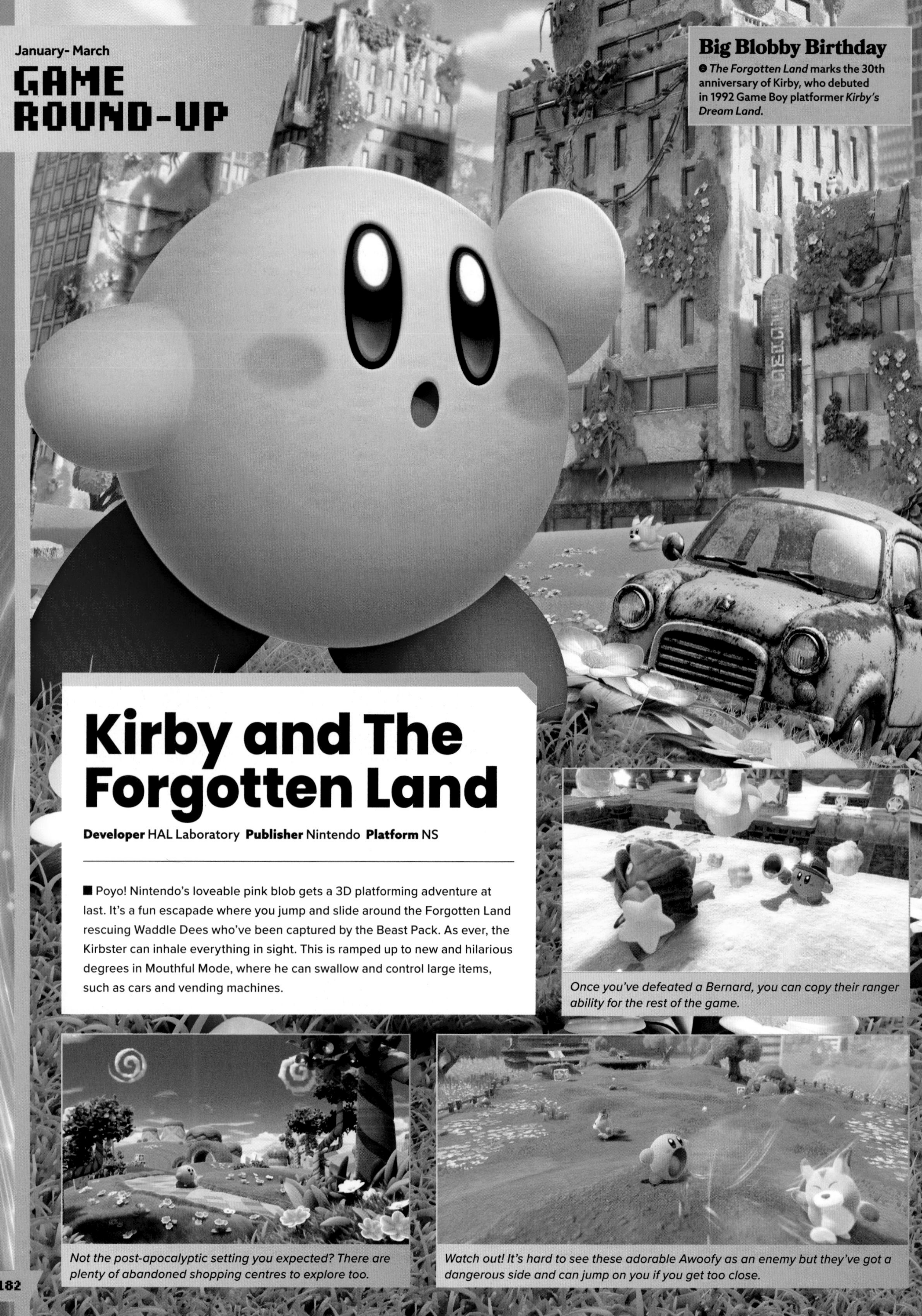

Big Blobby Birthday

The Forgotten Land marks the 30th anniversary of Kirby, who debuted in 1992 Game Boy platformer *Kirby's Dream Land.*

Kirby and The Forgotten Land

Developer HAL Laboratory **Publisher** Nintendo **Platform** NS

■ Poyo! Nintendo's loveable pink blob gets a 3D platforming adventure at last. It's a fun escapade where you jump and slide around the Forgotten Land rescuing Waddle Dees who've been captured by the Beast Pack. As ever, the Kirbster can inhale everything in sight. This is ramped up to new and hilarious degrees in Mouthful Mode, where he can swallow and control large items, such as cars and vending machines.

Once you've defeated a Bernard, you can copy their ranger ability for the rest of the game.

Not the post-apocalyptic setting you expected? There are plenty of abandoned shopping centres to explore too.

Watch out! It's hard to see these adorable Awoofy as an enemy but they've got a dangerous side and can jump on you if you get too close.

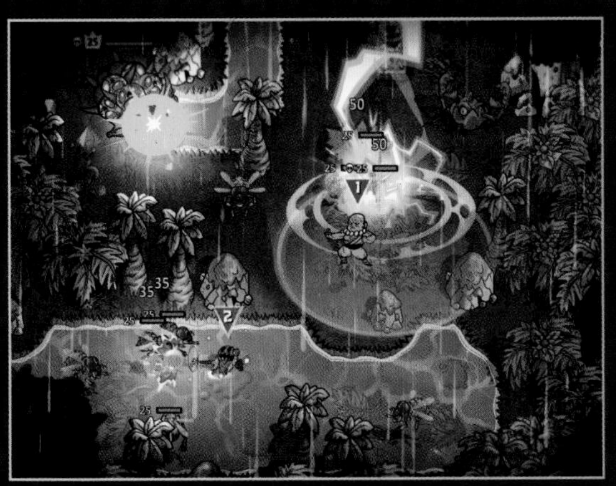

Nobody Saves the World

Developer DrinkBox Studios
Publisher DrinkBox Studios
Platform PC, PS4, PS5, XBO, XBX/S

■ You are Nobody. That's not an insult – just how you begin this dungeon crawler, with nothing other than a wand. As you work through the world, new abilities are unlocked. Use the wand to turn into seventeen different forms, such as a magician, mermaid, zombie or slug. Don't laugh! As a slug, you constantly excrete slime, slowing down nearby enemies who you can then take out with a move called Blob Lob.

Fiery Ambitions

Dragon is the ultimate form in *Nobody Saves the World*. To unlock it, you need to earn Rank C with both the Robot and Necromancer.

Rune Factory 5

Developer Hakama **Publisher** Xseed Games **Platform** NS

■ Farm, fight monsters and build friendships in a charming border town. Pick whether to play as Ares or Alice, then piece together your character's past after they lost their memory and joined up with a group of rangers. To solve the mystery, you'll need to team up with townsfolk who will help you protect Rigbarth. Along the way, you might pair off with one of the characters – such as half-elf Scarlett or apprentice carpenter Ryker.

Handheld History

Missed the previous games? That's not a huge surprise. *Rune Factory* was a DS exclusive back in 2006 and it's been a decade since *Rune Factory 4* was released.

Top Tips

There's a lot of loot hidden around The Lands Between that will help later on. Make sure you explore thoroughly before getting too far into the story.

Did You Know

The Dung-Eater has scabs all over his body that are actually horns that have been shaved down to the stump.

Elden Ring

Developer FromSoftware **Publisher** Bandai Namco **Platform** PC, PS4, PS5, XBO, XBX/S

■ **Last spring *Elden Ring* was everywhere. On the sides of buses, in a four-minute-long advert in Thailand, even on a continent-sized poster in Piccadilly Circus. The hype was huge, but the adventure made with *Game of Thrones* author George RR Martin matches it. Massive in size, scope and ambition, it quickly became the most exciting action RPG for next-gen's consoles.**

The game is linear to begin with but offers six main areas to freely explore. Each region is ruled by demigods who form the main bosses. Combat feels inspired by FromSoftware's legendary *Dark Souls* and *Demon's Souls* games. It also includes a stealth system and mounted battles atop your trusty steed Torrent. Riding remains awesome outside of combat and is the best way to explore, although fast travel through sites of lost grace is also an option.

Hell of a Ride

Elden Ring may look cheerier than earlier FromSoftware games, but this is still a challenging adventure. You're looking at fifty to seventy hours of character-building and enemy-slashing before you can work your way past every one of those bosses. Thankfully, you can add a co-op teammate by finding a yellow summoning sign or visiting a Summoning Pool. Just be wary of blood stains, these are a FromSoftware favourite that mark previous player deaths and could mean a hidden enemy is close.

Old Friends

● One of the fan-fave characters from previous FromSoftware games returns here. Patches, the beloved merchant, must be beaten in battle before he'll open his shop to you.

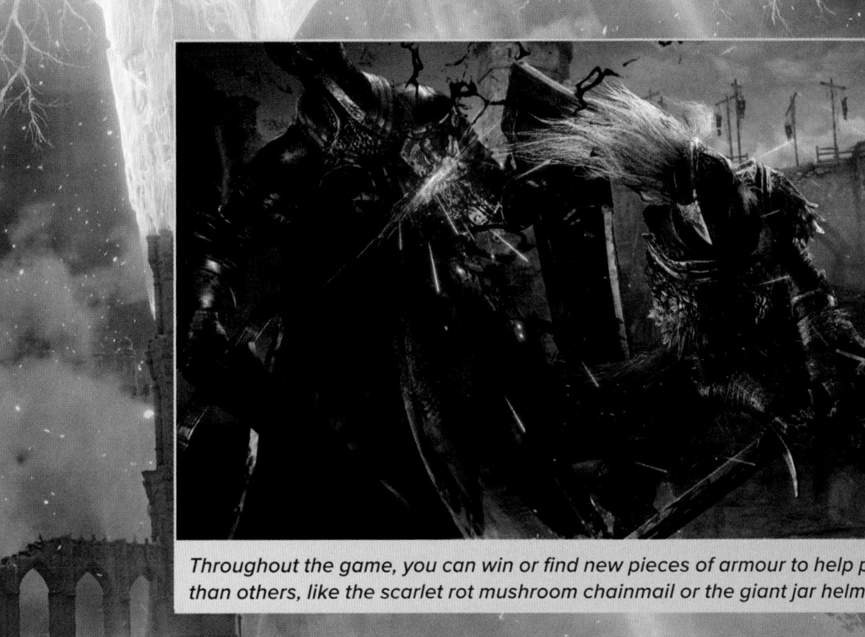

Throughout the game, you can win or find new pieces of armour to help protect you. Some are weirder than others, like the scarlet rot mushroom chainmail or the giant jar helmet.

Grow Your Own Way

There's no fixed main character in *Elden Ring*, you're simply a member of The Tarnished. Start out by picking a masculine or feminine body type, then you can make changes to the character to become gender-neutral, should you wish. Some of the classes for your avatar are Hero, Warrior, Prophet or Astrologer. The adventure's main joy is evolving your onscreen persona in thousands of varied ways as you progress. Fancy a giant beetle hat? Maybe you want to wear war paint?

Trolls are one of the earlier enemies you'll battle. They've got a long reach but are pretty slow so try using magic, or fight them on horseback to avoid their blows.

Exploring the Lands Between can take you to underground caverns. But watch out! They're a favourite spot for giant ants to nest.

Foul Horseplay

Even experienced *Souls* fans will find the horse-based combat refreshing. Four different attacks can be unleashed while riding Torrent, with the shoulder buttons used for light attacks and the triggers used for heavy attacks. Some weapons also have special mounted moves. Hold down the button while wielding a Greatsword to charge up an attack, drag the weapon along the ground to take out enemies then hit them with a giant upward strike.

FromSoftware highlights

Eight landmark games in the Japanese studio's illustrious history:

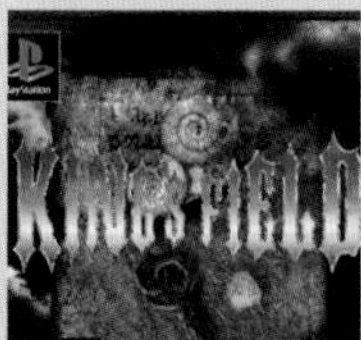

KINGS FIELD (1994)

ARMORED CORE (1997)

DEMON'S SOULS (2009)

DARK SOULS (2011)

DARK SOULS II (2014)

BLOODBORNE (2015)

DARK SOULS III (2016)

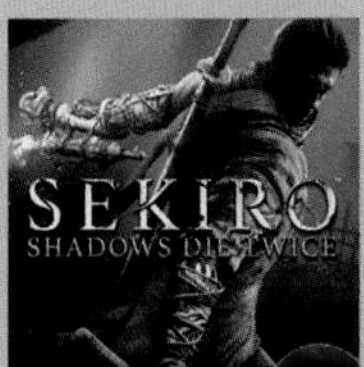

SEKIRO: SHADOWS DIE TWICE (2019)

NEWS FLASH

Big Games on the Move

It's not only football where mega-money transfers happen. All of these titles found new homes ...

Grabby New Year

January was a crazy month for studio purchases. **Industry giants spent $85 million buying up talent** – the same amount as all of 2021!

Destiny 2

Sony paid $3.6million to buy Bungie, creators of *Destiny 2*. It was a pretty shocking move as the studio found fame by making Xbox favourite *Halo*. Bungie is still an independent studio, but the deal means Sony teams can access its tools and resources. As well as future *Destiny* releases, Sony and Bungie are teaming up on ten live-service games. They'll launch between now and 2026.

Call of Duty & Overwatch

Two of the most popular gaming series are now owned by Microsoft. **The Xbox mastermind forked out $68.7 billion to buy publisher Activision Blizzard**. It's a move that makes them the third biggest gaming company on the planet. (Only Sony and Chinese company Tencent are bigger.) It could mean series like *Call of Duty* and *Overwatch* become exclusive to Xbox and PC in the future. However, Microsoft says they're committed to multi-format versions for now.

Oxenfree

The sequel to this spooky graphic adventure would be right at home with Sony or Microsoft. So guess who bought the studio that makes it? Netflix! Yep, **the video service grabbed Night School Studio**. It means future games from the developer will be free of charge as part of a Netflix membership. The sequel *Oxenfree II: Lost Signals* is still coming to Switch, PS4 and PS5.

High Heels

Mobile game *High Heels* scored an astonishing 129 million downloads in 2021. No wonder *Grand Theft Auto* publisher Take Two was keen to snap up its creator, Zynga. The company has a strong history with social games like *Farmville* and *Words with Friends*. **The deal went through for a huge $12.7 billion**. We might get a few more mobile games from series like *GTA* and *Borderlands* as a result.

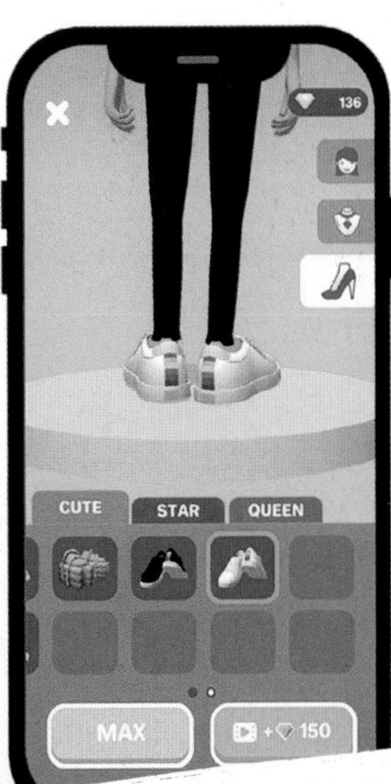

The Lord of the Rings: Gollum

In 2019, German developer Daedalic announced a new action-adventure game based on Smeagol's story. It's set before *The Fellowship of the Ring* and was due in 2021. That changed when French publisher **Nacon paid $60 million to own Daedalic** and oversee *LOTR*. With *Blood Bowl 3* and *Robocop: Rogue City* also on the way, it's set for a breakout year.

Assetto Corsa Competizione

Developer Kunos Simulazioni **Publisher** 505 Games **Platform** PC, PS4, PS5, XBX/S

Background | An Italian racer aimed at serious fans. It's similar to *Gran Turismo*. But *GT* is best played with a DualSense™ controller and the ultimate way to enjoy *Assetto Corsa* is with a gaming steering wheel. This edition emerged on PC in 2019 and got the PS5 and Xbox Series X treatment in February 2022.

Features | *Assetto Corsa* is stacked with options. *GT3* and *GT4* cars are the focus, with loads of real-life events. There's an offline career, custom races and authentic series like the Porsche Carrera Cup. Plus, you can save mid-race to return later. Online treats include hot laps, quick races and full race weekends.

Gameplay | You need a proper gaming rig to enjoy *Assetto Corsa* at its best. Driving feels realistic, right down to pit-stop experiences. Dynamic weather looks astonishing and forces you to rethink technical elements like tyres. It's hard, really pushing the difficulty of real-life competition. That makes wins even more rewarding.

Check out that view! While driving, the screen gives players all the info they need for a smooth drive.

Assetto Corsa Competizione *has twenty-five brand name cars for players to try out on the tracks.*

Trivia

● *Competizione* is a follow-up to 2014's *Assetto Corsa*. A full sequel, *Assetto Corsa 2*, is coming in 2024. Developer Kunos Simulazioni has its headquarters at a real-life racetrack: the Autodromo Vallelunga Piero Taruffi in Rome. Imagine if EA started making new series EA Sports FC at Old Trafford!

Trivia

G.O.A.T. Ricky Carmichael is included in the game as a tutor for new players. Online races offer up to twelve players, and the new split-screen mode is perfect for home-based racing. Still not enough bang for your buck? Check out *Supercross 5*'s DLC packs. These add both riders and tracks, and include a cool, retro 1974 version of Daytona.

Monster Energy Supercross 5

Developer Milestone **Publisher** Milestone **Platform** PC, PS4, PS5, XBO, XBX/S

Background | More Italian-made racing, this time on two wheels. *Monster Energy Supercross* first came out in 2018. There's been a new game every year since. Milan-based Milestone is considered racing masterminds in their home nation. Past successes include the *WRC* and *MotoGP* series. They also made the gem *Hot Wheels Unleashed.*

Features | Every rider from the 2021 Supercross season is in, like 450SX champ Eli Tomac and 250 SX East winner Colt Nichols. All tracks are here too, including the legendary Daytona. Injuries are added to Career mode, encouraging riders against risky moves. Creating and sharing tracks is also easier than ever.

Gameplay | Much of what's here was already in place for *Monster Energy Supercross 4*. Career mode is deep and detailed. It doesn't push next-gen machines to their limits, but still looks good at 60FPS. There's definitely more focus on pick-up-and-play fun. Casual difficulty levels offer more forgiving collisions and less aggressive opponents. Perfect for noobs!

Off the Tracks

If you get bored of the official tracks (unlikely!), **Monster Energy Supercross 5** also has a build-your-own mode. Get creative with your space and give your driver an imaginative view!

A new addition to the series is a multiplayer mode that lets groups of friends play through one console.

Courses don't just cover tracks, you can free-roam through a variety of new locations.

Top Tips

Although it's tempting to run away, you can still take damage if you try to escape an attack. Instead, try guarding, a defensive act with less chance of failure.

Stranger of Paradise: Final Fantasy Origin

Developer Team Ninja **Publisher** Square Enix
Platform PC, PS4, PS5, XBO, XBX/S

■ Square Enix has gone all out to mark *Final Fantasy*'s 35th anniversary. As well as releasing the beautiful collection of remasters on PC, they've created this alternate universe retelling of the very first game. It's built around Jack Garland, the bad guy back in 1987. Now he's the main character in a dark fantasy tale that explains how he found his evil side.

Stranger of Paradise adds modern elements to the original. Real-time battles now offer loads of freedom. Jack is able to use physical attacks, magical attacks, two assigned Jobs and deliver a final blow that crystallises an enemy. He can then harvest them and restore a portion of his magic points, in the same way you and I gain energy from our morning cereal.

Jack in the Box

Newcomers Jay and Ash join Jack on his quest. The story pits the crew against a knight who has taken on the role of Chaos and examines what being a Warrior of Light really means. The main game clocks in at twelve to fourteen hours, although you'll want to spend another ten hours taking in side quests too. All the questions you'll have throughout the game are nicely tied up with a startling yet satisfying climax.

Team up with Jay and Ash to fight and destroy Chaos. You'll get a range of different weapons to help you in the battle against evil.

Fun Fact

There are five difficulty levels: Casual, Story, Action, Hard and Chaos. The last one is unlocked when you complete the campaign on any of the other four.

Job Centre

The Job system – *Stranger of Paradise*'s version of classes – is a real highlight. There are twenty-seven in total, with eight basic ones unlocked as you get new weapons. Find an axe to become a Marauder, or a mace to become a Mage. Ten Advanced and ten Expert Jobs are then gained by working your way up the skill tree. Plus, you can switch between your two equipped Jobs in battles, seamlessly going from fist-pounding to sword-slashing, and back again.

Check Out

***Nier: Automata* is another Square Enix game featuring real-time strategy elements. If you liked *Stranger in Paradise*, then give it a go!**

One of the Great Malboro's special powers is having smelly breath. No really! Watch out or the toxic gas will knock your health down.

Crystal-clear Inspirations

This may be a dark remake of the first *Final Fantasy* but there are loving references to later games too. The palatial Crystal Mirage stage is an homage to the Crystal Tower from *Final Fantasy III*, and the wooded Refrain Wetlands are based on the Sunleth Waterscape. A high-security factory is based on the Mako Reactors from *Final Fantasy VII Remake*, and there's a nod to *Final Fantasy XIV*'s introductory in a pirate cove filled with Sahagin enemies.

GAME ROUND-UP

Unbound: Worlds Apart

Developer Alien Pixel Studios
Publisher Alien Pixel Studios
Platform MAC, NS, PC, PS4, PS5, XBO, XBX/S

■ Soli is a selfless and completely silent mage who can open portals with their magic to transform the surroundings and win battles. Some portals change foes from one creature into another, others reverse gravity or turn light to darkness. There aren't any weapons in the game, so boss battles rely on working out how to use an enemy's own habitat against it. Tricky!

A Whole New World

The levels are hand-drawn. As is Soli, who was designed to be easily drawn by a four-year-old.

OlliOlli World

Developer Roll7 **Publisher** Private Division **Platform** NS, PC, PS4, PS5, XBO, XBX/S

■ *OlliOlli 2* was absolutely unputdownable. And now the skateboarding game gets a follow-up! *OlliOlli World* replaces pixels with a cartoony hand-drawn art style. There's loads of fun experimentation to be done using the millions of levels found within sandbox mode. If your aim is to rack up big scores, then try grinding rails, riding walls and unleashing combos. It's also fully customisable, for those who want to skate in flip-flops while dressed as an alien.

A Rad Ride

The bizarrely named Radlandia forms *OlliOlli World*'s setting. It has five regions to play through in Campaign Mode before reaching Gnarvana.

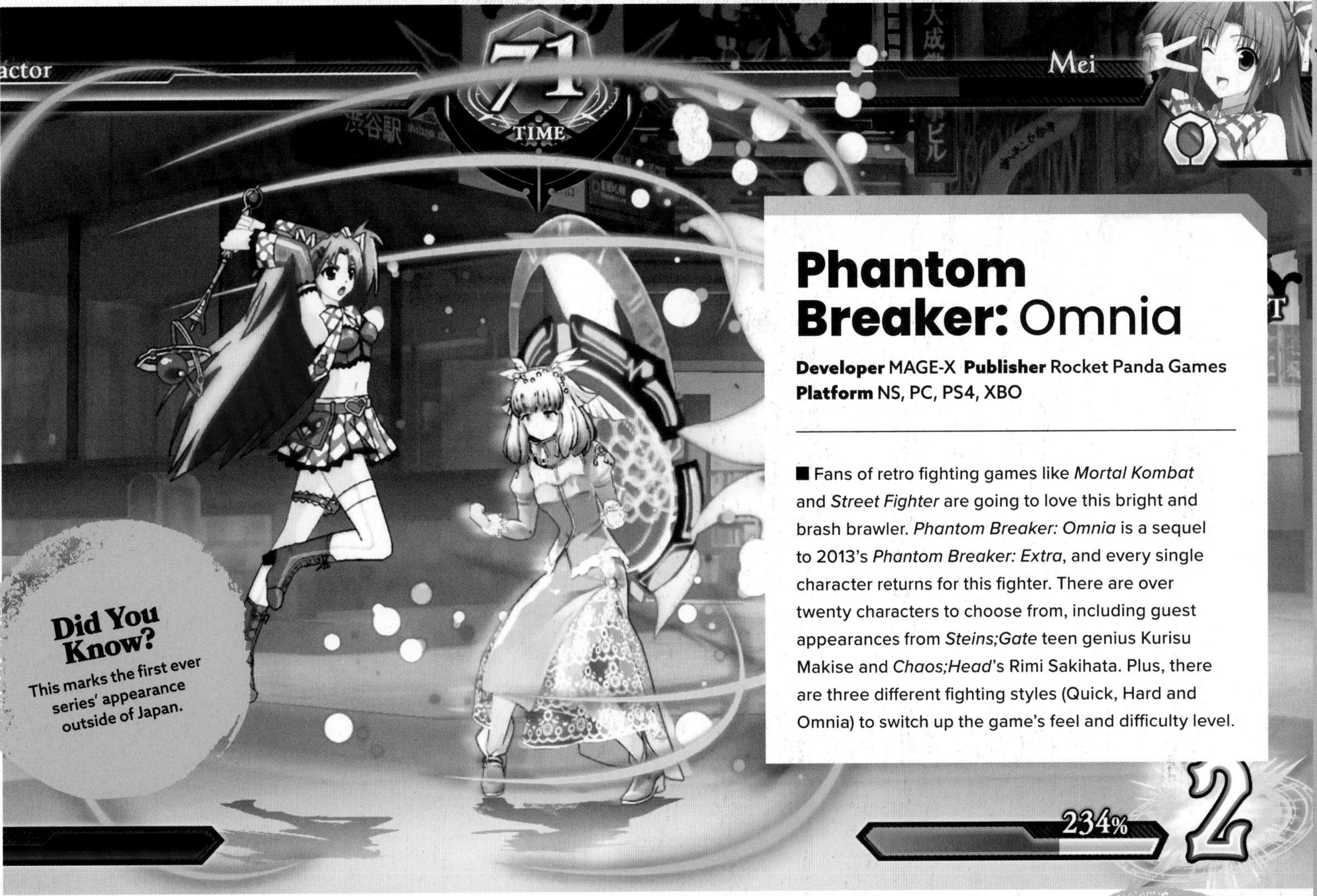

Phantom Breaker: Omnia

Developer MAGE-X **Publisher** Rocket Panda Games **Platform** NS, PC, PS4, XBO

■ Fans of retro fighting games like *Mortal Kombat* and *Street Fighter* are going to love this bright and brash brawler. *Phantom Breaker: Omnia* is a sequel to 2013's *Phantom Breaker: Extra*, and every single character returns for this fighter. There are over twenty characters to choose from, including guest appearances from *Steins;Gate* teen genius Kurisu Makise and *Chaos;Head*'s Rimi Sakihata. Plus, there are three different fighting styles (Quick, Hard and Omnia) to switch up the game's feel and difficulty level.

Did You Know?
This marks the first ever series' appearance outside of Japan.

Did You Know?
SNK's short-lived Neo Geo Pocket Color handheld was available from 1999 to 2001 and featured eighty-two games in total.

SNK vs Capcom: Card Fighters' Clash

Developer SNK **Publisher** SNK **Platform** DS

■ Now's your chance to try out this retro game! *SNK vs Capcom* is a card-based battler featuring characters from *Street Fighter, Resident Evil, Metal Slug* and many more. It originally appeared on Neo Geo Pocket Color in 1999. Although it's over two decades old, the Switch conversion is perfect. Players get three card slots for each fight and win *Pokémon*-style treats in return for victories. There's even a new rewind function, so you can go back and erase a costly mistake.

STATE OF PLAY

The Best of MINECRAFT

The World's Biggest Block Party Keeps on Rolling!

Building Up

The block-building game is a global phenomenon. **Minecraft** sees almost **140 million users every month.**

Check Out

A brand new game is soon to be hitting platforms. Get ready for **Minecraft Legends**, an exciting new action strategy where players must defend against the hungry piglins.

Stay Up to Date

The team at *Minecraft* headquarters has brought out some exciting new releases. The most recent was The Wild Update. Two biomes were included, plus loads of fauna and flora. Frogs are a new peaceful mob and *Minecraft*'s first ever cold-blooded creature. An even more exciting addition is the Allay mob. These cute blue blocks help you transport items by flying. They were voted into the game after winning a Minecraft Live fan poll. *Minecraft Dungeons* also had some cool new updates! Joining *Echoing Void* in their list of paid DLC is *Hidden Depths*. It was released to celebrate the game's first anniversary and takes place in an underwater biome.

The Wild Update

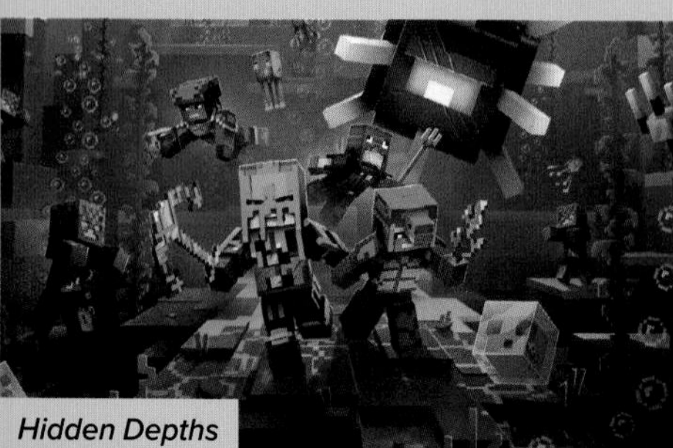

Hidden Depths

Echoing Void

Legends

Croco Island Arrives

New DLC is always welcome but *Minecraft* added something extra special. The free Croco Island map added a tennis court, parkour course and thirty skins. But what's the point of the crocodile? Well, it's the mascot of a very famous clothing company. See, the DLC launched *Lacoste x Minecraft*, a crossover that also includes real-life apparel and footwear. There are loads of in-game outfits to unlock as a result, just in case you can't get enough green-and-black.

Did You Know

Lacoste wasn't the only fashion brand to get a crossover. In February, a **Minecraft x Puma** campaign delivered cool new trainers.

The Big Minion Invasion

Minecraft is massive. *Minions* are massive. It was only a matter of time until someone blended the two. Last July, it finally happened. *Minions x Minecraft* added a ton of familiar characters to the block-based world. Lucy, Margo, Edith and Agnes were all included. As were all six of the Vicious 6, the villainous troupe from *Minions: Rise of Gru*. The DLC pack includes twenty-nine skins, as well as a Minions Adventure Map.

Minecraft Live Mob Vote

Three were nominated, only one could win. Here's what happened:

Glare	Allay	Copper Golem
11.2%	**51%**	**37.8%**

In-game English Lessons

Homeschooling has become normal over the last two years. Now it's part of *Minecraft. Adventures in English with Cambridge* is a new story-driven world found in the Minecraft Marketplace. It was created by the famous university. The aim is for younger players to practise their language skills using puzzles, mini-games and a fairy sidekick. It's just as fun as it is educational.

THE EIDOS TOUCH

Eidos-Montréal

■ The studio behind *Marvel's Guardians of the Galaxy* is based on the upper floors of a downtown Montreal building. More than 500 staff work there. Its focus isn't only on perfecting Quill, Drax and Nebula. The company also hosts sports events, trivia quizzes and board game nights for its teams. Eidos-Montréal is owned by Square Enix Europe. Those guys were famous for *Tomb Raider* and *Championship Manager*.

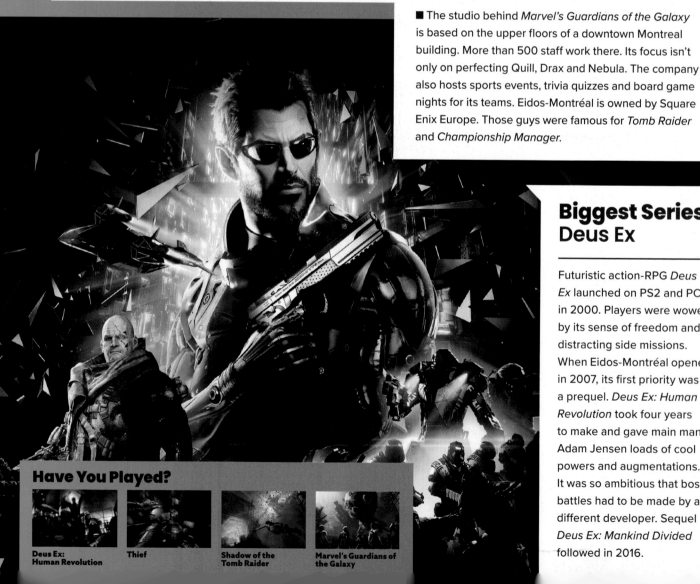

Biggest Series: Deus Ex

Futuristic action-RPG *Deus Ex* launched on PS2 and PC in 2000. Players were wowed by its sense of freedom and distracting side missions. When Eidos-Montréal opened in 2007, its first priority was a prequel. *Deus Ex: Human Revolution* took four years to make and gave main man Adam Jensen loads of cool powers and augmentations. It was so ambitious that boss battles had to be made by a different developer. Sequel *Deus Ex: Mankind Divided* followed in 2016.

Have You Played?

- Deus Ex: Human Revolution
- Thief
- Shadow of the Tomb Raider
- Marvel's Guardians of the Galaxy

RACECAR ROCKSTAR

Polyphony Digital

■ Japan's kings of racing are world-famous for making *Gran Turismo*. However, their first game was nothing like that legendary series. It was called *Motor Toon Grand Prix* – and it wasn't very good! The game arrived in 1994 with a cast of OTT characters and was considered a *Mario Kart* wannabe. It took three years to perfect *Gran Turismo*. Since then, it's only ever made two non-*GT* games. They are 1999 shooter *Omega Blast* and 2006 motorbike simulation *Tourist Trophy*.

Biggest Series: Gran Turismo

GT creator Kazunori Yamauchi is now a legend in the driving world. His team was known as Polys Entertainment when *Gran Turismo* came out in 1997. It sold 10.85 million copies, and the studio changed its name to something much cooler. Its success with *Gran Turismo* led to real-life car projects. In 2007, the studio was tasked with designing the in-car display for the new Nissan GT-R. This let drivers monitor G-forces, brake pedal pressure and steering angles.

Have You Played?

Gran Turismo 6

Tourist Trophy

Gran Turismo Sport

Gran Turismo 7

Codemasters Hall Of Fame

The UK developer is renowned for its racing excellence. Here's why:

MICRO MACHINES (1991)

TOCA TOURING CAR CHAMPIONSHIP (1997)

COLIN MCRAE RALLY (1998)

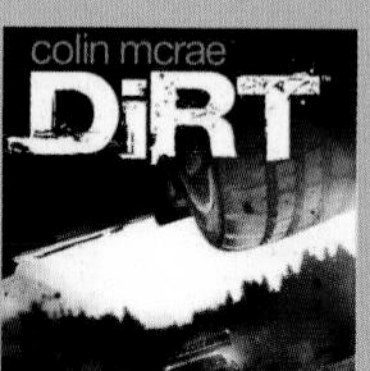
COLIN MCRAE: DIRT (2007)

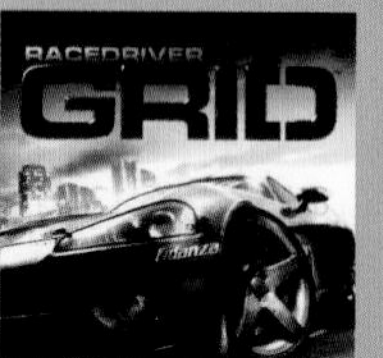
RACE DRIVER: GRID (2008)

DIRT RALLY (2015)

F1 2021 (2021)

Grid Legends

Developer Codemasters **Publisher** EA
Platform PC, PS4, PS5, XBO, XBX/S

■ *Grid Legends* is an incredibly realistic driving simulation. Not only are the hairpin turns flawless, the errors are too! Codemasters have added human-style error to the game. Rival AI drivers suffer punctures or spin out when under pressure, adding an anything-can-happen feel which is often missing in other simulation games. It gives a sense that you always have a shot at a late comeback.

Power and Glory

Despite the title, there are no real-life icons on offer here but the choice is still huge! Over 100 cars – such as trucks, Minis and electric vehicles – and 130 tracks, including Indianapolis and Suzuka International. The heart of the game is the Driven to Glory story mode. Your underdog team of Seneca Racing looks to overcome the big bucks (and hype!) of Ravensport Racing and its cocky lead driver, Nathan McKane.

Zoom zoom! Try out the incredibly realistic racing game to feel like you're actually behind the wheel.

Go bumper to bumper with your rival driver and prove that the underdog always wins.

McKane and Able

Rival competitor Nathan McKane has been mentioned throughout the series in voiceovers and background racing reports right back to 2008's *Race Driver: Grid*, but this is his first physical appearance.

Total War: Warhammer III

Developer Creative Assembly **Publisher** Sega
Platform MAC, PC

■ *Total War* is a giant in real-time strategy games. It started out as a history-focused series, but the team up with *Warhammer* has taken it in unexpected fantasy directions. This final game in the trilogy adds four otherworldly realms packed with armies to conquer, each ruled by a Chaos God. You have one of eight factions to choose from and must race other factions to claim four Daemon Princes' souls and try to save the imprisoned bear-god Ursun.

Total Score

● For an insane amount of fun, choose the Daemons of Chaos faction. You can customise your own Daemon Prince with body parts like scythe hands, and access units from all four Chaos Gods.

Chocobo GP

Developer Arika **Publisher** Square Enix
Platform ANDROID, NS

■ *Mario Kart* with a *Final Fantasy* makeover? Well, yes! This racer featuring favourites such as Chocobos, Moogles and Mages is definitely worth a test drive if you're a fan of *Final Fantasy*. Courses include the Gold Saucer from *Final Fantasy VII* and Alexandria from *Final Fantasy IX*. Iconic hero Cloud Strife is playable – if you pay extra for a Season Pass.

Free Wheelin'

● There's a free version of the game called *Chocobo GP Lite*. You get a Story Prologue, GP mode and three characters to try out.

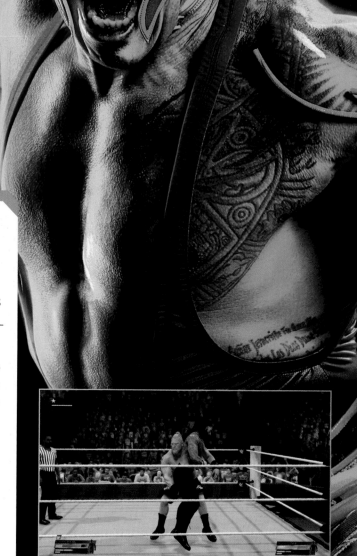

DLC

Get access to New World Order stars including Hulk Hogan, Scott Hall and Kevin Nash in the **nWo 4-Life Bonus Pack.** Also includes the nWo Wolfpac Championship, as well as 2 classic arenas.

WWE 2K22

Developer Visual Concepts **Publisher** 2K **Platform** PC, PS4, PS5, XBO, XBX/S

■ Get ready to rumble! Wrestling's biggest series returns with a ton of new names. This is the muscle-bound grappler's first release onto PS5 and Xbox Series X. Universe Mode is back, giving players the chance to control all of WWE. Here you get to plan every single show, match, feud and storyline decision, without the worry of a rival character trying to outshine you.

Get a ringside seat to the action in GM Mode, where you build your own show and compete against rival managers for ratings and popularity. Now known as MyGM, the mode lets you plan fights and book matches for wrestling shows Raw, Smackdown, NXT or NXT UK. In MyGM, players have tons of weird and wonderful possibilities. What British fan hasn't dreamed of The Rock being exclusive to NXT UK?

Brock Solid

Inside the ring, *WWE 2K22*'s has a revamped control system with extra focus placed on combos. Reversals have been simplified to one button and it's now possible to dodge opponents. There's also a weightiness to monster-sized combatants such as Bobby Lashley and Brock Lesnar. It's great to have *WWE 2K* back after two years in the wrestling wilderness.

Playing Brock Lesnar as he takes down Roman Reigns in a triumphant KO is almost like seeing it in-person.

Becky Lynch enters the ring in a dramatic cinematic. The crowd goes wild.

Rey of Light

WWE 2K22 has lots of new faces, but a very familiar masked one fronts its Showcase Mode. It lets you replay classic WWE bouts, and they all feature leaping luchador Rey Mysterio. Among these are two timeless matches with best pal Eddie Guerrero, plus clashes against JBL, Kane, Shawn Michaels and The Undertaker.

Did You Know

In the Showcase mode, you play out famous fights from Rey Mysterio's career. If he loses against Eddie Guerrero, he gets unmasked!

Does he seem a little overdressed for a wrestling match? Don't worry, the Edge takes his floor-length jacket off before he gets in the ring.

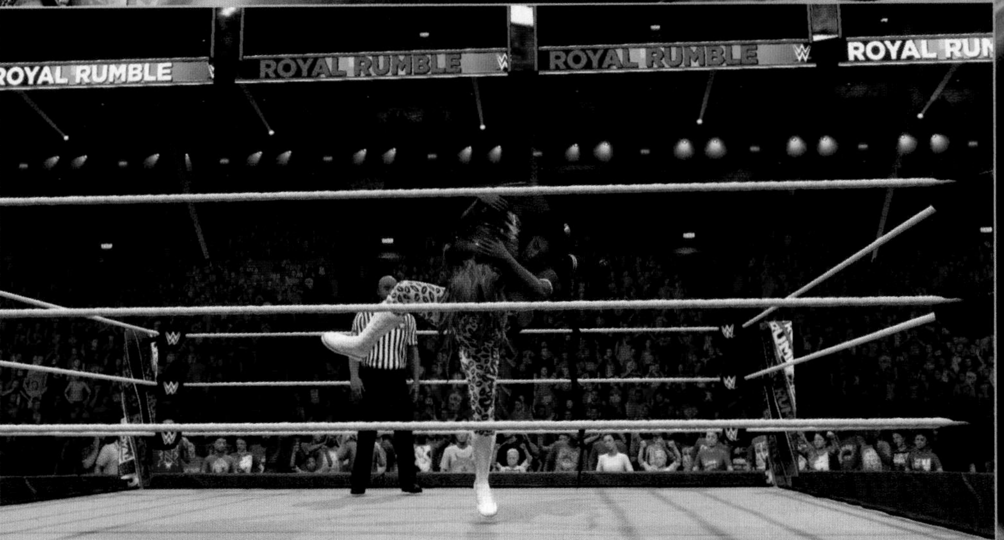

Two of the biggest female fighters, Becky Lynch and Bianca Belair, put on a Royal Rumble show worth tuning in for.

Even Hollywood legends The Rock and John Cena are available to play. Who doesn't want to see Maui go head-to-head with the Peacemaker?

Must-know Newcomers

Austin Theory

WWE 2K22 wrestlers include former Evolve champion Theory. He was fast-tracked to the main roster when he was twenty-three and has already had numerous interactions with owner Mr McMahon.

Kay Lee Ray

Scottish scrapper Ray moved to the US in to compete on WWE's American TV shows. She is the longest-reigning NXT UK Champion as he held the title for 649 days.

Kushida

Kushida is undefeated in MMA. He retired in 2005 to embark on an illustrious wrestling career in his homeland of Japan. In 2019, she signed for WWE and is a former Cruiserweight Champion.

Shotzi

The green-haired wrestler is another to have been with WWE since 2019. Her tag partner Tegan Nox left WWE before the game's release, but remains on the roster as another first-timer.

Ever thought you'd be taking on a robotic dragon that spits fire? Now you can with the range of insane melee weapons!

Tiny Tina's Wonderlands

Developer Gearbox Software **Publisher** 2K Games
Platform PC, PS4, PS5, XBO, XBX/S

■ If you love crazy characters and lots of loot then check out the *Borderlands* series. Spin-off *Tiny Tina's Wonderlands* brings those goodies to PS5 and Xbox Series X in style. You can play with up to three mates, both online and off. The main Fatemaker character is completely customisable. Are you a Graveborn, happy to sacrifice health in order to wield extra damage? Or a Robin-Hood-like Spore Warden, less powerful but able to unleash seven arrows at once?

Little Mix

There are six classes available. Handily, it's possible to mix and match skills from different types. As well as picking what your Fatemaker looks like, their personality is user-selected too. They can be Gallant, Clever, Gruff or Strange. There are also two voice options, both with adjustable pitch.

Loot is what you'll want to focus on. It gives you boundless options when it comes to spells, guns and weapons. You can donk enemies with a hammer. Or whack them with an axe. Or wave swords around, or wield machine guns and assault rifles, or get clever with magic! Enemies include a great pink shark with legs, as everything you loved about *Borderlands* gets an even more over-the-top second life.

Mythic Guest

● The actor who voices Tiny Tina, Ashly Burch, stars in the game developer sitcom *Mythic Quest* and also voices Aloy in the *Horizon* series.

Tiny Teenager

Who exactly is Tiny Tina? She's a thirteen-year-old explosives expert, with a love of bunnies and sugar. And big bangs, obvs. Tina appeared as an NPC in *Borderlands 2* and *Borderlands 3*. She even got her own *Borderlands 2* DLC. It was called *Tiny Tiny's Assault on Dragon Keep*, and she narrated it throughout. You can't actually play as her in *Wonderlands*. Instead, it's her own personal playground.

Top Tips

Loot rarity is a big deal. Items drop in one of five colours: Common (white), Uncommon (green), Rare (blue), Epic (purple) and Legendary (orange).

These monstrous mushrooms (and their visible bums) are one of the reasons the game has a teen rating, if only they were wearing trousers!

The Clawbringer class is born with the blood of a dragon in their veins and will have a wyvern (a type of dragon) companion that can breathe fire.

Unicorn With A Difference

The main character is user-created, but the surrounding cast is what you'd expect from a *Borderlands* spin-off. There's a horse-like Queen made of diamonds, who's a binicorn (two horns!) rather than a unicorn. She's called Butt Stallion. The power of Magic is protected by the wrestler-sized Fairy Punchfather. Torgue, meanwhile, roams around in sunglasses, carrying a lute capable of unpredictable spells.

There are a bunch of different locations to explore. A fan favourite is Wargtooth Shallows, a pirate cove filled with hidden loot to be discovered.

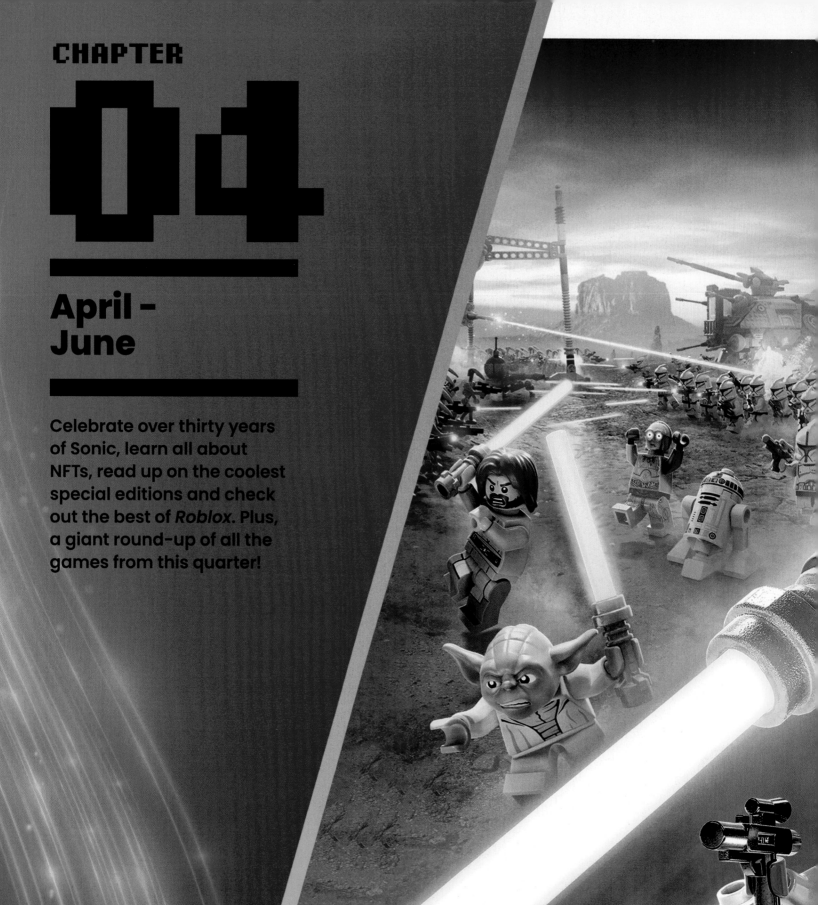

CHAPTER 04

April - June

Celebrate over thirty years of Sonic, learn all about NFTs, read up on the coolest special editions and check out the best of *Roblox*. Plus, a giant round-up of all the games from this quarter!

Page 239

Super-Sonic Travel

April Fools' Day brought news of an iconic hog being spotted on the Heathrow Express. It had to be a prank, right? Incredibly, it wasn't! To mark the release of *Sonic the Hedgehog 2*, the film's creators built a custom boarding area at London Paddington station. A life-sized version of the speedy blue guy welcomed travellers onto the train, kicking off their holidays with a unique twist. No word on where Sonic himself was off to. There are no flights from Heathrow to Green Hill Zone!

STATE OF PLAY

Catch Up With Sonic

The Big Blue Blur's Been Busy

■ The world's most famous ball of spikes is zooming all over the world. There was the new movie, and another announced, plus collaborations with *Two Point Hospital* (below left) as well as *Monster Hunter Rise*. Sonic also celebrated thirty years since the original game landed on the Sega Genesis. To celebrate, the FILMharmonic Orchestra Prague played Sonic's theme tunes in concert (below right). Check out what else the Blue Blue has been up to ...

Sonic the Movie-Hog

Get ready for even more Sonic! Paramount Pictures announced that **Sonic the Hedgehog 3** is now under development, as well as a **Knuckles** spin-off series starring **Idris Elba**.

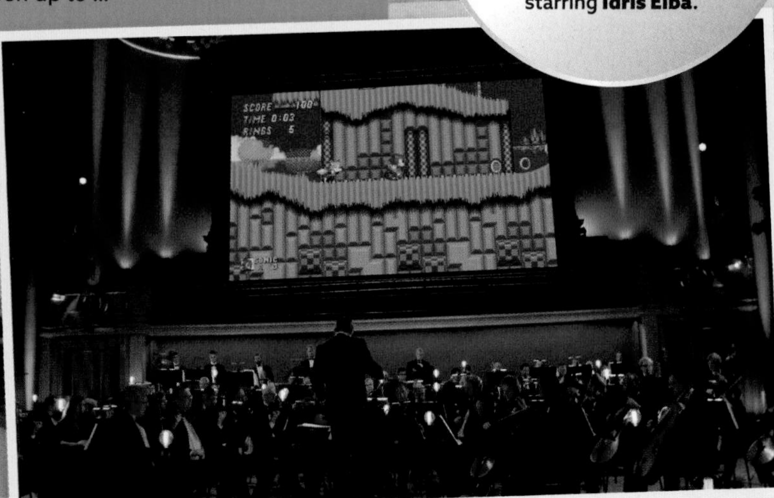

Genesis of a Hedgehog

In the UK, Sonic was ushering families off on holiday. Over in America, the super spiky speedster was part of the third-biggest auction in gaming history. An early copy of *Sonic the Hedgehog* for Sega Genesis sold for $360,000. It was part of a massive video game sale by Heritage Auctions, which made almost $5 million. One of the first ever copies of 1987 classic *Metroid* also scored a massive price. Twenty-five bids were made on it, with the winner paying a whopping $168,000.

Furry Controllers

Our favourite red-shoed mascot returned to cinemas in *Sonic the Hedgehog 2*. The movie was hilariously good, and inspired an especially kooky piece of merch. Microsoft teamed up with filmmakers Paramount to produce furry Xbox Wireless Controllers. They come as a pair – one red, one blue – along with a customised Xbox Series X console, bearing a shiny gold ring. Only one machine and set of controllers were produced. It was given away in a competition on Twitter.

Classics on Next-gen

The most exciting news for retro gamers was the announcement of *Sonic Origins*. Released in June, it contains a beautiful remastered version of the first *Sonic The Hedgehog* for PS5 and Xbox Series X. *Sonic 2, Sonic 3, Sonic & Knuckles* and *Sonic CD* are all super fun to play, too. New options include infinite lives and fresh missions to earn even more gold coins. It's also out on PC, PS4 and Xbox One.

> **Check Out**
> If you're into motorcycle simulations, then take a look at *Ride 4*. It's created by the same team so shares a lot of mechanics.

MotoGP 22

Developer Milestone **Publisher** Milestone
Platform NS, PC, PS4, PS5, XBO, XBX/S

■ Finding online match-ups in niche sports games can be super hard. *MotoGP 22* tackles this with an old-school split-screen mode. It breaks the screen up into two vertical halves. The result: all the fun of multiplayer at Le Mans, without worrying about server speeds. Perfect!

Back to 2009

That's not the only way this two-wheeler farms the past for inspiration. Its main mode is set around the back-and-forth 2009 motor racing season. You get seventeen tracks, nineteen racers and thirty-seven challenges from that year, bound together by a step-by-step documentary. That's on top of seventy historic greats available to race with elsewhere. Plus twenty-one circuits from across the globe.

There's modern-day depth, too. Start a managerial career and all manner of bike-tweaks are yours to toy with. Aerodynamics and electronics are adjustable in minute detail, and there's even the option to start from the ground up with a junior team in Moto3.

Up your speed and take corners like a pro! The game's realistic art style feels like you're watching the real thing.

MotoGP 22 *has all the best bike brands, like Yamaha, Lenovo and Ducati.*

Check out the huge range of bikes (and their bikers!) from across the world, and also back in time. MotoGP 22 *has seventy different historic drivers.*

Happy Valentino's Day

● Four GP legends feature prominently in Season 2009 mode: Valentino Rossi (Italy), Jorge Lorenzo (Spain), Dani Pedroza (Spain) and Casey Stoner (Australia).

SIFU: Vengeance Edition

Developer Sloclap **Publisher** Sloclap **Platform** PC, PS4, PS5

■ After a kung fu master is murdered, his son grows up with an appetite for revenge. You play as that son. He's now an adult, armed with more than 150 unique attacks in the hunt for daddy's killer.

The adventure packs in Japanese tradition. A real kung fu expert even helped choreograph fights. Yet there's also a cunning twist. Our main man wields a magical talisman that plays havoc with time in innovative ways. Don't worry, after every death, you're resurrected. You're now slightly older, with more power but less health – until it's no longer possible to be revived. It's a neat way of modernising old-school gaming's focus on a certain number of lives.

Slowcap imitated real-life kung fu fights to create the combat system.

Don't just kick and flip in open spaces! Use your surroundings, a table, chair or basket, to attack enemies.

The small space of the cafe kitchen makes this one of the toughest fights to beat, but as you fail, you learn how to win.

All About the Benjamin

● 'Sifu' means 'master' in Cantonese. The game's kung fu expert is called Benjamin Colussi. He is indeed a 'Sifu', in Bak Mei.

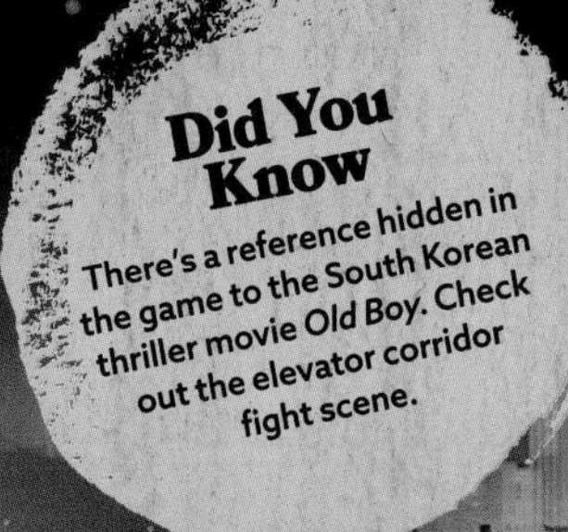

Did You Know

There's a reference hidden in the game to the South Korean thriller movie *Old Boy*. Check out the elevator corridor fight scene.

Quest for Vengeance

The physical *Vengeance Edition* emerged in May, three months after *SIFU*'s digital-only release. As well as the game, you get a steelbook case, three lithographs, a digital soundtrack and fourty-eight-page artbook. It's the best way to own 2022's biggest beat-'em-up surprise.

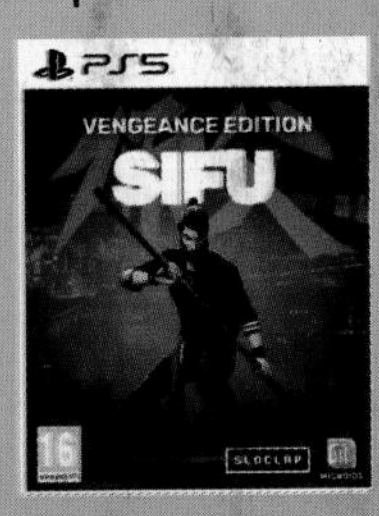

The NFT Era Arrives

And What Exactly Are They?

■ NFTs have turned the world over and they're the hottest topic in gaming. The name stands for non-fungible token. It's a piece of data that you own in digital, rather than physical, form. The first ever post on Twitter, by creator Jack Dorsey, sold for $2.9 million. Check out how the gaming world has reacted to this new tech.

Art Attack

The most expensive NFT ever isn't a game, but a piece of art. **Beeples' *Everydays: The First 5000 days*** is a digital composition of 5,000 images. Singapore-based programmer Vignesh Sundaresan paid **$69.3 million** for the token.

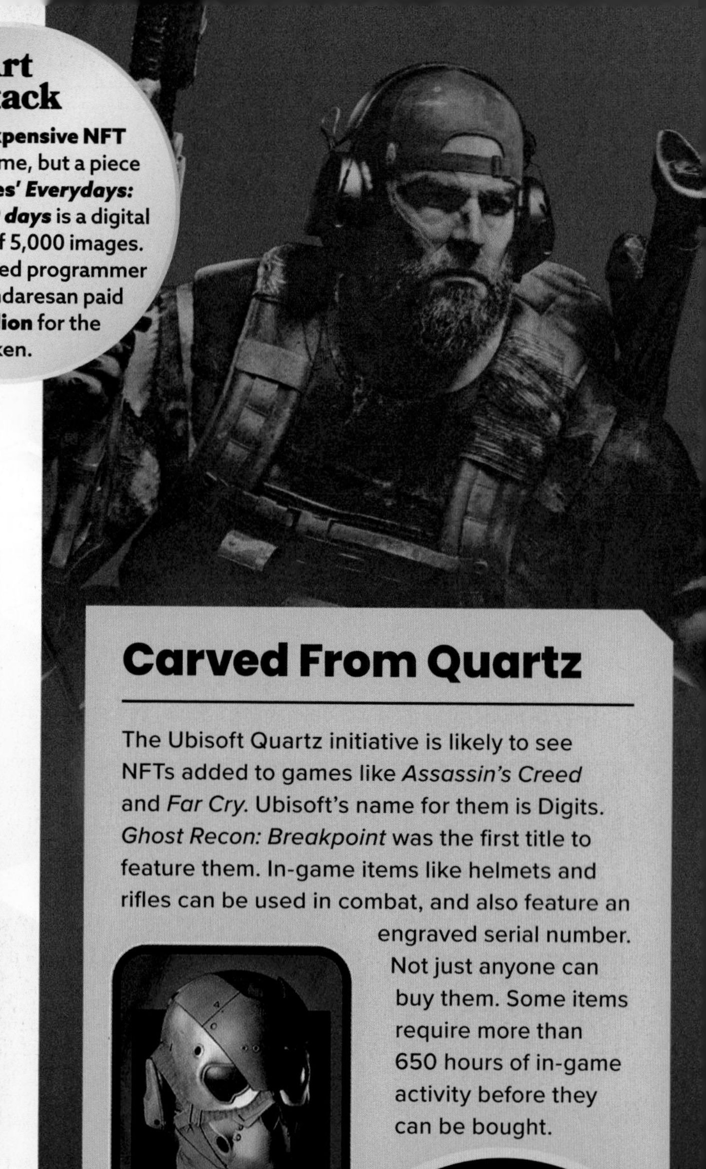

The First NFT Game

Etheria was released in 2015 and players bought and sold plots of land, using a currency called ETH. When released, one plot cost one ETH – roughly $1. Six years later, a plot sold for 70 ETH – the equivalent of £130,000. You can see why some publishers are keen for a bite of the NFT pie.

Carved From Quartz

The Ubisoft Quartz initiative is likely to see NFTs added to games like *Assassin's Creed* and *Far Cry*. Ubisoft's name for them is Digits. *Ghost Recon: Breakpoint* was the first title to feature them. In-game items like helmets and rifles can be used in combat, and also feature an engraved serial number. Not just anyone can buy them. Some items require more than 650 hours of in-game activity before they can be bought.

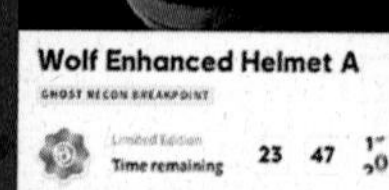
Wolf Enhanced Helmet A
Time remaining
Claim your free Digit!
To celebrate the launch of Ubisoft Quartz, redeem the first three Editions for free! These Editions are limited, grab them while you can!
CLAIM MY DIGIT NOW

M4A1 Tactical | Wolves
Time remaining
Claim your free Digit!

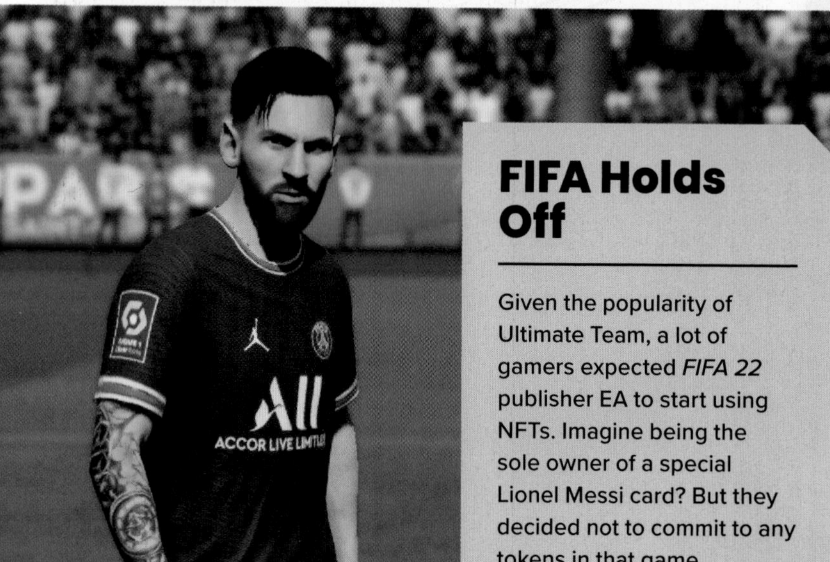

FIFA Holds Off

Given the popularity of Ultimate Team, a lot of gamers expected *FIFA 22* publisher EA to start using NFTs. Imagine being the sole owner of a special Lionel Messi card? But they decided not to commit to any tokens in that game.

Sony's Epic Plans

Lego and PS5 creator Sony look to be considering big NFT plans. In April, they each invested $1 billion in Epic Games' metaverse project. Epic is the maker of *Fortnite*, and the metaverse is where gamers meet online to socialise and potentially trade NFTs. This could mean digital-only content in *Uncharted* or *Horizon* in the future.

Card Sharks

Splinterlands is the most popular NFT-focused game. Players use cards in battle, aiming to outdo opponents using magic, speed and unique abilities. All of these cards are limited edition NFTs, usually with catchy names. Alpha cards, Beta cards, Untamed cards, Dice cards. The market is huge! 450,000 gamers play it every single day.

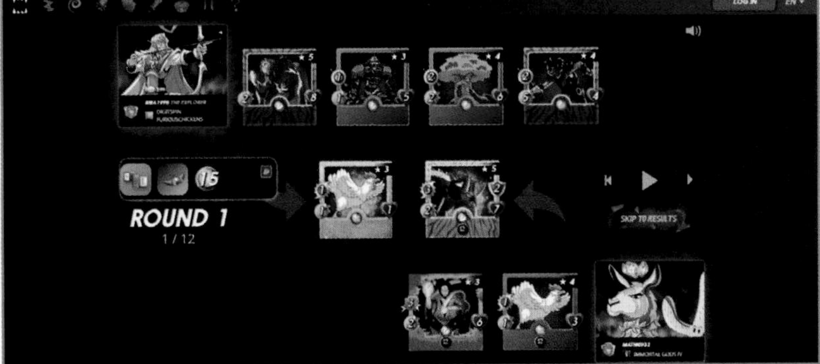

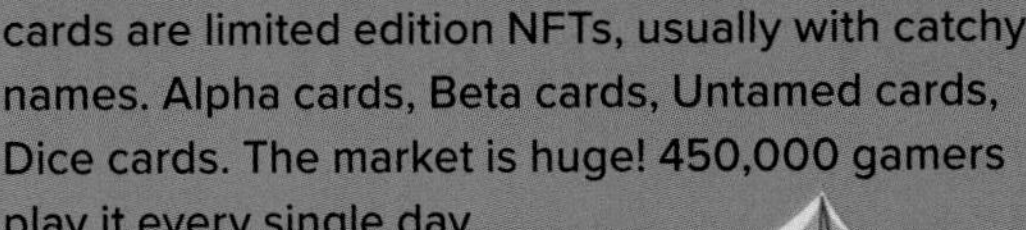

THE INSIDER TAKE

Developers Share Highlights from a Memorable Year

Becky Crossdale
Senior Game Designer on Grid Legends

What's the best thing you played in the last year?
Resident Evil Village had me terrified but gripped. There's great tension-building and exploration, punctuated with intense action horror – delivered at just the right frequency to allow appreciation of calmer moments!

What element of Grid Legends are you most proud of?
I feel the combo of multiclass racing and the hop-in feature makes interesting, edge-of-the-seat racing. Being able to have a full grid of cars racing, whilst allowing players to hop into an AI seat, really keeps the multiplayer momentum going.

What game are you most looking forward to?
Lord of the Rings: Gollum sounds like it could have intriguing mechanics, with both personalities of Sméagol and Gollum coming into play. Also *Dead Space* [fear emoji!].

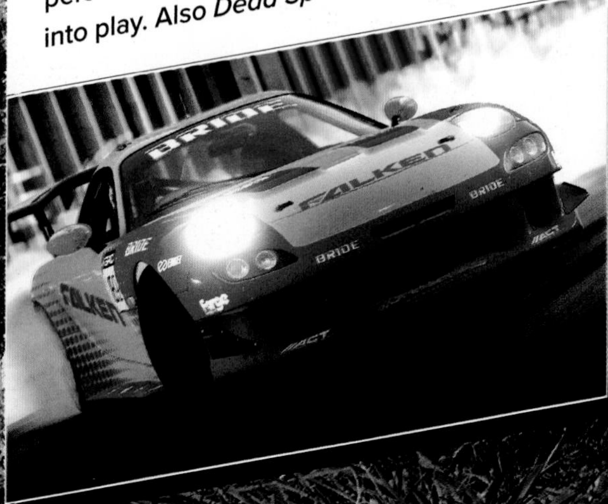

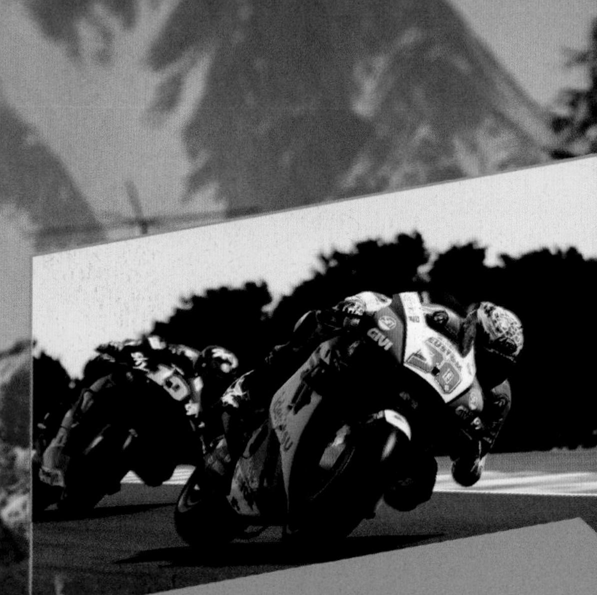

Matteo Pezzotti
Producer on MotoGP 22

What's the best thing you played in the last year?
Dungeons & Dragons! I love video games, but after the pandemic, I prefer to spend my free time in social games. If I have to choose a video game, I'll say *Mario Kart*, because he kept me company during the pandemic!

What element of MotoGP 22 are you most proud of?
The Nine – Season 2009 game mode. Thanks to the support of famous film maker Mark Neale, we managed to create a crossover between a video game and a movie, telling the story of one of the most exciting championships of the modern era.

What game are you most looking forward to?
Definitely the sequel to *Breath of the Wild*. I've been a *Zelda* fan since I was a kid, and can't wait to play it!

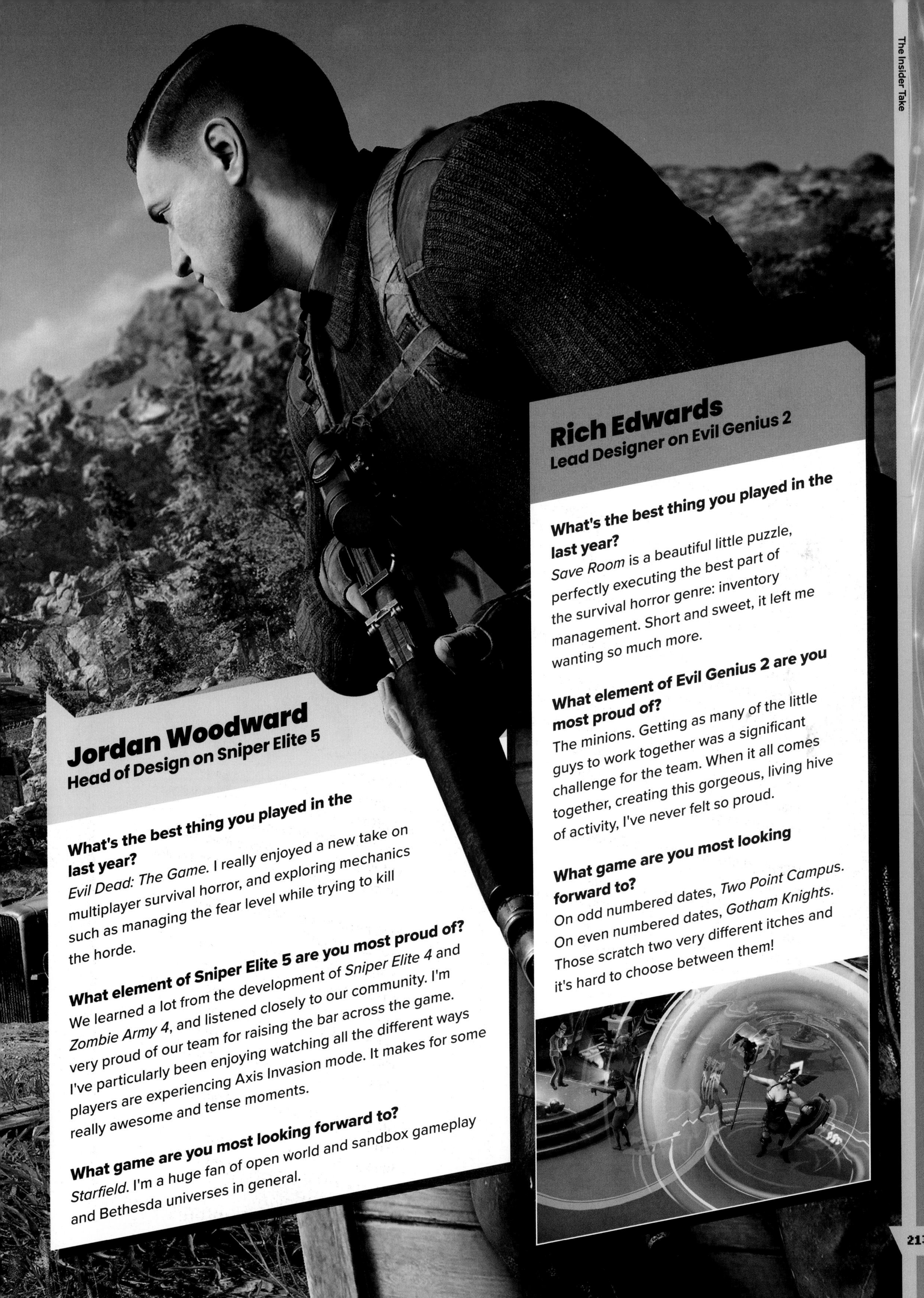

Rich Edwards
Lead Designer on Evil Genius 2

What's the best thing you played in the last year?
Save Room is a beautiful little puzzle, perfectly executing the best part of the survival horror genre: inventory management. Short and sweet, it left me wanting so much more.

What element of Evil Genius 2 are you most proud of?
The minions. Getting as many of the little guys to work together was a significant challenge for the team. When it all comes together, creating this gorgeous, living hive of activity, I've never felt so proud.

What game are you most looking forward to?
On odd numbered dates, *Two Point Campus*. On even numbered dates, *Gotham Knights*. Those scratch two very different itches and it's hard to choose between them!

Jordan Woodward
Head of Design on Sniper Elite 5

What's the best thing you played in the last year?
Evil Dead: The Game. I really enjoyed a new take on multiplayer survival horror, and exploring mechanics such as managing the fear level while trying to kill the horde.

What element of Sniper Elite 5 are you most proud of?
We learned a lot from the development of *Sniper Elite 4* and *Zombie Army 4*, and listened closely to our community. I'm very proud of our team for raising the bar across the game. I've particularly been enjoying watching all the different ways players are experiencing Axis Invasion mode. It makes for some really awesome and tense moments.

What game are you most looking forward to?
Starfield. I'm a huge fan of open world and sandbox gameplay and Bethesda universes in general.

Did You Know
The word chambara means "sword-fighting" in Japanese and it's the name of a movie genre. In English, it's called samurai cinema.

Nintendo Switch Sports

Developer Nintendo **Publisher** Nintendo **Platform** NS

■ ***Switch Sports* combines the best bits of *Wii Sports, Wii Sports Resort* and *Ring Fit Adventure* – then sprinkles new stuff on top! Check out our guide to the six sports currently available to play at the moment, and get ready for golf to be added later in the year.**

Play football without getting muddy, swing a tennis racket without breaking windows or go bowling without having to change your shoes. Then wrestle with your sibling when they want the telly back to watch Netflix!

On the Ball!

Were you wondering how to play football virtually? *Nintendo Switch Sports* has an add-on accessory to make your World Cup dreams come true. Wrap the leg strap around your ankle and all your kicks and flips will be transmitted.

Classic Sports

Tennis

Unleashing your inner Andy Murray is super simple. Raise the Amiibo™ up and forwards to serve, then swing like a real racket to unleash shots. There's depth too. Twist the controller from right to left mid-shot to add backspin, or the opposite way for topspin. Matches are two-on-two and get mega intense when you're controlling the player closest to the net!

Chambara

Swordplay was the best bit of Wii Sports Resort, and it's back for *Switch Sports* – with a new name! You hold the Amiibo™ upright in front of you and move it left and right to block, then swing it forward to catch your opponent off guard. Timing is critical! There are three types of sword to choose from,and you can control two at once.

Bowling

Sadly, Nintendo hasn't recreated the smell of burgers at your local bowling alley. But *Switch Sports* nails everything else about a ten-pin round. You stand upright in readiness to bowl, then hold ZR and motion the Amiibo™ forwards. Like a pro, spin can be added by twisting your wrist while releasing the ball. Watch out for obstacles like square blocks, and moving lanes!

Listen to the squeak of your opponents' rented shoes as they line up their shots in the virtual bowling alley.

Check out that view! The courts in Switch Sports *are as luxurious as any Olympic stadium, maybe even fancier.*

New Sports

Football

Footy in *Switch Sports* has the leg strap. It's in a mode called Shoot Out, you've probably worked out that the idea is to swing your leg to score goals. Prefer a Amiibo™ kickabout? Then jump into four-on-four or one-on-one footy. You shoot by flicking the right controller upwards, or perform a diving header by pushing two Amiibo™s forward.

Badminton

It's slightly calmer than tennis, but only just. These matches are one-on-one, so there's nobody to cover your mistakes but that means you keep the glory to yourself. Like in real life, the harder you swing, the more power in your shots – but it's worth trying to catch your opponent out with subtle drop shots too. Hold ZR while swinging to attempt one of those hits.

Volleyball

This requires real skill and teamwork. It helps if you're good at the real thing! You bring your wrists together at waist height then thrust upward to bump the ball in the air, and push them high together to 'set' the ball above the net. The really fun part is slamming your arm downwards to spike the ball and hopefully win the point! Devilishly competitive chaos.

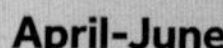

Did You Know
Matt Vasgersian retired from commentating *The Show* this year, he's had the job since 2006. His replacement is ESPN regular John Sciambi.

MLB The Show 22

Developer San Diego Studio **Publisher** Sony
Platform NS, PS4, PS5, XBO, XBX/S

■ Sony's baseball sim is a blast. For newcomers, it's all about flinging fastballs and swatting huge home runs. Experts get subtle nuances like varied pitch types and strategic options. Whatever your experience, no other game is so good at making you feel in control of pro sports.

Shortened Seasons

Baseball seasons are 162 matches long, in the past this meant a serious time commitment. That's changed this year. The popular franchise option is back, but casual players will prefer March to October mode. It shortens the season down to your team's key pitches and at bats. This way, you can breeze through weeks at a time. Fans loved last year's game, but you could only play one season. Now multiple campaigns are included. You can also sign players to improve your team.

All thirty major league teams are here, along with their affiliated clubs. Baseball works differently from football. Each team in the minor league's top two levels (AAA and AA) is tied to an *MLB* team. This leads to fun dream match-ups and lots of in-season options, like promoting AAA players to your *MLB* roster. It's comprehensive yet super fun. Mashing homers just never gets old.

A Hero's Welcome

Nervous about playing a baseball game for the first time? Sony hears you. It's added two difficulty settings to *The Show 22*. These are sure to transform you from 'inquisitive noob' to 'full-time addict'. Once you've grasped the beginner setting, the new amateur and minor settings introduce extra hints and subtleties. It's then on to rookie, where you should feel comfortable flying solo. There's a practice mode too, just in case.

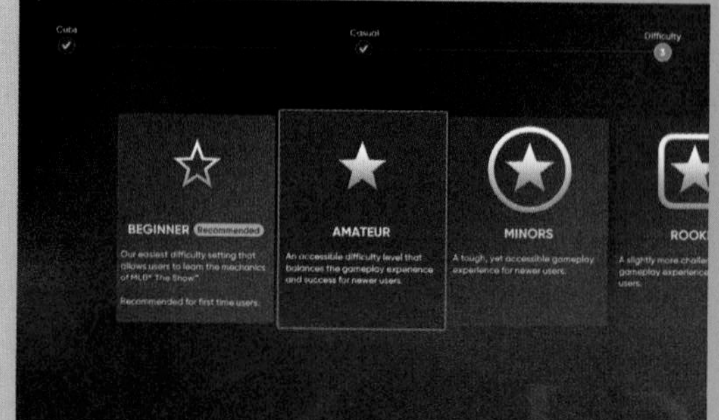

Check Out

Love *MLB The Show* but want to play it on the go? Try *Baseball 9*, it's available on iOS and Android phones.

Check out the mini display board in the left corner of your screen for helpful stats to make your pitching even better.

As well as the celebration moves, your players also act out their dismay at losing a run or being called out.

The HUD (heads-up display) on MLB The Show 22 gives you all the details you need to manage the best team.

The fields, known as diamonds in baseball, are insanely realistic. Each one comes with a digital stat screen plus the more traditional manual scoreboard.

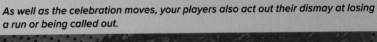

Watch your players as they celebrate home runs with their teammates, each one has their own moves.

Searching for Diamonds

The Show's version of *FIFA*'s Ultimate Team is called Diamond Dynasty. It has a reputation for being more generous than *FIFA* in dishing out legendary player cards. Building a dream squad only takes a month or two. This year's favourites include Prince Fielder, who whammed 319 home runs between 2005 and 2016. Red Sox legend David Ortiz is another popular icon. He was elected to the Baseball Hall of Fame shortly before the game's release.

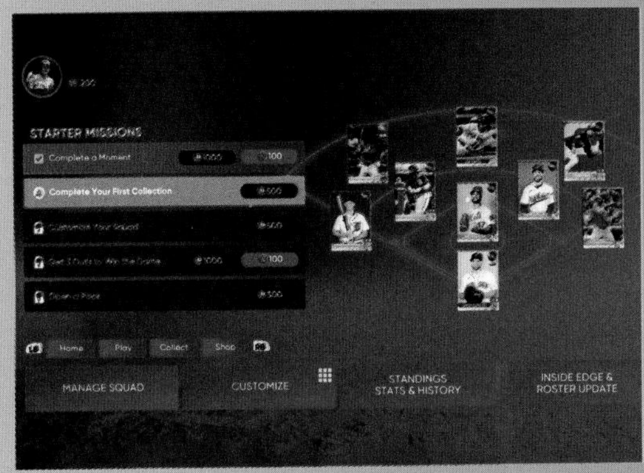

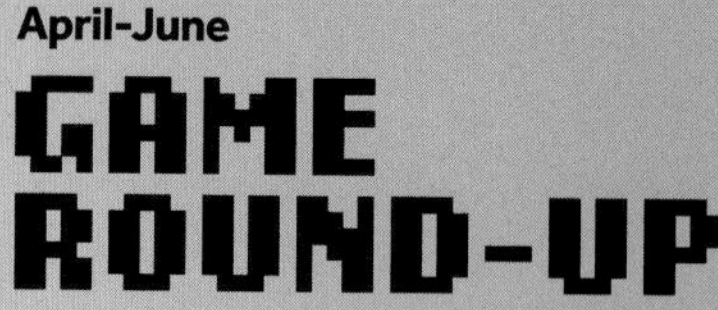

Road 96

Developer DigixArt **Publisher** Plug In Digital
Platform NS, PC, PS4, PS5, XBO, XBX/S

Ever dreamed of playing a hitch-hiking simulator? Hmmm, probably not. Here's one anyway! A great game, too. With the nation of Petria struggling under a tyrannical regime, a bunch of teens decide to flee. It's up to the player to decide whether their character focuses on crossing the border or influencing an upcoming election.

Bored Games

Drivers share stories and secrets as you traverse Petria. If you try multiple runs as different characters, you'll discover more about the election and unlock abilities such as lock picking. Not all player choices are critical, however. There are more fun ones like deciding what to buy from a petrol station vending machine. Playing Connect Four while in the back of a car is another amusing distraction, as is a cheeky game of air hockey.

If you loved Telltale's interactive stories such as *Game of Thrones* and *The Walking Dead*, this is the closest equivalent for PS5 and Xbox Series X.

Check Out

Set in 1986, *Lake* is a narrative adventure where you play Meredith Weiss. Deliver post to the local characters and get to know them one by one.

Each car or truck you try to wave down could contain your ticket across the border or a dangerous encounter.

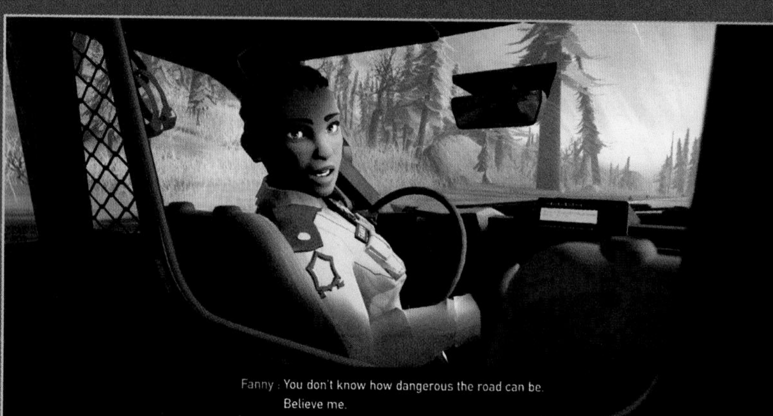

Fanny : You don't know how dangerous the road can be.
Believe me.

Plenty of the side characters are perfectly friendly and happy to help out, but working out which ones to trust is the tricky part.

The game was inspired by road-trip movies and TV shows, and even includes diners and pitstops.

On the Road

Road 96 is set in 1996, hence the title. There are seven major NPCs who crop up in different locations with each playthrough.

Snowrunner

Developer Saber Interactive
Publisher Focus Home Interactive
Platform NS, PC, PS4, PS5, XBO, XBX/S

■ Plough sixty trailer trucks over rocks, hills and snow-capped peaks. The aim is to move cargo across challenging terrain. Each of the fifteen locations is based after a disaster, like a flood or volcano. Not only do these backgrounds look realistic, so does the damage done to your vehicle. This off-road driver has been out a while but just landed on PS5 and Xbox Series X. It's an open-world game like none you've played before.

Did You Know

Snowrunner is a sequel to 2014's *Spintires* and 2017's *Mudrunner*. Both games were based in unpaved areas of Russia.

Tropico 6

Developer Limbic Entertainment
Publisher Calypso Media
Platform MAC, NS, PC, PS4, PS5, XBO, XBX/S

■ Ever played *Sim City* and wanted more of a beach vibe? This Caribbean city-builder launched to happy reviews in 2019 and it's now on next-gen with 4K visuals. The tools for laying roads and building houses are very user-friendly. There's also some political complexity here too. Not to mention funny, mission-based twists. For example, you can engage in piracy – and even steal the White House!

Lucky Number Six

● There really have been five previous *Tropico* games. The first launched on PC and Mac in 2001, and *Tropico 5* hit consoles in May 2014.

Back to Valhalla

A Bountiful Year for Viking Assassins

■ No new *Assassin's Creed*? No problem. *Assassin's Creed Valhalla* continues to get love from gamers young and old. This is the first *AC* game to receive a second year of support from creators Ubisoft. It's meant a free crossover mission with *Assassin's Creed Odyssey*, new expansion, and more ...

Valhalla vs Odyssey

Assassin's Creed Odyssey came out in 2018. You could choose your main character from two Spartan siblings: Alexios or Kassandra. A crossover event brought Kassandra to *Assassin's Creed Valhalla*. Called *A Fated Encounter*, it set Eivor loose in a new location, the Isle of Skye. While investigating a plague of nightmares, she comes face-to-face with Kassandra! She's looking for an ancient artefact. The quest line lasts a couple of hours and blends the pair's tales.

A New Dawn

Dawn of Ragnarok is the game's biggest ever expansion. The story sees Eivor becoming the Norse god Odin. Sounds mad, but it makes sense. It means exploring the phenomenal new realm of Svartalfheim. Enemies are made of ice and flame, like the unkillable fire giant Surtr. The best bit: you get the powers of a god to tackle them. Becoming immune to fire and lava is pretty handy. And who doesn't enjoy a spot of teleportation?

Not-so-little Miss

Main hero Eivor's popularity has expanded beyond the video game. She was added to the Epic Store as a *Fortnite* skin alongside original *Assassin's Creed* main character Altair. There are hood-up and hood-down options and items include her twin axes and longboat. She's also a Mr Men and Little Miss character now. The book *Mme Eivor* was released in France, and penned by series author Adam Hargreaves.

Hall of Heroes

Assassin's Creed has a rich history of brilliant main characters ...

Altair
Assassin's Creed

Ezio
Assassin's Creed II

Aveline
Assassin's Creed III: Liberation

Edward
Assassin's Creed IV: Black Flag

Alexios
Assassin's Creed: Odyssey

Kassandra
Assassin's Creed: Odyssey

Dice Dice Baby

The dice game of Orlog is played by Norsemen in Valhalla. So Ubisoft licensed a Kickstarter campaign for a real version. More than 12,000 fans backed it, to the total of 1.1 million Canadian dollars. It's pretty cool, with acrylic dice, sturdy tokens and Norse art. The dice are rolled to attack, acquire tokens and earn God favours.

Forgotten Saga

Ubisoft have announced a new update for **Assassin's Creed Valhalla. The Forgotten Saga** is a rogue-like game mode, that lets players take on enemies in their hordes!

What in the Weird?

Wild and Weird Gaming Stories From Across the World

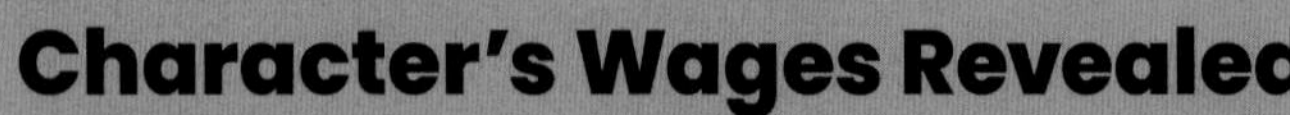

Character's Wages Revealed

Ever wondered what Mario would earn as a plumber in real-life? A study took the time to figure it out. The online gaming platform Solitaired researched salaries to figure out how much characters would earn. As a martial arts instructor, *Street Fighter*'s Ryu would be on £21,273, or $28,212. Mario would take home £32,895/$42,721. The richest character of all would be *Borderlands 2* bad guy Handsome Jack. As CEO of Hyperion Corp, his annual salary would be £333,043 or $432,524.

Xbox Series S(tar Wars)

Custom consoles have become a clever way of marking a new game's release. On 4 May – AKA Star Wars Day – they unveiled twelve different Xbox Series S consoles to promote *Lego Star Wars: The Skywalker Saga*. Each one is themed on a popular character, like Chewbacca, Kylo Ren and R2-D2. The colour of each console also matches its inspiration. Darth Vader is black, Yoda is green and so on. They were all given away for free in a Twitter sweepstake.

FaZe Clan Turns Blue

FaZe Clan's bid for world domination got even stronger. Premier League giants Manchester City hosted a pop-up event dedicated to the *Call of Duty* and *Counter-Strike* favourites. Kevin de Bruyne appeared alongside Mew and Santana, and eSports fans packed the Etihad Stadium. A special FaZe Clan x Man City gaming PC was also created for the occasion. It's half red and half blue to represent the two heavyweights' main colours and was given away to a very happy twelve-year-old.

Saved By a Headset

A pair of Razer Kraken headphones miraculously saved a gamer's life. Eighteen-year-old Jonathan Gonzalez was gaming at home in California when a stray bullet flew through his window and struck the headset. Some were cynical when he shared the story, complete with photos, on Reddit. But Razer took Gonzalez on his word. The company sent him a free, brand-new set of replacement cans.

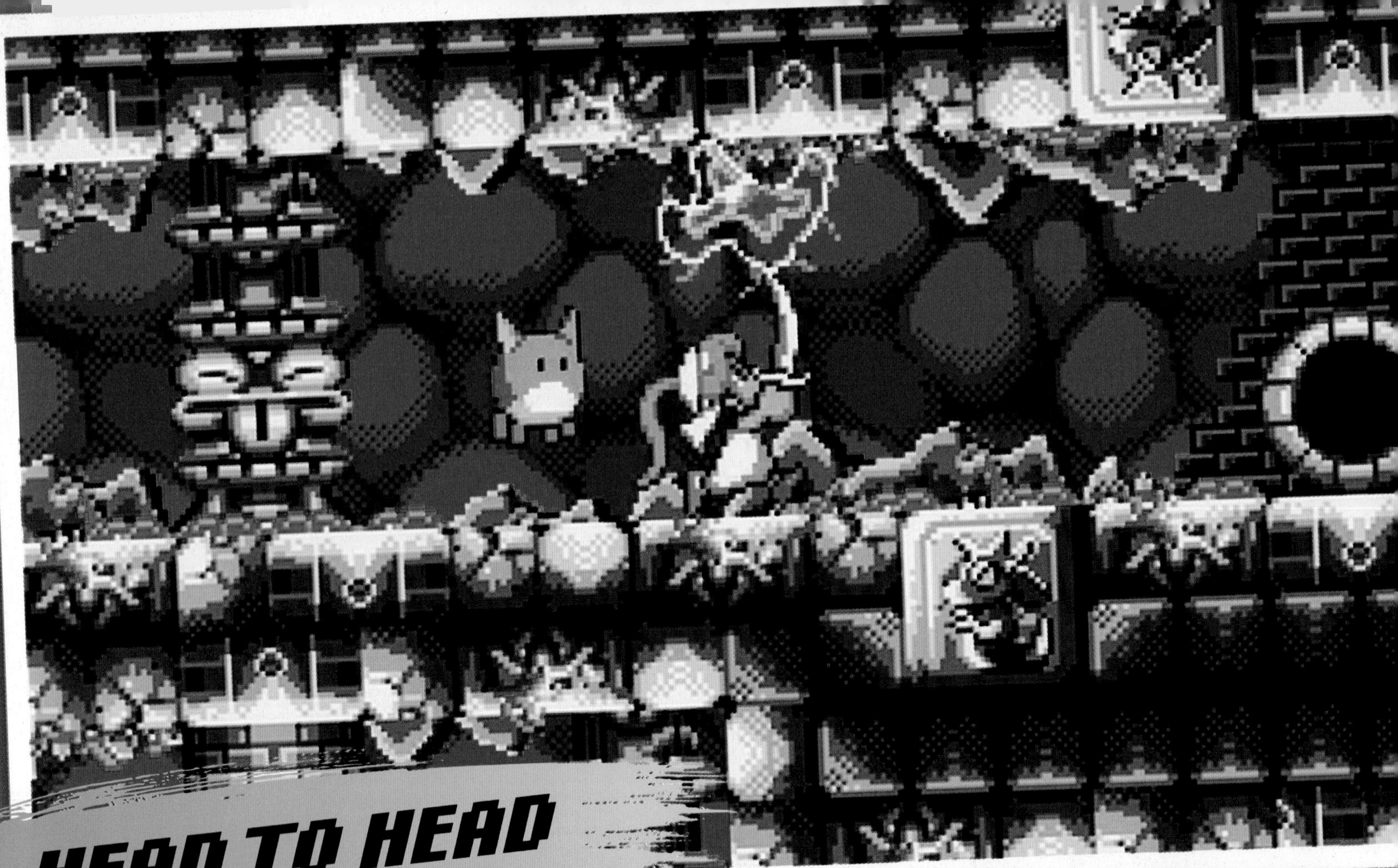

HEAD TO HEAD

Wonder Boy Collection

Developer Westone Bit Entertainment
Publisher United Games **Platform** NS, PS4

Background | *Wonder Boy* rewrote the platforming rulebook in 1986. The best bits? Skateboarding, stone-throwing and an always-decreasing vitality metre that forces you to find energy to stay alive. This collection brings together that classic with *Wonder Boy in Monster Land* (1987), *Wonder Boy in Monster World* (1991) and *Monster World IV* (1994).

Features | The pixel art style remains true to the originals, and captures the simplistic and moreish games. There are modern touches too. A rewind option lets you undo mistakes, while an art gallery brings together classic *Wonder Boy* imagery. Even the graphics can be fiddled with, using shading and filter options.

Gameplay | This is all about the retro. The series is famous for its frantic platforming and RPG elements, and all four games stay true to those origins. Playing all of them in a row is a lot of fun. The first *Wonder Boy* feels fairly easy, but by *Monster World IV* new character Asha can swing her sword in loads of directions and summon her pet Pepelogoo to access hidden areas.

Tom Tom the wonder boy gets around faster on his skateboard, but watch out for obstacles! You'll need to master some speedy button skills.

Trivia

● The first *Wonder Boy* was known as *Super Wonder Boy* in Japan (cool!), and *Revenge of Drancon* when rereleased for Sega's Game Gear in the USA (weird!). The main character is actually called Tom Tom. The last truly new entry in the series was 2018's *Monster Boy and the Cursed Kingdom*, for PS4, Xbox One and Nintendo Switch.

Trivia

The other five titles are shooters *Space Seeker* and *Wild Western*, run-and-gunner *Front Line*, platformer *Chack'n Pop* and *Elevator Action*. That last one is about being a spy, rather than skateboarding down moving staircases. Taito still makes new games occasionally, like cute Switch platformer *Bubble Bobble 4 Friends*.

Taito Milestones

Developer Taito **Publisher** United Games **Platform** NS

Background | *Space Invaders* is known as the first essential arcade game. Taito was the publisher, all the way back in 1978. This collection focuses on ten of Taito's 1980s releases. It starts with 1981 puzzler *Quix* and finishes on side-scrolling 1987 beat 'em up *The Ninja Warriors*.

Features | *Taito Milestones* does a great job of emulating the ten originals, right down to their unique quirks. *The Ninja Warriors* experimented with a ground-breaking widescreen display that keeps it distinct from the other nine games. Plus, there are several basic manuals included to help you work it out.

Gameplay | There's loads here for anyone looking to check out gaming classics from the era of shoulder pads, Madonna and *The Breakfast Club*. *Alpine Ski* offers a trio of basic and fun events in downhill ski, slalom and ski jump. *The Fairyland Story* serves up gentle platforming in the shoes of witch Ptolemy. *Halley's Comet* is a top-down shooter with tons of *Space Invaders* vibes.

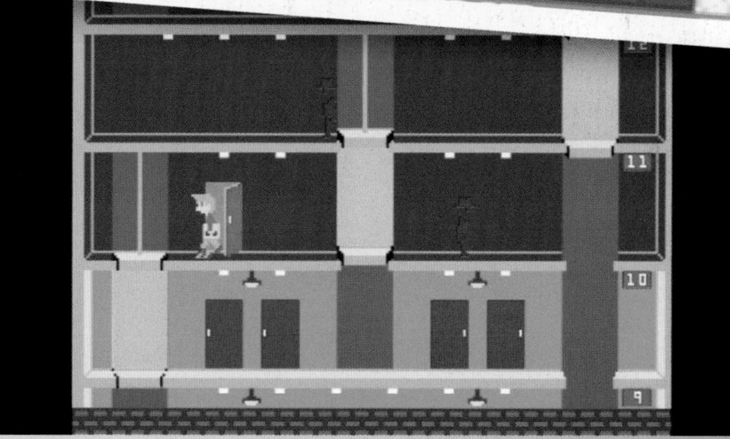

Try out classic arcade game Elevator Action *and sneak into a thirty-storey building as agent 17.*

Fast-paced side-scroller The Ninja Warriors *lets two players work together to take down the bad guys. One as Ninja and the other gamer plays as Kunoichi.*

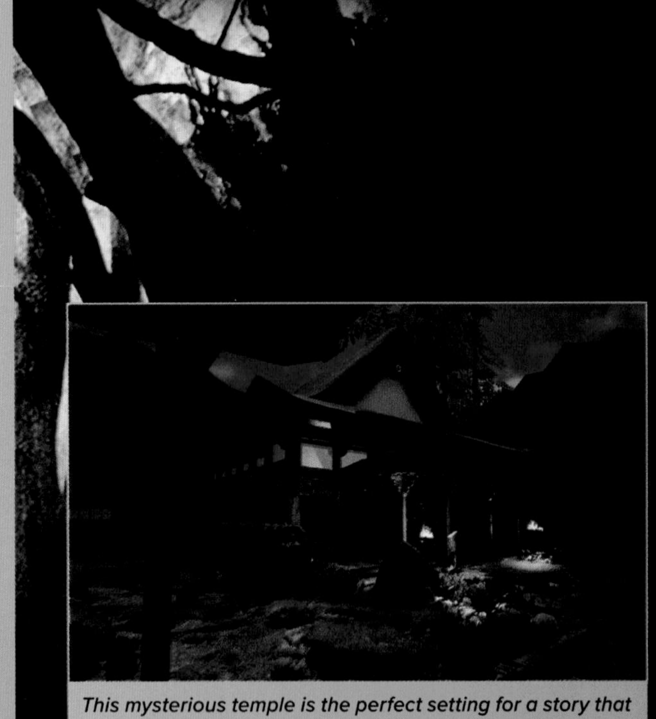
This mysterious temple is the perfect setting for a story that focuses on Japanese horror.

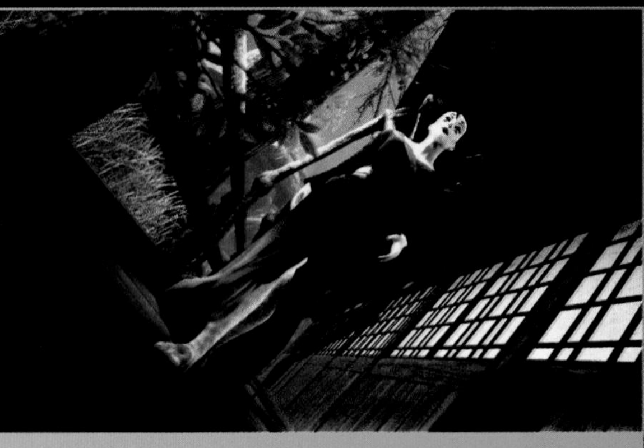
Wander the halls, search for clues and listen up for any tips your host may be feeding you.

Did You Know
Part of the game is learning to draw Japanese banishment symbols. You trace the icon out on special paper and they ward off evil spirits.

Ikai

Developer Endflame **Publisher** PM Studios
Platform NS, PC, PS4, PS5, XBO, XBX/S

■ *Ikai* is an absolutely nerve-jangling survival horror that explores traditional Japanese demons and ghosts. Feudal princess Naoko lives in a temple surrounded by artefacts. Studying these gives you clues about the monsters you face and her voiceover helps you solve spooky puzzles.

These tips are super handy as there are no weapons to fight the enemies, which look insanely creative. If you want to get further in the game, then try acting stealthy. And don't forget: you always have the option to run away. Much like real life, the best option is often to confront your fears and the game becomes less scary as you settle into it. To help, developer Endflame throws in mundane tasks like sweeping floors and picking up dirty laundry.

Seal Spotting

Ikai's most interesting element is drawing. The only way to banish evil is to draw a protective seal, then place it over a cursed item. This works best when you have a bit of skill with your virtual paintbrush, and is a world away from fending off Yōkai (monsters) with fists or swords.

Feudal Ghosts
❶ Yōkai are also known as ayakashi, mononoke and mamono. Many have animal features and the kappa is similar to a turtle.

Zorro: The Chronicles

Developer BKOM Studios **Publisher** Nacon
Platform MAC, NS, PC, PS4, PS5, XBO, XBX/S

■ Teenage Zorro gets his own game! *Zorro: The Chronicles* is based on the animated TV show. Much like the inspiration, it's all about dishing out justice in nineteenth-century California. You get to play as either Don Diego or his sister Ines. Whiplash enemies, nail spectacular moves and stealth around on rooftops. Want to add a final flourish to combat? Use the tip of your sword to mark foes with the shape of a Z.

Z Marks the Spot

Like in the TV show, Zorro never kills opponents. Instead, he chooses to ridicule them to teach them a lesson.

Sniper Elite 5

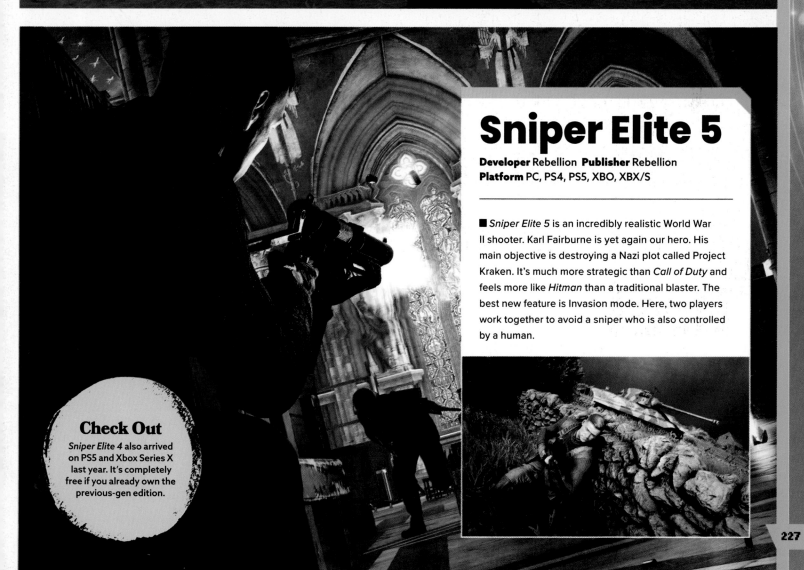

Developer Rebellion **Publisher** Rebellion
Platform PC, PS4, PS5, XBO, XBX/S

■ *Sniper Elite 5* is an incredibly realistic World War II shooter. Karl Fairburne is yet again our hero. His main objective is destroying a Nazi plot called Project Kraken. It's much more strategic than *Call of Duty* and feels more like *Hitman* than a traditional blaster. The best new feature is Invasion mode. Here, two players work together to avoid a sniper who is also controlled by a human.

Check Out

Sniper Elite 4 also arrived on PS5 and Xbox Series X last year. It's completely free if you already own the previous-gen edition.

April-June

GAME SPOTLIGHT

Evil Dead: The Game

Developer Saber Interactive **Publisher** Saber Interactive
Platform NS, PC, PS4, PS5, XBO, XBX/S

■ The only game in this book that lets you kill enemies using toxic farts. Yes, really! The *Evil Dead* story first began with a 1980s movie that's become a cult classic. Fans fell in love with the equal mix of humour and horror. The new game is no different. There's gore for sure but laughs too.

Ashes to Ashes

Longstanding main character Ash Williams plays a major role. As Ash, or Kelly Maxwell, or Lord Arthur, you fight alongside three pals against demonic zombies called Deadites. There are loads of nods to the movies, and the more recent TV show. You can explore the ramshackle cabin from the classic original film or motor around in Ash's famous yellow car.

Evil Dead offers loads of pick-and-and-play amusement as well as a story you'll want to finish. Four Survivor classes offer you the chance to experience the game in different ways: Leader, Warrior, Hunter and Support. Plus, you can upgrade through the skill tree.

Vomit Comet

Evil Dead's clever twist is that you can control the main enemy, if you want. And four-versus-one isn't as lopsided as it sounds. The Kandarian Demon can possess Deadites, set traps and unleash powers – like those toxic farts. Not gross enough? Try taking down one of the good guys with a jet stream of green vomit. As voice actor Bruce Campbell says in the trailer: "It was no accident that Ash always wore brown pants."

DLC

A free to download add-on map named **Castle Kandar** is planned as the first DLC. Adding to the existing two maps, Remington Rapids and Cleaver County.

Old Timer

Evil Dead has been around longer than any gamer under forty! The first film came out in 1981. It was followed by *Evil Dead II* (1987) and *Army of Darkness* (1992). A reboot of the original dropped in 2013, and the TV show *Ash vs Evil Dead* ran from 2015 to 2018. Its first video game came out in 1984 and was a blocky adventure for Commodore 64 and ZX Spectrum.

As well as the overall goal (stay alive!), you'll also find smaller quests that help you unravel the plot.

Pick which characters you want on your team based on their Survivor class, skills and abilities.

The Deadites, or zombies, look similar to vampires from the nineties' TV show Buffy the Vampire Slayer.

Ash's famous ride, it stands out when he's racing away from the murderous mob.

Ace of Spades

Gore is big on the menu. You can take enemies down with shotguns, chainsaws and cleavers. Or axes. Or a massive garden spade! But you need to search as well as shoot. Track down enough artefacts to access a spell that ends the Kandarian Demon for good. Or until your next play, anyway ...

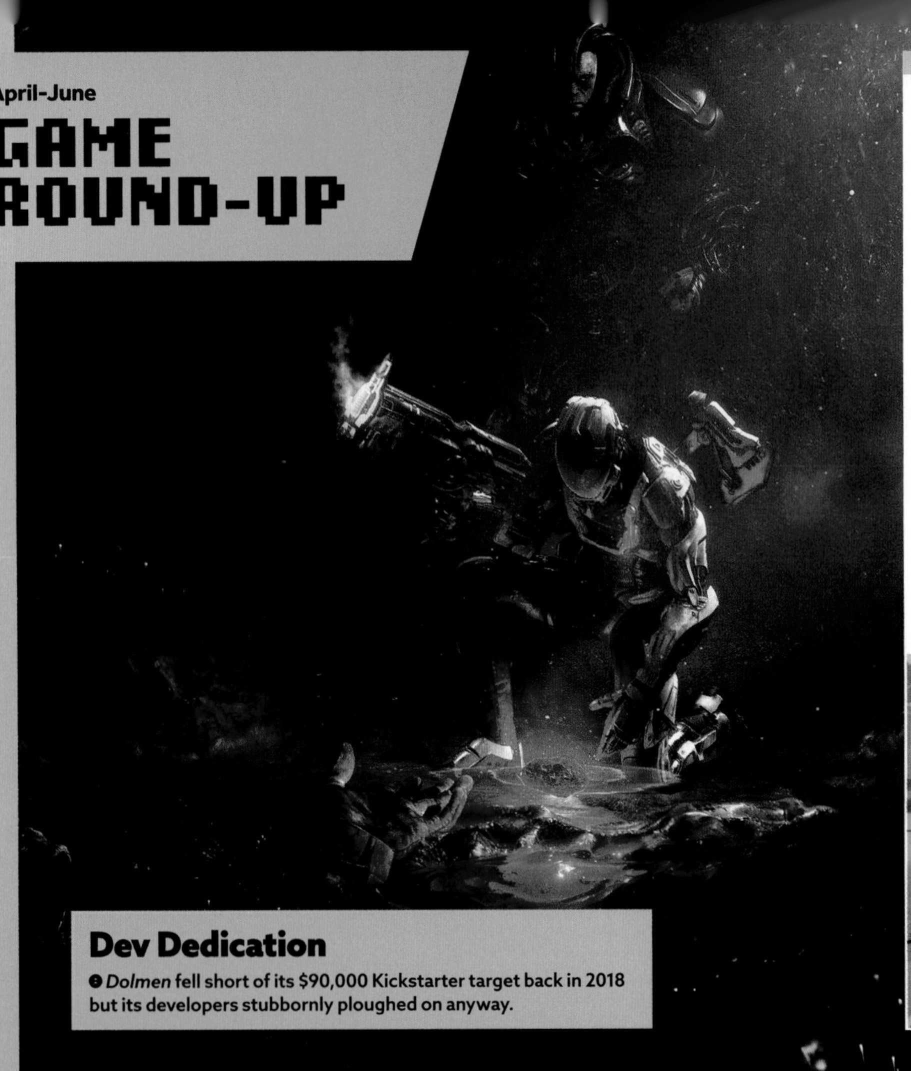

Dolmen

Developer Massive Work Studio **Publisher** Prime Matter **Platform** PC, PS4, PS5, XBO, XBX/S

■ Uh oh. The mining station of Revion Prime is infested with ugly, otherworldly creatures. Naturally, it's your job to wipe out the hive. There are loads of cool weapons to go slaying with. Enjoy dropping enemies with speed and shiftiness? Unleash the zoan axe and shield combo. Prefer the direct, powerful approach? Whip out the two-handed, sword-like driller killer. *Dolmen* plays like *Dark Souls* meets *Dead Space* meets *Alien*, in a good way!

Dev Dedication

Dolmen fell short of its $90,000 Kickstarter target back in 2018 but its developers stubbornly ploughed on anyway.

Stat Attack

The *Pac-Man* games have sold 44.5 million copies since the series launched in 1980.

Pac-Man Museum +

Developer Now Production **Publisher** Bandai Namco Entertainment **Platform** NS, PC, PS4, XBO

■ Fancy trying out this arcade classic but find forty years of games daunting? *Pac-Man Museum +* is for you! There are fourteen cherry-munching, ghost-chasing games in the retro collection. The original is in, of course. So are the sequels *Super Pac-Man* (1982) and *Pac & Pal* (1983). The weirdest game is Super Nintendo gem *Pac-In-Time*. Instead of being based on a maze-style board like the others, you solve puzzles in side-scrolling levels. The most recent game here is 2016's *Pac-Man 256*. It lets the little guy loose in an endless maze, with lasers and tornadoes as weapons.

Cotton Fantasy

Developer Studio Saizensen
Publisher Sega **Platform** NS, PC, PS4

■ Check out this crazy cartoony blaster! Fly through the sky as broom-riding witch Cotton, unleashing fireballs at enemies. The sixteen levels pack in gothic design and insane inventiveness. Imagine a planet in the shape of a skull! Bosses are bonkers, and there are five other playable characters for when you want to switch things up. Plus, completing the game with each character unlocks a new level just for them. Neat.

Mouthful of Cotton

❶ This had a more tongue-twisty name when released in Asia. Ready? *Cotton Rock 'n' Roll Superlative Night Dreams.*

Salt and Sacrifice

Developer Ska Studios **Publisher** Ska Studios **Platform** PC, PS4, PS5

■ All mages must die. That's the rule you live by as a marked inquisitor, sworn to take out all enemies and defend your once-peaceful kingdom. This is the sequel to 2016's *Salt and Sanctuary*, one of the best games inspired by Demon's Souls. There are eight classes to choose from when exploring its 2D levels: Highblade, Paladin, Assassin, Cleric, Dualist, Fighter, Ranger and Sage. Whichever you choose, battles with wandering spooks and super-sized mages are guaranteed. Downing a mage lets you harness its abilities, improving your skills for the tougher fights to come.

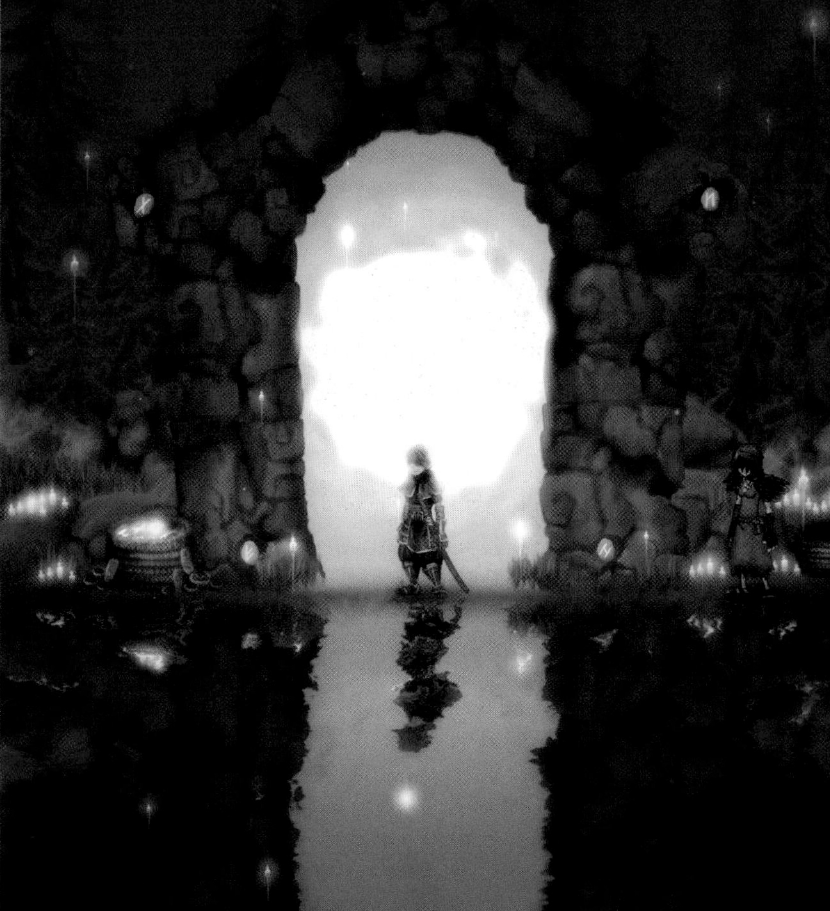

Pass the Salt

❶ Unlike its predecessor, *Salt and Sacrifice* has multiplayer. You can buddy up in co-op or join a faction for PvP match-ups.

The Best Special Editions

From Soundtracks to Statues, Check Out the Most Exciting Bonus Treats

Elden Bling

If you like collecting figurines of all your favourite gaming characters, then take a look at Bandai Namco's Elden Ring figurines. There are mini versions of Melina and Raging Wolf.

Elden Ring

Two months after it came out, *Elden Ring* had sold twelve million copies. Very few of them were this hard-to-find collector's edition. It came with a statue of boss character Malenia, Blade of Miquella. It stands an impressive 23cm tall. Also included are a steelbook box, forty-page-artbook plus the digital soundtrack.

Tiny Tina's Wonderlands

Borderlands and *Wonderlands* are all about loot and the Tiny Tina Treasure Trove has lots of it. You get a Butt Stallion plush and papercraft booklet. The cloth *Wonderlands* map is a cool tie-in, and the enamel companion pins and illustrated tarot cards are also ace. There's a standalone Bunkers & Badasses module to use in-game too. The bizarre bit? The collection doesn't include the game itself!

Tales of Arise

Bandai Namco's action-RPG has a dark side, but its Hootle edition is full-on cuteness. This one does give you a copy of the game, plus other treats. Its 15cm Hootle plush can be customised with four different accessories. Stickers featuring major characters should please fans of all ages, as will a physical soundtrack CD. Also inside are three art prints and a sixty-four-page artbook, plus in-game accessories.

Horizon: Forbidden West

This hefty collector's edition has an art book, steelbook case and statues of Aloy and Tremortusk. Everything else is digital. Both PS4 and PS5 versions of the game are included, along with a soundtrack and comic book. There's a photo mode, Carja Behemoth and Nora Thunder outfits, and a couple of new weapons too.

Final Fantasy XIV Endwalker

The *Endwalker* collector's edition is more colossal than any in-game boss. Like *Wonderlands*, there's no actual game included. You do get a breath-taking Paladin figure and super cute Loporrit plush, as well as a special art box featuring Hydaelyn and Zodiark. Also included is a collection of ten art prints, a frame to showcase your favourite print and an Azem crystal pin.

STATE OF PLAY

The Best of ROBLOX

All the Hot Happenings From the Playground Favourite!

Check Out

Overlook Bay is another **Roblox** game, which has plenty of cute critters for you to adopt. Plus, you can play mini-games with your pets and win prizes.

Purrfect Pets

Roblox has a huge range of different games for every type of player. The most popular *Roblox* title, *Adopt Me!*, gives gamers the chance to adopt adorable pets. Second-placed *Tower of Hell* is correctly named! Try getting to the top of a tricky obstacle course without a checkpoint.

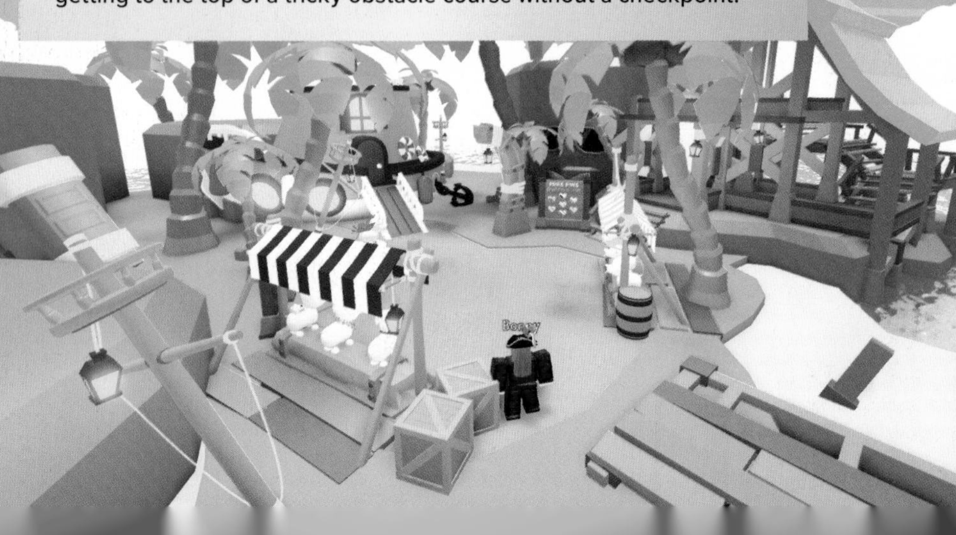

Tower of Hell

Roblox Top Ten

1. Adopt Me!
2. Tower of Hell
3. Brookhaven
4. Meep City
5. Piggy
6. Murder Mystery 2
7. Royale High
8. Welcome to Bloxburg
9. Jailbreak
10. Blox Fruits

Kick It

Roblox celebrated women's football in a cool way. Ahead of UEFA Women's EURO 2022, it launched content dedicated to the tournament. Kai, Robyn and Ashley are likeable mascot characters and you train with them before taking on Obbys (obstacle courses). You can get national team colours for your avatar. And the three mascots appear in a YouTube video series, alongside twelve big real-life names. These include Alexis Putellas (Spain), Vivianne Miedema (Netherlands) and Lucy Bronze (England).

Hello He-Man

He-Man and *Roblox* crossover? Who knew! *Masters of the Universe: You Have The Power* launched in 2022. You can collect favourite characters, fight other players and explore Castle Grayskull. Hello Kitty is also working with Roblox now, too. Her game is called *My Hello Kitty Cafe*. It's based around real-life restaurants in America and Asia. You create and customise your own cafe, serving customers and making friends.

Did You Know

There's even an exclusive Sonic skin that unlocks on *Sonic Speedc Simulator* if you managed to get 10,000 likes.

Sonic's 'blox Party

First, he was on the Heathrow Express. Then he sold for big bucks at an American auction. Sonic's huge year got even more massive when he appeared in *Roblox* for the first time. *Sonic Speed Simulator* is the fastest game in *Roblox*, ever. You can dash around in any direction, launching spin attacks and grinding on rails. You can also race against friends to earn pets and rewards.

Bakugan's Big First

Roblox launched in 2006, so genuine firsts are hard to come by. But the makers of *Bakugan* achieved one. For the first time ever, a full-length TV show episode premiered on *Roblox*. Specifically, it was season three, episode 317 of *Bakugan: Geogan Rising*. Even Netflix viewers had to wait another week to watch it!

Top Tip
Button bashing works! If your opponent is getting too close, you can speed up your hyper strike by mashing A.

Mario Strikers: Battle League

Developer Next Level Games **Publisher** Nintendo **Platform** NS

■ **Bored of Ultimate Team? Decided *eFootball* isn't for you? Then your goalscoring dreams are about to be answered by the most unlikely of Ronaldo rivals. Mario's first football game in fifteen years offers end-to-end five-on-five action. It's just like a kick-about on the playground or down the local park. Only with electric fences. And banana peels. And Princess Peach.**

Bowser Ball

All your favourites are here to build a team around. You can storm forward with Bowser, flanked by Toad on the left and Rosalina on the right. That trio can do something even the Premier League's best players can't. Grab a glowing orb, power it up and unleash a hyper strike to earn a two-point goal. Wonderful – unless you're on the receiving end in the last minute!

Local multiplayer supports up to eight players. Each gamer uses a single Amiibo™, and the two goalkeepers are AI-controlled. It's exactly as chaotic as *Mario Kart* or *Mario Party*, with the same just-one-more-match factor as car-footy classic *Rocket League*.

Squad Goals

Nintendo confirmed ten characters when *Battle League* was announced. They are Mario, Luigi, Bowser, Yoshi, Wario, Waluigi, Toad, Princess Peach, Donkey Kong and Rosalina. All have individual stats, just like in *FIFA 22*. But you can customise their stats using gear, like a new pair of shoes to increase Mario's speed. Power-ups you'll recognise from *Mario Kart*, like mushrooms and green shells, also affect how a match unfolds.

Hyper Hits

Two-point hyper strikes are true game-changers. So it's only right that they're individual to each character. Mario boots the ball high into the air, then leaps up and unleashes a bicycle kick. Bowser slings the ball forwards after engulfing it in flames. Yoshi's is hilarious. The dynamic dino lays a giant egg, which bounces around randomly before firing itself into the goal.

The Power of Three

This is the third *Mario Strikers* game, although it's a decade and a half since his last footy outing. *Super Mario Strikers* kicked its way onto Gamecube in 2005. It was followed up in 2007 by the still-beloved *Mario Strikers Charged* for Nintendo Wii.

Mario Strikers: Battle League *is an explosive game to play with all your friends and family.*

Pick your team line-up carefully, each member has different abilities through their kit.

Tourist Bus Simulator

Developer TML Studios
Publisher Aerosoft
Platform ANDROID,PC, PS5, XBX/S

■ Is this the weirdest simulation game to come out in the last year? You decide! Explore Fuerteventura by bus. It's surprisingly realistic, with twenty real-life cities and beaches. As well as sightseeing, the aim of the game is to build a travel empire. You'll be in charge of the routes, hiring the right staff and buying buses.

Whistle-stop Tours
Roads in *Tourist Bus Simulator* are set at 1:5 scale. This means you can explore all of Fuerteventura faster than in real life.

World of Final Fantasy Maxima

Developer Tose
Publisher Square Enix
Platform NS, PC, PS4, XBO

■ Lann and Reynn are twins and monster tamers in the towns and dungeons of Grymoire. The battle system in *World of Final Fantasy Maxima* mimics old-school Final Fantasy games, and the monster-capturing borrows heavily from *Dragon Quest*. You can even go fishing with Noctis from *Final Fantasy XV*! It's cute and quirky plus really funny too – you'll swiftly grow to love the scrappy siblings.

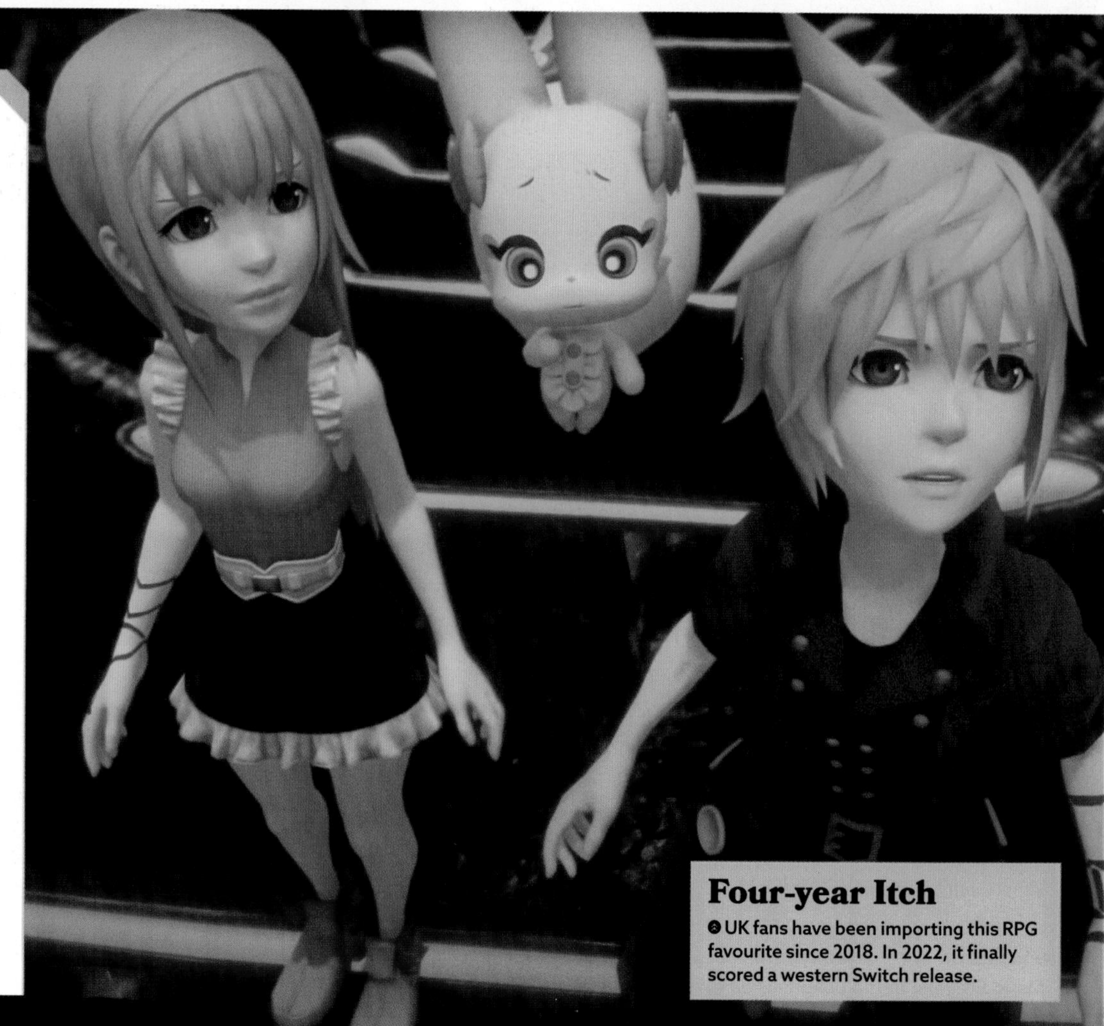

Four-year Itch
UK fans have been importing this RPG favourite since 2018. In 2022, it finally scored a western Switch release.

Did You Know

The in-world language Aurebash can be translated. Some of the more odd shop signs are Arm and a Leg or Crispy Fried Dewback.

Lego Star Wars: The Skywalker Saga

Developer Traveller's Tales **Publisher** Warner Bros **Platform** NS, PC, PS4, PS5, XBO, XBX/S

■ Long before Harry Potter and Jurassic Park, Star Wars was the first ever Lego game. Now it's back, with all nine movies playable in brick-based form. There's especially good news for those who've played its predecessors. Rather than restart every trilogy from scratch, you can jump into any film. (In the past you had to finish *A New Hope* and *The Empire Strikes Back* to unlock Return of the Jedi.)

Jack in the Box

While gamers got to play the seventh film in 2016's *Lego Star Wars: The Force Awakens*, this is the first appearance of *The Last Jedi* and *The Rise of Skywalker*. That's not the only cool new feature. Characters with lightsabers can mix light and heavy attacks and Force moves. There's also the odd choice between real voice acting or mumbling, as happened in the early games.

The package is a Star Wars fan's wildest dream. Every film is packed with lore and charm. And challenges, too! The puzzles here make you think, and tease you back for additional plays. Especially with 380 characters to unlock. There've been dozens of Lego games over the years. This one is the very best.

Relive some of your favourite scenes from the sensational spacefaring movies.

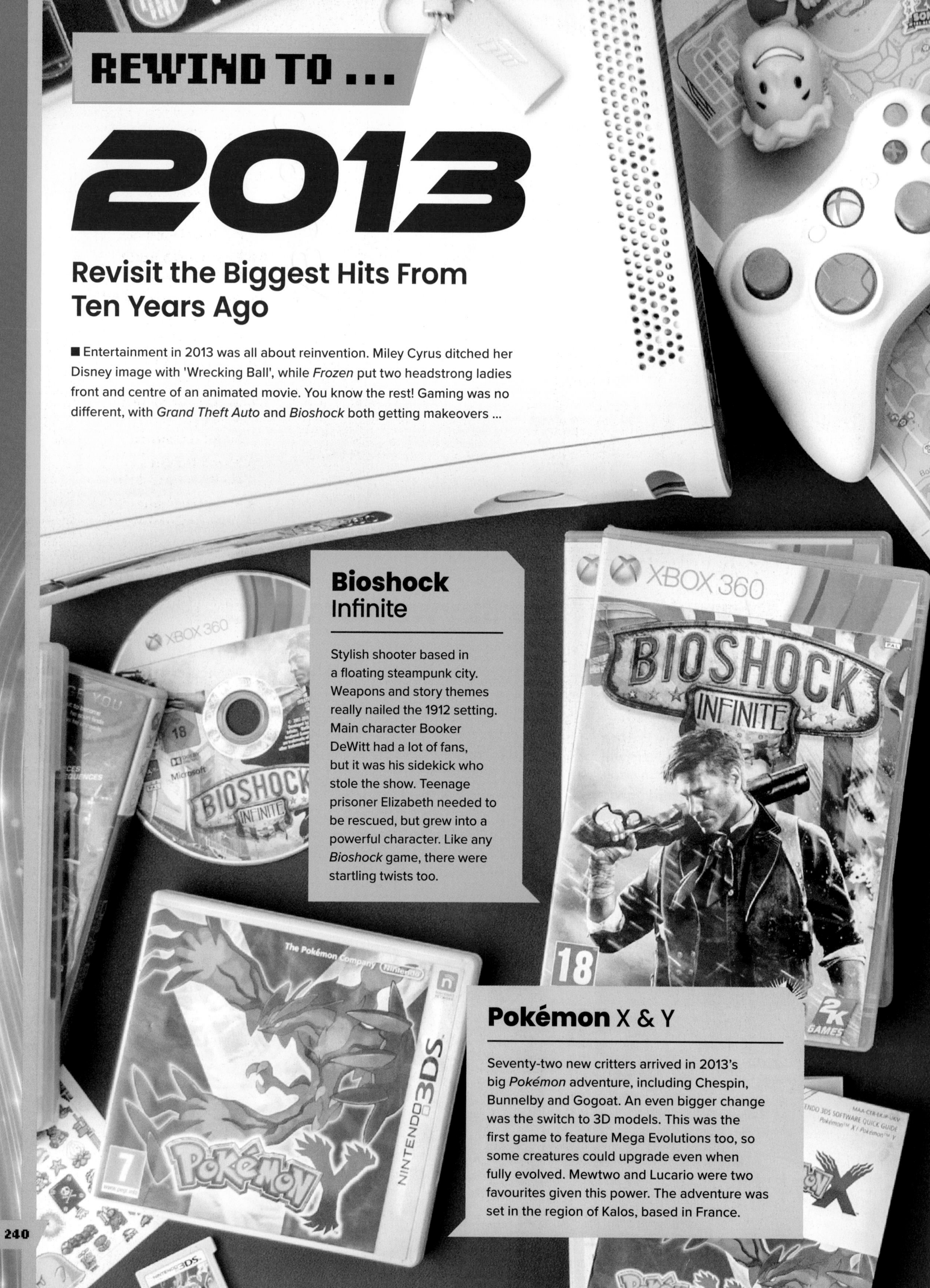

REWIND TO ...

2013

Revisit the Biggest Hits From Ten Years Ago

■ Entertainment in 2013 was all about reinvention. Miley Cyrus ditched her Disney image with 'Wrecking Ball', while *Frozen* put two headstrong ladies front and centre of an animated movie. You know the rest! Gaming was no different, with *Grand Theft Auto* and *Bioshock* both getting makeovers ...

Bioshock Infinite

Stylish shooter based in a floating steampunk city. Weapons and story themes really nailed the 1912 setting. Main character Booker DeWitt had a lot of fans, but it was his sidekick who stole the show. Teenage prisoner Elizabeth needed to be rescued, but grew into a powerful character. Like any *Bioshock* game, there were startling twists too.

Pokémon X & Y

Seventy-two new critters arrived in 2013's big *Pokémon* adventure, including Chespin, Bunnelby and Gogoat. An even bigger change was the switch to 3D models. This was the first game to feature Mega Evolutions too, so some creatures could upgrade even when fully evolved. Mewtwo and Lucario were two favourites given this power. The adventure was set in the region of Kalos, based in France.

Grand Theft Auto V

When *GTA V* came out, it changed the game completely. The open-world sandbox had three different main characters: Michael, Franklin and Trevor. You could switch between them at any time, giving the sense of leading three separate lives. Combat felt satisfying. Driving brought a real thrill. And missions tied the trio of lead characters' stories together brilliantly. It made $800 million in its first day on sale.

Biggest-selling Games of 2003

01. **Grand Theft Auto V**
    Publisher Rockstar Games
02. **Call of Duty: Ghosts**
    Publisher Activision
03. **FIFA 2014**
    Publisher EA Sports
04. **Pokémon X and Y**
    Publisher Nintendo
05. **Assassin's Creed IV: Black Flag**
    Publisher Ubisoft
06. **The Last of Us**
    Publisher SCE
07. **Animal Crossing: New Leaf**
    Publisher Nintendo
08. **Tomb Raider**
    Publisher Square Enix
09. **Monster Hunter IV**
    Publisher Capcom
10. **Bioshock Infinite**
    Publisher 2K Games

The Next Generation

2013 also saw the next generation of consoles unleashed on the world, with Sony's **PlayStation 4** and Microsoft's **Xbox One** both coming out in November.

The Last of Us

Everyone loves a post-apocalyptic tale. *The Last of Us* is possibly the most believable of the bunch. Made by the studio behind *Uncharted*, you travelled across a lawless United States as smuggler Joel and teenage orphan Ellie. Their odd friendship builds through the story. And it's a really great story. Salvaging items to craft weapons or medkits was also a highlight. As for its settings: ruined versions of Pennsylvania and Colorado looked and sounded eerily real.

HOME OF HORIZON

Guerrilla Games

■ The creators of *Horizon: Forbidden West* are based in a Californian skyscraper looking out over the Pacific, right? Nope! In fact, Aloy's masterminds are from Amsterdam. Guerrilla Games' beautiful office is close to the famous Dam Square. It has state-of-the-art audio booths and a special effects studio. The studio was formed in 2000 as Lost Boys Games, and initially worked on kid-friendly Game Boy titles, like *Dizzy's Candy Quest, Rhino Rumble* and *Black Belt Challenge*.

Have You Played?

Killzone 3

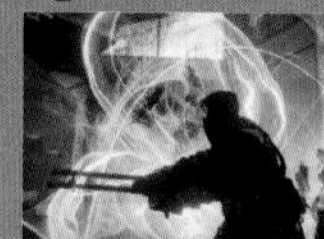
Killzone: Shadow Fall

Horizon: Zero Dawn

Horizon: Forbidden West

Biggest Series: Killzone

Horizon is relatively new for Guerrilla. From 2004 to 2013, it focused on PlayStation-exclusive shooter *Killzone*. The futuristic franchise focused on the interplanetary war between two fictional factions. The Vektans, led by Jan Templar, were a force for good. Red-eyed enemies the Helghan, fronted by dastardly Scolar Visari, were the opposite. Tight, precise gunplay made it one of the best single-player series going before multiplayer shooters came to rule.

LANDS OF LOOT

Gearbox Software

■ In 1975, Randy Pitchford's dad brought home a computer he'd developed himself. Pitchford was five, and soon began writing his own games. As a young adult, he worked on *Duke Nukem 3D* and *Shadow Warrior*, before setting up his own studio. Based in Texas, Gearbox became one of the world's most successful developers. Gritty shooter *Brothers in Arms* brought joy to World War 2 nerds. *Borderlands* was spun off into *Tiny Tina's Wonderlands* in 2022.

Biggest Series: Borderlands

Loot, loot, loot. The joy of Gearbox's shooter has always been unearthing new goodies. Over the years this has been in the form of money, bullets, weapons, class mods and more. But it wouldn't have lasted more than a decade without sound mechanics, too. The series perfectly married larger-than-life shootouts with RPG elements. It's so beloved that even six years after release, a million gamers were still playing *Borderlands 2* every month. Wow!

Have You Played?

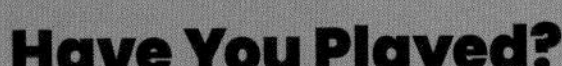

Tiny Tina's Wonderlands

Borderlands 2

Aliens: Colonial Marines

Borderlands 3

LOOKING FORWARD

››

The last year has delivered some incredible games. Which is the entire point of this book! But, with PS5 and Xbox Series X just a couple of years old, the future is even brighter. In the coming pages we round up the best new games coming soon. The future of football will be transformed by *EA Sports FC*. *Hogwarts Legacy* is set to reinvent the *Harry Potter* franchise. Plus, there are sequels from *Street Fighter, Breath of the Wild* and *Kingdom Hearts* on the horizon. Not to mention even more from a blue hedgehog who's absolutely everywhere right now ...

Sonic Frontiers

Developer Sonic Team **Publisher** Sega **Release** Christmas 2022

You'd figure Sir Spins-A-Lot might want a year off after his manic twelve months. Nope! Sonic is another classic character who's about to roam an open world for the first time. That world is called the Starfall Islands.

It's made up of biomes based around classic Sonic levels. You can check out flowery fields, ancient ruins and pretty forests in early footage. These locations are the gateway to everything you'd expect from your favourite blue hedgehog. Ring collecting is important, obvs, to go along with rail grinding and bopping robot enemies.

What's really cool is that you don't just zoom left and right around this fully 3D world. It's also about moving vertically, with Sonic speed-running up walls to reach higher areas. These contain more puzzles and secrets, and the type of awe-inspiring views usually associated with games like *Breath of the Wild*.

Also Coming Soon

Sonic isn't the only classic Sega game that's getting a makeover. The studio has also announced reboots of **Jet Set Radio** and **Crazy Taxi**.

EA Sport FC

Developer EA Canada **Publisher** EA **Release** Autumn 2023

EA has published the *FIFA* series since its Mega Drive inception in 1992. But *FIFA 23* will be the last entry made by the sports juggernaut. In the spring of 2023 it's launching its own brand called *EA Sports FC*. All the modes you love, like Ultimate Team and Volta, are already guaranteed. The sports-mad company has also announced 19,000 players, 700 teams, 100 stadiums and 30 leagues.

The name *FIFA* will continue too, with football's governing body branching out into non-sim games. For example, there's a mysterious new game from a different studio coming just before the 2022 World Cup in Qatar. *FIFA 24* and *FIFA 25* are on their way too – but they won't be made by EA.

Street Fighter 6

Developer Capcom **Publisher** Capcom **Release** 2023

Ryu, Ken and Chun-L are back. You've never played a *Street Fighter* like this, though. There's still plenty of fireball throwing and dragon punching, but the solo world tour lets you roam an open world between fights. Just wanna hadoken other humans? Head straight for the online battle hub.

Kingdom Hearts IV

Developer Square Enix **Publisher** Square Enix **Release** TBC

Square Enix's latest Disney-blended RPG is top-secret to the point that there's no release date. They have released a sneak peek of a redesigned Sora waking up in the Tokyo-inspired world of Quadratum, then taking on a car-wielding devil-beast. Plus, Donald and Goofy get cameos!

The Legend of Zelda
Breath of the Wild 2

Developer Nintendo **Publisher** Nintendo
Release 2023

Every new *Zelda* game is a big deal. But a sequel to the universally worshipped *Breath of the Wild*? For Switch owners, there's simply nothing that can match this for hype.

Development began in 2017, with famed director Hidemaro Fujibayashi back for his seventh *Zelda* game. Fans have predicted that it'll be a darker series entry, akin to *Majora's Mask*. Link's got a cool new haircut, and a cybernetic arm. He can use this to fire green energy shots, and freeze and reverse enemy fire. As for Hyrule, Link's homeland has been expanded vertically. Our main man-boy can get around by paragliding through the skies to explore clusters of land set high above the clouds.

Also Coming Soon

Nintendo has a big year ahead with new releases including **Splatoon 3, Bayonetta 3, Mario + Rabbids Sparks of Hope** and **Advance Wars 1+2: Re-Boot Camp.**

Pokémon Scarlet & Violet

Developer Game Freak **Publisher** Nintendo
Release November 2022

Another pair of *Pokémon* adventures will soon be fighting for your affections. Three new starter *Pokémon* are confirmed to get you going: Sprigatito, Fuecoco and Quaxly. Excitingly, you can now explore in a party of four, in the first ever Pokémon open-world RPGs. Mega!

God of War Ragnarök

Developer Santa Monica Studio **Publisher** Sony
Release Christmas 2022

The sequel to 2018's *God of War* takes Kratos and son Atreus back into ancient Scandinavia. The story picks up from a massive twist at the end of the first game, bringing Atreus into conflict with thunder god Thor. There's no Chris Hemsworth here – just glorious scenery and meaty combat.

The Best of 'Busters

Ghostbusters (1984)

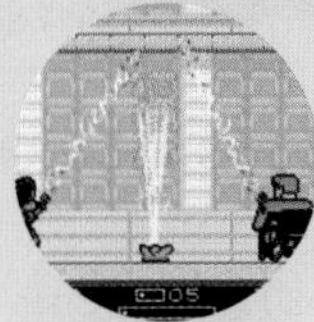

Extreme Ghostbusters (2001)

Ghostbusters: The Video Game (2009)

Lego Dimensions: Ghostbusters (2015)

Ghostbusters: Puzzle Fighter (2015)

Ghostbusters: Spirits Unleashed

Developer IllFonic **Publisher** IllFonic **Release** Christmas 2022

A whole new 'bustin crew gets to wield proton packs and drive Ecto-1. Pals can fill out the spots in your team, or – how cool is this? – you can play as a ghost instead! Movie originals Winston (Ernie Hudson) and Ray (Dan Ackroyd) also feature in the spooky co-op blaster.

Spider-Man 2

Developer Insomniac Games
Publisher Sony **Release** 2023

You might need a next-gen machine to play this Spidey sequel, as Sony says it's exclusive to PS5. We know that Venom plays a major role. Uh oh! Plus, Peter Parker tries out the Iron Spider suit, so expect more cool powers to boost your web-slinging and goon-thwacking.

Also Coming Soon

If you're a fan of Marvel video games, **Midnight Suns** is due to release in October. It was created by Firaxis Games and is the first modern Marvel strategy game.

Hogwarts Legacy

Developer Avalanche Software
Publisher Warner Bros
Release Christmas 2022

Wipe everything you know about *Harry Potter* games. This open-world RPG is set in the late 1800s, with your character starting their fifth year at Hogwarts. There are loads of charms, potions and spells at your disposal, in familiar locations like the Forbidden Forest and Hogsmeade Village.

The Hottest New Gaming Movies

The Division
Jake Gyllenhaal
2022

Super Mario Bros
Chris Pratt
2023

Borderlands
Cate Blanchett
2023

Minecraft: The Movie
Jason Momoa
2023

Metal Gear Solid
Oscar Isaac
2023

Tomb Raider 2
Alicia Vikander
2023

Splinter Cell
Tom Hardy
2023

Call Of Duty
Dwayne Johnson
2024

Overwatch 2

Developer Blizzard Entertainment **Publisher** Blizzard Entertainment **Release** Autumn 2022

Blizzard's hotly-anticipated sequel to the super popular team-based shooter. Get ready for a ton of exciting new heroes, maps and modes, as the publisher has announced free seasonal updates for *Overwatch 2*. The PvP game will be hitting stores in October and the PvE will be released in 2023.

WHAT'S NEXT?

››

Exciting times ahead, right? And the games showcased here are just the beginning. Also on the way are *Call of Duty: Modern Warfare II*, *Gotham Knights*, *Lord Of The Rings: Gollum* and *Starfield*. 2023 should also see a brand-new *Assassin's Creed* game, while *Wonder Woman* and *Wolverine* are getting next-gen adventures too. As for *Fortnite*, *Minecraft* and *Roblox*, that big three will continue to drop fresh content throughout the next twelve months.

You can look forward to checking these out in *Next Level Games Review 2024* ...

INDEX

CREDITS

Ratchet & Clank: Rift Apart, Razer Kraken, Real Madrid, Resident Evil, Resident Evil 4, Resident Evil Village, Return to Monkey Island, Returnal, Riders Republic, Riders Republic, RiMS Racing, RimWorld, Ring Fit Adventure, Rise of the Tomb Raider, Road 96, Roblox, Rocket League Championship Series, Rocket: Robot on Wheels, Rocky Legends, Roller Champions, Rune Factory 5, Saints Row, Salt and Sacrifice, Sea of Thieves, Sekiro: Shadows Die Twice, Shadow of the Tomb Raider, Shaun White Skateboarding, Shaun White Snowboarding, Sherlock Holmes: Chapter One, Shin Megami Tensei V, Shooting Hoops, SIFU: Vengeance Edition, Sly Cooper, Sniper Elite 4 , Sniper Elite 5, SNK vs Capcom: Card Fighter's Clash, Snowrunner, Sonic Colours Ultimate, Sonic Frontiers, Sonic Mania, Sonic the Hedgehog, Spider-Man, Spider-Man 2, Spider-Man: Miles Morales, Splinter Cell, Splinterlands, Sports Party, Starfield, Steam Deck, Steep, Stranger of Paradise: Final Fantasy Origin, Stranger Things 3: The Game, Stranger Things: 1984, Street Fighter, Street Fighter 6, Streets of Rage 4: Mr X Nightmare, Summer in Mara, Super Mario Bros , Super Monkey Ball: Banana Mania, Switch Sports , Synth Riders, Tails of Iron, Taito Milestones, Tales of Arise, Tales of Arise, Team Liquid, Teeter, Tetris Effect Connected, The Artful Escape, The Dark Pictures Anthology: House of Ashes, The Division, The Forgotten City, The Great Ace Attorney Chronicles, The International, The Last of Us, The Legend of Zelda: Breath of the Wild, The Legend of Zelda: Breath of the Wild 2, The Legend of Zelda: Majora's Mask, The Legend of Zelda: Skyward Sword, The Legend of Zelda: The Wind Waker, The Lord of the Rings: Gollum, The Quarry, The Riftbreaker, The Sims 4: Cottage Living, The Six Invitational, Time Loader, Tiny Tina's Wonderlands, TOEM, Tomb Raider, Tomb Raider 2 , Tomb Raider Chronicles, Tomb Raider II, Tomb Raider III, Tomb Raider: Legend, Tomb Raider: The Angel of Darkness, Tomb Raider: The Last Revelation , Tomb Raider: Underworld, Toronto FC, Total War: Warhammer III, Tottenham Hotspur, Tourist Bus Simulator, Tribes of Midgard, Tropico 6, Two Point Campus, Two Point Hospital, Unbound: World's Apart, Uncharted, Uncharted 2: Among Thieves, Uncharted 3: Drake's Deception, Uncharted 4: A Thief's End, Uncharted: Drake's Fortune, Uncharted: Fight for Fortune, Uncharted: Golden Abyss, Uncharted: The Lost Legacy, Unpacking, Until Dawn , Warioware: Get it Together, Wii Sports, Wii Sports Resort , Windjammers 2, Wonder Boy Collection, World Champion Cup, World of Final Fantasy Maxima, WWE 2K22, Wytchwood, Xbox Series X/S, Zephyr Mouse, Zombie Army 4, Zorro: The Chronicles

Picture Credits

Front Cover Blizzard Entertainment, Electronic Arts, Nintendo, Sony Interactive Entertainment, Square Enix, Ubisoft, Xbox Game Studios

Back Cover Electronic Arts, Nintendo, Sega

Photography
014 Koelnmesse / gamescom
015 Koelnmesse / gamescom
054 Andrew Leung
066 Roman Kosolapov / Shutterstock.com
068 Sipa US / Alamy Images
069 Roman Kosolapov / Shutterstock.com
070 REUTERS / Fabrizio Bensch / Alamy Images
071 REUTERS / Tom Jacobs / Alamy Images
072 Roman Kosolapov / Shutterstock.com
073 Roman Kosolapov / Shutterstock.com
160 Gorodenkoff / Shutterstock.com
160 Vantage_DS / Shutterstock.com
171 logoboom / Shutterstock.com
207 Paramount Pictures / Strike Media Ltd
223 wagner_umezaki / Shutterstock.com
223 Cosmin Iftode / Shutterstock.com
242 Andrew Leung

Acknowledgements

The Expanse team would like to thank the following people for their help and contribution towards Next Level Games Review 2023:

Becky Crossdale, Ben Wilson, Charles Cecil, Craig Jelley, Domenico Celenza, Jase Wan, Jonathan Zimmerman, Jordan Woodward, Julia Hardy, Kris Doorga, Lauren Scott, Lynell Jinks, Matteo Pezzotti, Mike Mahar, Nick Pearce, Rich Edwards, Russ Seal, Susie Rae, Tom McBrien, Wren Brier

LEVEL COMPLETED

DO YOU WANT TO CONTINUE PLAYING?

> YES NO

NEXT LEVEL